ART-BASED SUPERVISION

Art-Based Supervision is a unique text for graduate supervision classes and seminars as well as a resource for postgraduate supervisors and practitioners. It offers a new view of supervision, one that incorporates both images and words as tools to investigate and communicate the interactions that occur in therapy and in the systems in which clinicians work. The fundamental principles of supervision provided in the book are useful for anyone interested in exploring the use of images to support reflection, understanding, and empathy in their work. Full-color images further enrich the narrative.

In addition to supervision courses, *Art-Based Supervision* may be used for introductory art therapy, psychology, social work, and counseling courses for readers interested in a broad range of intimate examples of the challenges of therapeutic work and the use of response art to grasp nuanced communication.

Barbara J. Fish, PhD, is an artist, art therapist, clinical counselor, supervisor, and educator serving on the faculty of the School of the Art Institute of Chicago. Dr. Fish specializes in working with trauma, program development, and art-based supervision. She is currently exploring the use of response art in art-based research.

ART-BASED SUPERVISION

Cultivating Therapeutic Insight Through Imagery

Barbara J. Fish

Routledge
Taylor & Francis Group

NEW YORK AND LONDON

First published 2017
by Routledge
711 Third Avenue, New York, NY 10017

and by Routledge
2 Park Square, Milton Park, Abingdon, Oxon, OX14 4RN

Routledge is an imprint of the Taylor & Francis Group, an informa business

© 2017 Barbara J. Fish

Library of Congress Cataloging-in-Publication Data
Names: Fish, Barbara J., author.
Title: Art-based supervision : cultivating therapeutic insight through
    imagery / Barbara J. Fish.
Description: New York, NY : Routledge, 2016. | Includes bibliographical
    references and index.
Identifiers: LCCN 2016000791 | ISBN 9781138814363
    (hbk : alk. paper) | ISBN 9781138814370 (pbk : alk. paper) |
    ISBN 9781315747538 (ebk)
Subjects: LCSH: Psychotherapists—Supervision of. | Psychotherapy—
    Study and teaching—Supervision.
Classification: LCC RC459 .F57 2016 | DDC 616.89/140076—dc23
LC record available at http://lccn.loc.gov/2016000791

ISBN: 978-1-138-81436-3 (hbk)
ISBN: 978-1-138-81437-0 (pbk)
ISBN: 978-1-315-74753-8 (ebk)

Typeset in Bembo
by Apex CoVantage, LLC

Printed and bound in the United States of America by Publishers Graphics,
LLC on sustainably sourced paper.

For those who work to restore broken imaginations and for those who guide their practice.

CONTENTS

FIGURES

ABOUT THE AUTHOR

Barbara J. Fish, PhD, ATR-BC, LCPC is an art therapist and clinical counselor with more than thirty years of supervisory, clinical, teaching, and administrative experience. As a faculty member, she has provided supervision for those in graduate training at the School of the Art Institute of Chicago, the Adler School of Professional Psychology, and the University of Illinois at Chicago.

Barbara provides supervision through her private practice and on-site for a wide range of professionals including expressive therapists, counselors, social workers, psychologists, nurses, and milieu staff. These clinicians are employed in hospital, day treatment, school, residential, and community-based settings. She offers oversight for those developing new programs and practicing in well-established agencies where the challenges of day-to-day clinical demands are the focus, supporting them as they work toward professional credentials, strengthen their ongoing practice, and sharpen their own supervisory skills.

Barbara has written about her use of response art and has melded her focus on art-based supervision with her interest in art-based research. She recently published "Painting Research: Opportunities in Intimacy and Depth," a chapter in Shaun McNiff's edited text *Art as Research: Opportunities and Challenges*, published by the University of Chicago Press. Her future publications include a forthcoming chapter, "Drawing and Painting Research," in Patricia Leavy's edited text *Handbook of Arts-Based Research*, published by Guilford Press.

FOREWORD

Art-Based Supervision: Cultivating Therapeutic Insight Through Imagery describes the process of artistic inquiry within supervisory relationships and models it with sensitivity and imagination. The images shown throughout the book and every element of the process of creating them involve a discipline of feeling, shaping, and allowing forms and expressions to emerge in ways that are simply inaccessible through our more linear and narrative speech.

This is the first full-length book on art therapy supervision and, without in any way questioning the clear distinction that is made between supervision and therapy, I feel that it is also an important new book on art therapy practice and its underpinnings in creative expression. The contextual purpose and professional responsibilities of therapy and supervision are different, but the operational processes of artistic inquiry may not be so far apart. What we do in one setting informs others with good ideas and methods crossing over from one domain of practice to another. As much as convention and professions might insist on strict separations and silos of experience, reality does not oblige.

In my book *Educating the Creative Arts Therapist*, where I said that the arts therapies "must initiate art-based modes" of supervision (McNiff, 1986, pp. 163–164), I also addressed the idea that "supervision is a therapy of therapy; in other words, it is a metatherapy" (Abroms, 1977, p. 82). It pleases me greatly to see Barbara Fish dealing in a comprehensive and inspirational way with these issues in relation to art therapy.

While agreeing that there is a porous separation between supervision and therapy, I want to take this opportunity to once again affirm that supervision is supervision and not therapy. The same applies to more general distinctions between training and therapy. Everything we do professionally is determined by the purpose of the context. The roles we play and the missions of the places where we work and our contractual relations define what is and is not therapy. Yet everything is connected to everything else, and the core process of artistic inquiry has transcontextual qualities; it is for me a *metaprocess* that can be applied across the broad spectrum of life situations.

What I see as the most fundamental and important feature of this book is the way the author and others use the process of personal artistic expression in the presence of another professional person, the defining feature of art therapy practice, to understand and perfect what is happening in the art therapy experience. Barbara Fish succinctly says how artmaking furthers insight—"Since my earliest experiences as a therapist I have used imagery to understand my practice. I make response art when an incident strikes me powerfully, when I feel overwhelmed, confused, or have a reaction that seems overly intense or does not make sense for the situation. Working with imagery makes it possible for me to take the event and give it form so that I can look at it outside of myself."

This focus on accessing "innate knowledge" through artistic expression in order to reflect upon art therapy is a logical extension from, and affirmation of, the art therapy process. I have always asked, how can we be complete and consistent in art therapy without engaging art as a primary way of understanding? If we believe that artistic expression generates insights inaccessible to spoken language, why do we exclusively use the latter in supervision? How can we begin to know what art does unless we experience it ourselves and actively experiment with the process? How can we ask others to do something unless we do it ourselves?

But there is a distinct divide within art therapy where many are not involved in personal artistic practice and where art is not used as a primary way of knowing in supervision, education, and research. The conventional and perhaps dominant paradigm assumes that artistic processes ultimately need to be translated into psychological concepts in order to be understood and accepted. Professional art therapy presentations and publications have adopted social science formats for just about everything they show and thus do not look, feel, and sound like what I experience as the unique character of the worldwide practice of the discipline (McNiff, 2014). This book makes a major contribution to correcting the imbalance between art and psychology, showing how the former can lead from time to time within the relationship rather than always be secondary.

I repeatedly discover through my own experience with making art how the process and the emerging imagery are always a few steps ahead of the reflecting mind. Thoughts and words have an important place in art therapy, but ideally we relax the need to know the end at the beginning, accept uncertainty, and learn how to do a better job witnessing creative expression without judgment and preconception and with a sense of purpose that guides and sustains the overall process.

The use of artistic expression to understand experience is demonstrated throughout this book by a wealth of varied and vivid vignettes offering a sense of what happens in art-based supervision sessions with a broad spectrum of professionals from art therapy to nursing and child care. The artworks made by the author and the people she supervises include aesthetically crafted works by experienced artists and the authentic, equally sensitive expressions of beginners. The overall presentation of artworks has a strong impact on me as a reader and arguably says as much about the value and appeal of the process as the verbal descriptions. I am not in any way questioning the complementary verbal dialogue and explication. It is the one-sided hegemony pervading even art-based professions that is the problem. Art is more than a supplier of "data" and raw materials for analysis by other modes of thought and communication. It is, as Barbara Fish says, a way to understand experience and is uniquely capable of compassionately engaging disturbing emotions. The chapter "Harm's Touch: How We Are Affected by What We Witness" shows how art-based supervision does something creative with "the intensity and impact of therapy," the tendency to absorb the pain and tumult of others that challenges the ability of many to stay involved with therapeutic practice.

With regard to the written word, Barbara has a special ability to write about complex processes and expressions in a terse way that is free of academic formalities. I see the same subtle and sensitive directness and precision in her artistic expressions. The pages feel closely attuned to her readers; no doubt this is an extension of the way she is with the people she supervises, and their art. The book explicitly shows this attentiveness in the section where Barbara reflects upon when it might be useful to show her own art and also when it might interfere with the process. I envision her witnessing it all carefully and trying to assure that whatever she initiates helps to further the particular situation.

A recent experience with Barbara where we were supervising a doctoral candidate's work crystallizes for me how the process of artistic inquiry works in all aspects of the arts in therapy, including practice, training, clinical supervision, and research. Sarah Hamil, an art therapist working in a Memphis art museum, was questioning how she might use her personal artistic expression to interpret a series of interviews about art therapy in museum settings. Like any significant lived experience, the interviews were a "complex" of materials that lent themselves to multiple and varied interpretations, some more capable than others in identifying meaning and new possibilities for understanding. Verbal discussion, and in some cases numbers, can be indispensable modes of interpretation, but they can also obscure more subtle processes that operate within alternative paths and sensibilities of knowing. Discursive responses follow certain rules and narrative structures that advance their communication by selecting certain contents and not others. The capacity to augment expression, communication, and understanding is one of the major reasons why the arts in therapy came into existence, but as I say above there are clear gaps and inconsistencies between what we may do in sessions and how we reflect on the experiences and communicate what we think happened.

Sarah was aware of the prejudicial aspects of textual analysis and the limitations of the literal quantitative coding of words and phrases permeating contemporary social science, and she devised a method of restating what she considered to be poignant words, phrases, and sentences into an aesthetically organized form, constructed in relation to what we might call a "feel" for the material and its expression (McNiff, 2015, p. 58). The method involved a careful and sustained reading of the text by the researcher. However, rather than marginalize personal and emotional interpretative responses, they were maximized as one of many ways of understanding the interviews that lived on in memory with their cadences, emphases, and numerous sensory dimensions.

Yet even this interpretive method was still limited to words. Sarah also wanted to use the visual artmaking process to reflect on the work but did not have a clear sense of how to go about doing this. Barbara suggested that she simply make art on a regular basis as a parallel process while conducting and reflecting on the interviews without a particular objective but with an intention to enhance understanding. I was struck by how this recommendation affirmed the most fundamental qualities of artistic inquiry and how they differ from more linear logical and verbal analysis.

Every life situation or process of inquiry such as the one that Sarah was conducting includes a multifaceted mix of thoughts, memories, feelings, hopes and aspirations, challenges and difficulties, and many things both inside and outside conscious awareness. The stories we tell about what we think happened in an experience both highlight significant processes and keep others outside consciousness. The use of open-ended and spontaneous artistic expression to further insight expands the range of interpretive possibilities. It complements discursive analysis and in some cases provides a vital alternative when the more conventional thought processes are blocked, entangled, or unable to open to perspectives outside of themselves.

The direct and basic artistic advice that Barbara gave contrasts to the general assumption that therapy, research, or any other form of professional experimentation has to involve preestablished and sanctioned technical procedures that inevitably make themselves the primary outcome of the activity. Similarly, I find that even those who might be considering the use of art to further understanding (McNiff, 1998) feel the need for formal technical methods rather than simply making art in relation to a given situation. There is too much emphasis on control and following fixed, step-by-step operations that prevent the intrusion of anything outside them.

Conceptual certainty may limit the creative process by solidifying patterns that do not best serve our ultimate purpose. Pat Allen, in response to her classic book *Art Is a Way of Knowing* (1995), is also saying today that "art is a way of *not* knowing" (Personal communication, February 21, 2013). Accepting what we do not know helps us more completely open to forces moving through present experience unseen, perhaps innately searching for new ways of being organized and presented in awareness.

Art-Based Supervision: Cultivating Therapeutic Insight Through Imagery gives readers an opportunity to witness and practice a way of imaginative inquiry that allows for the emergence of meaning outside the already established and often impermeable structures of thought that guard against change and threats to the way things already appear to be known. It demonstrates from start to finish how open-ended artistic expressions will reliably support the process of discovery, creative change, and the perfection of practice in the supervision of art therapists or any other discipline open to these methods. In showing art therapy how to complete itself by practicing its own essential methods within the supervision process, Barbara Fish makes a historic contribution to the future of the field and its impact on the world.

by Shaun McNiff

Shaun McNiff, University Professor, Lesley University, Cambridge, MA, is the author of Imagination in Action, Art as Research, Integrating the Arts in Therapy, Art Heals, Art as Medicine, Trust the Process: An Artist's Guide to Letting Go, *and many other books.*

References

Abroms, G. (1977). Supervision as metatherapy. In F. W. Kaslow (Ed.), *Supervision, consultation, and staff training in the helping professions* (pp. 81–99). San Francisco: Jossey-Bass.

Allen, P. (1995). *Art is a way of knowing: A guide to self-knowledge and spiritual fulfillment through creativity.* Boston: Shambhala Publications.

McNiff, S. (1986). *Educating the creative arts therapist.* Springfield, IL: Charles C Thomas.

McNiff, S. (1998). *Art-based research.* Philadelphia, PA: Jessica Kingsley Publishers.

McNiff, S. (2014). Presentations that look and feel like the arts in therapy: Keeping creative tension with psychology. *Australian and New Zealand Journal of Arts Therapy, 9*(1), 89–94.

McNiff, S. (2015). *Imagination in action: Secrets for unleashing creative expression.* Boston: Shambhala Publications.

PREFACE

I walked into a classroom filled with nursing students who were discussing their first training encounters. When I told them that we would be making response art to help them manage their experiences as part of their work, they looked at me like I was crazy. After the seminar I reflected on what they shared about their experiences, making a drawing about one of the nurse's account of sitting with a family in hospice while the father died. The following week, after I shared my drawing with the nurses, they picked up art supplies and vigorously began to make imagery to express their own experiences.

We can understand ideas, one another, and ourselves by making art. Creativity and imagination are resources that are available to everyone. Images can range from quick expressions made with the materials at hand to fully expressed pieces. Art-based supervision engages the therapist in training, the new professional, and the supervisor in the creative process. This approach to supervision is rooted in the belief that artmaking supports deep knowing. Imagery has the potential to show our responses, giving us the opportunity to explore and comprehend them. Art-based supervision supports image-based exploration and critical discussion, helping to bring theoretical concepts to life and integrate theory into practice.

Art therapy texts present casework by discussing the imagery created by the client. Although that work is an important part of supervision, this book focuses on the creative investigation of the supervisee and the supervisor. Art-based supervision introduces the use of imagery to reflect on therapy, bringing new resources for oversight and the support of treatment. This method provides ways to engage in the exploration of clinical issues by transforming them into metaphors, physically handling them through media, and providing a place to put them.

Images, like words, are tools for investigation and communication. Art-based supervision offers a vehicle for self-reflection, helping both supervisors and supervisees investigate countertransference and supporting their nuanced understanding of the people, places, and interactions that comprise therapeutic work. While making imagery, and after the expression is formed, the supervisor and new therapist have the opportunity to use it as a resource to consider treatment and related issues. This use of media offers fresh perspectives and rich sources for investigation. This method holds opportunities for participants who are willing to engage their imaginations to explore their practice.

For more than three decades I have employed the creative process, and the images that come from it, to explore and understand my practice as an art therapist. In addition to my work providing supervision during graduate training and postgraduate work, most of the supervision that I provide takes place in an interdisciplinary milieu within psychiatric hospitals, therapeutic residential programs, and schools. This gives me an opportunity to use imagery to investigate and share information and concerns across disciplines. Art-based ways of knowing are fundamental to my practice. When my niece asked me what an art therapist does, I responded that I help to repair broken imaginations.

Bringing imagery into my work as a supervisor feels natural because I find it so useful in my practice as a therapist. As I engage in supervision, the use of creativity and imagination fosters therapeutic insight as well. In supervision I set an example by making imagery, demonstrating my dedication to art-based investigation. I help supervisees recognize its value, supporting the ongoing use of their artwork in their practice. There are precedents for the use of imagery in supervision, but little attention has been paid to the value of the supervisor's images to support the practice.

Within the history of human service supervision, dialogues have traditionally been verbal. While this may not be surprising in fields such as counseling, social work, and psychology, it has often been the case in art therapy as well. There is enormous potential to deepen communication and expand the understanding of relationships and the content of therapeutic work through art-based investigation and discourse. Dialogues in images, like the practice of art therapy itself, have the advantage of offering an alternative to more widely used verbal methods of interacting and investigating concerns. Imagery can hold a space for what is sensed but not known. Images can literally contain the intolerable and represent the unspeakable. As in art therapy, artwork made in supervision often expresses information that is not yet conscious or "known" in the cognitive sense. At its best, the unfolding process of supervision promotes the supervisee's developing understanding. The image can contain challenging content until the supervisee is emotionally and intellectually ready to fully apprehend its meaning.

Making images to explore case material is an integral part of art-based supervision, offering diverse perspectives on the internship experience and the complexities of human encounters. Art-based supervision relies heavily on the use of response art, a process-based form of investigation. When used with a well-defined purpose, this way of working with imagery can help to unpack experiences, effectively exploring and communicating about them. It supports self-reflection, critical investigation, and the appreciation of nuanced didactic and interpersonal material.

This is not a text about how to do art therapy. The art therapy profession encompasses extensive education about the use of materials and their application. While this way of working does not require high levels of artistic skill or training, those providing it should be familiar with the media they offer to others. The intrinsic qualities of materials can settle or stir the therapist in search of clarity in the same way that they can affect clients. Personal experience with a medium is critical before proposing that it might be helpful to someone else. The same is true of supervision assignments. The ability to offer this resource is informed by the supervisor's familiarity with the use of imagery and metaphor in his or her own work.

As supervisors we must work within the scope of our training and the professional standards of our fields. Art-based supervision asks only that you select materials that are familiar to you and use them to stir your imagination and creative resources in the service of developing a fuller understanding of treatment.

This book is intended for supervisors of all levels, from beginning practitioners to those who are advanced in their careers. Art-based supervision offers fresh resources for exploring and managing therapeutic work. Seasoned clinicians, striving to refine their understanding, will find the use of imagery to be a fresh lens to reflect on their practice. This text is also helpful for professionals who anticipate providing supervision in the future, offering fundamental information and creative approaches to hone and deepen their practice. I envision those about to take on a supervisee for the first time using this book as a guide to infuse their work with creative resources. The practice of art-based supervision, introduced early in training, helps new therapists gain an appreciation for how creative expression can facilitate their work. Students and new therapists will also find information about what they can expect from this complex and important relationship. I picture teachers and supervisors reading the book together with those they supervise, engaging the material as a springboard for their discussions and creative investigations.

ACKNOWLEDGMENTS

This work is the culmination of many years of collaborative experience. I am grateful to those that I supervise for allowing me to share their journeys and their images. Their creativity and dedication is a privilege to witness, and I have grown by working beside them. Supervision is at its best when both supervisor and supervisee learn from the process. I want to thank Pat Allen, Randy Vick, Leah Feldman, and Elizabeth Savage for their support and encouragement at the inception of the project and as it unfolded. I appreciate Jordan Pigott and Sze-Chin Lee for their help with the digital representations of the images. Special thanks to Laurie ShoulterKarall, whose editorial help and friendship sustained me throughout the challenges I encountered while writing. Finally, I want to thank Joan Fish, my mother, for cultivating the artist in me and paying attention to every page of the book.

INTRODUCTION

Art-Based Supervision is a text that advocates for creative work in any discipline for those striving for therapeutic insight. Counselors, social workers, psychologists, and other clinicians can all venture into their imaginations to find deeper meaning in their work. This text introduces response art, used for investigation and communication, and presents examples of work with imagery as a venue for self-reflection, feedback, and support.

Chapter 1 begins a discussion of the essential elements of supervision with a description of some of the fundamentals. A history of art-based supervision is provided in Chapter 2. Suggestions are offered for creating space that facilitates work with media and strategies are provided for engaging images in Chapters 3 and 4. We move into a discussion of the challenges and opportunities of supervision, including examining power in the supervisory relationship and managing and learning from the toxicity of the content that we witness, in Chapters 5 and 6. We look at the use of art-based supervision during and after formal training in Chapters 7 and 8. We explore its use to deepen understanding and interdisciplinary communication in fields beyond art therapy in Chapter 9. In Chapter 10 we discuss the use of imagery for closure, drawing a comparison between the importance of termination in supervision and in therapy.

Art-based supervision is a rich resource for supporting therapy. Examples of assignments and vignettes describing the work are included throughout the text, demonstrating the potential of art-based supervision to facilitate and expand the options for the investigation of clinical practice. The people in the stories and images included here have been identified according to the wishes of the supervisee involved. This includes the way that race, class, gender, age, religion, sexuality, and physical, emotional, and intellectual agency and other demographics are described. I have been careful to protect the confidentiality of clients and the anonymity of the agencies where these experiences have occurred. I hope the thoughtful presentation of this material will provide inspiration and practical ideas for those looking to bring fresh tools to this important work.

1

FUNDAMENTAL PRINCIPLES OF SUPERVISION

Keys to Supervision

A therapist I supervised for some time came to see me because she was struggling with her new role as an administrator in a day treatment program for adults with chronic mental illness. As we talked about her efforts to find her personal style for supervising the staff, she began painting a hand holding a key. When she returned the following week to resume our discussion, she brought another image, *Keys to Success* (Figure 1.1). She painted this image at home after supervision as she continued to explore her concerns.

The therapist's watercolor and ink painting depicted an array of keys that she labeled with the skills that she thought were necessary to effectively supervise others. The image was her "key" to recalling and accessing her own strengths, supporting her successful work with those in her charge. As we painted and talked together, she worked to recognize that she had the qualities that she needed. Her challenge was one of finding confidence and remembering to believe in her own abilities.

There are parallels between the work of therapy and that of supervision (Wilson, Riley, & Wadeson, 1984). Both are intimate relationships with important boundaries and guidelines. This chapter provides fundamental information to clarify expectations for supervisors, those who are considering supervising in the future, and for supervisees wanting to understand what to expect from this important relationship.

Supervision is a form of support and oversight that is provided in all mental health professions. Beginning in training, we learn to rely on a colleague with more experience to guide and direct our work. Seasoned practitioners often revisit supervision throughout their careers to ensure the clarity of their practice.

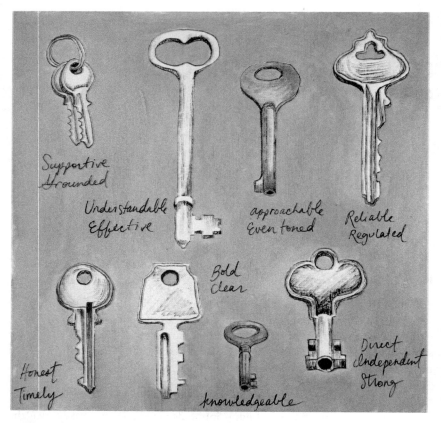

FIGURE 1.1 Keys to Success

Anonymous

As professional relationships evolve, former students become supervisees, colleagues, and often friends. I am happy to say that those who helped me find my way as a therapist early in my career continue to be resources for me to this day.

Supervisor Training

There are some aspects of supervision that come naturally. Reflecting on his or her own early work, the advanced clinician can empathize with the new therapist's experiences. As a supervisor it is gratifying to support earnest work to understand the complexity of treatment planning, explore interpersonal dynamics, and investigate the systemic issues that have impact on treatment. However, there are responsibilities in this multifaceted practice that may be less evident to the new supervisor. The evaluative component, intrinsic in supervision, requires accountability for the quality of care provided by the new therapist to the client and the agency where he or she provides services. This calls for the supervisor to be firm as well as supportive when addressing supervisory issues, compliance with policies and procedures, and standards of practice.

In the past, therapists have taken on supervisory roles with only their own experience as a guide. Recently many professions, such as counseling, have begun to include supervisory coursework as part of their degree requirements. State credentialing boards have begun to require the acquisition of formal supervisor training to maintain licensure. Some organizations monitor experience, training, and years of supervisory practice as well as offer advanced certification for "master" supervisors. Training opportunities can address the challenges and complexities of this role and offer guidance on how best to provide support for the ongoing quality of care for clients.

Literally meaning "to oversee," supervision entails a complex set of skills; whether acquired formally, through experience, or intuitively, these skills can be sharpened. Supervisors may take advantage of seminars and other training opportunities offered through formal education programs and local and national professional associations as a way to develop a keener skillset.

Professional Credentials

It is the supervisor's responsibility to guide the new therapist through professional requirements and milestones, providing information about expectations and helping him or her to become a professionally sound, informed consumer of supervisory services. When working with those in graduate training, the supervisor must be knowledgeable and able to inform students about the training guidelines and postgraduate qualifications established for programs that are approved by their corresponding professional associations and credentialing bodies.

Many programs that provide training are approved or accredited and regularly reviewed by their corresponding professional associations or state licensing boards to ensure ongoing compliance with guidelines established to assure the quality of training and best practices. During graduate school, the expectations for site and faculty supervision are regulated, including the credentials of the supervisors, size of the fieldwork class, and number of hours spent weekly with clients and in supervision. As the requirements for credentials vary from state to state, supervisors should direct individuals considering training to contact their state and national professional associations in the location where they intend to practice to ensure that the educational program they choose meets the required educational standards.

After graduation, during the early years of professional practice, new therapists seek supervision as they work toward professional credentials and licensure. A supervisor who is well versed in the specific discipline's requirements in the state of intended practice can facilitate the navigation of these specialized milestones.

The qualifications for obtaining credentials vary by professional discipline and location. For example, art therapists are credentialed through national regulation and may be licensed according to the state. Graduates from art therapy training programs that are approved by the American Art Therapy Association (AATA) may apply for art therapy registration (ATR) and board certification (BC) with the Art Therapy Credentials Board (ATCB) after one thousand supervised post-graduate art therapy contact hours. Graduates from unapproved programs must complete two thousand supervised postgraduate contact hours to earn the ATR.

License titles, qualifications, and training requirements vary from state to state as do the requirements for supervisors. New therapists should confirm that their selected supervisor has current, appropriate credentials in order to ensure that their supervision hours qualify them for their own credentials.

There are also discipline- and location-specific guidelines for the ways new therapists may gain postgraduate experience. Depending on state law, working as a consultant is often prohibited until the clinician is a licensed professional. Until that time, the therapist must accumulate the hours required for licensure by working as an employee of an agency. This is intended to protect the public. A consultant is an independent contractor that is paid on an hourly basis and is responsible for his or her own liability. Most often as a credentialed professional, the consultant has years of postgraduate, supervised experience in preparation for independent practice. As an employee, the new therapist is held responsible for following the agency's policies, procedures, and practices while working under the oversight and supervision of the agency. Some professions count hours of volunteer experience toward credentialing as long as a credentialed professional provides the supervisee with supervision; others do not.

Supervisory Functions

Supervisors are gatekeepers and guides, overseeing the quality of client care and facilitating new therapists' professional development. While managing the work of new therapists, the two main functions of supervision are clinical and administrative. These tasks are not mutually exclusive. The supervisor guides and evaluates the work, ensuring sound practice and overseeing the documentation of services. The supervisor provides support, direction, and evaluation while ensuring adherence to professional standards. At the same time he or she is an ally, supporting and advocating for the new therapist within the agency.

Clinical Supervision

Clinical supervision focuses on the nuances of working with clients and new professionals' unfolding understanding of therapeutic practice. Here the supervisee brings information about his or her work, discussing what transpired in order to reach a deeper understanding of the services provided. The overarching goal of this aspect of supervision is fostering ethical and effective clinical work. The focus of clinical oversight varies widely. One strategy is to take a broad view that allows for the examination of questions or crises that have arisen since the previous session. A more in-depth approach may track a single challenging case or group over a period of time. Whatever the strategy, it is best that the participants agree upon a method that is suitable to the supervisee's needs in order to maintain a constructive focus. This approach should be evaluated periodically as skills and needs evolve.

In addition to the planning and interventional components of clinical work, relational issues are a key dimension of mental health practice. Countertransference and other personal responses to clients and coworkers are frequently encountered in the course of treatment. Helping supervisees to unravel these challenges can remove interpersonal impediments and bring clarity. While this facet of clinical supervision comes closest to therapy, it is this very closeness that necessitates sensitive exploration of issues of power and cognizance of professional boundaries.

Supervisory oversight takes different forms. For example, in art therapy training supervision is provided from two vantage points, those of the field site supervisor and the faculty supervisor. Within this paradigm, the field site supervisor has the proximity to observe treatment directly. With firsthand experience of clients and the setting, this supervisor can be an essential resource for support, feedback, and direction. The faculty supervisor provides oversight within a class format, helping students understand what to expect from supervision and facilitating their application of academic content to real-world practice. In this forum, student therapists engage alternative perspectives and are exposed to work with a wide range of client, systemic, and interpersonal concerns encountered in the field.

These ways of working may be replicated after graduate training. Some new therapists participate in supervision on-site that may focus on administrative and clinical issues that arise in treatment. Many seek additional supervision from a professional outside of the agency to supplement and deepen their understanding and skills, supporting their professional goals. This is often the case for new art therapists when there is not a senior art therapist employed on-site. In fact, art therapists must receive supervision from a registered art therapist for at least half of their postgraduate hours to qualify for their own registration as an art therapist.

This is one profession's model of supervision. Others vary by discipline and have corresponding requirements for oversight. Working across disciplines has advantages. However, the development of competency in a professional scope of practice and appreciation of clinical nuances may be best supported by someone working within the same paradigm.

Administrative Supervision

Administrative supervision focuses on the communication of information and assures that professional standards of practice and agency policies and procedures are followed. Schedules, budgets, and projects are discussed, feedback is provided, guidelines are communicated, documentation is reviewed, and performance evaluations are conducted. While therapists are in training, the field site supervisor plays a central role in providing administrative direction, introducing the new therapist to the agency, supporting his or her evolving working relationships, helping to mediate conflict, and facilitating successful work with others. After graduation, new therapists working in agencies are typically assigned to a specific staff member who provides administrative supervision. This same person may or may not provide clinical oversight.

Supervisors are role models, demonstrating professional engagement with colleagues. They guide new therapists' professional development as well, promoting involvement in professional organizations, encouraging new therapists to seek peer support and other resources on- and off-site, and supporting participation in continuing education, conferences, and other professional activities. The supervisor recommends readings, training opportunities, and conferences related to practice and often gives advice regarding career choices and professional credentials. The supervisor is typically called upon to play a formal role in documenting clinical performance as a part of licensure or other credentialing processes.

Scope of Supervision

The open discussion of expectations supports sound supervision during therapist training and postgraduate work. To clarify this complex relationship, it is critical to have an understanding of mutual responsibilities, establishing a supervisory agreement that delineates what each person can anticipate from this unique relationship.

When an intern is placed at an agency during training, a supervisory agreement is made between the academic institution and the fieldwork site. This written document clarifies roles and expectations for the intern, the school, the supervisor, and the agency. It reflects the supervision partnership between the school and the agency and establishes parameters for the frequency and duration of supervision and the key responsibilities of the site supervisor, the faculty supervisor, and the intern. This agreement clarifies the student's academic schedule and the requirements for internship hours. It specifies methods for evaluation and observation and includes the forms and a schedule for written evaluations. It also delineates the expectations for the duration and frequency of on-site supervision.

Professionals providing postgraduate supervision should develop their own written agreement, delineating mutual expectations and spelling out parameters for their work. This document includes specifics such as the time and structure of meetings, fees and cancellation policy, the method and frequency of evaluation, and the limits of confidentiality. It conveys the supervisor's training and credentials, specifies areas of competencies, identifies the supervisor's theoretical approach, and provides contact information in the event of a complaint. Discussing this agreement helps new therapists to appreciate the importance and complexities of the informed consent process that they engage in with clients.

Postgraduate professionals and those in training are expected to follow the professional ethics and standards of practice of their discipline as well as the day-to-day policies and procedures of the agency where they work with guidance from the supervisor. These include clinical procedures for reporting recipient abuse or neglect, policies regarding the dress code, and expectations for calling in sick and scheduling time off. The supervisor is responsible for the new professional's practice. He or she is charged with ensuring the client's well-being by guiding, managing, evaluating, and communicating critical feedback to the supervisee about his or her work. The effective transmission of expectations is critical. For that reason, individual learning goals and objectives should be established early to help guide the new therapist.

Evaluation

The supervisor is responsible for evaluating the supervisee's performance to ensure the quality of care that is provided for clients and to encourage the new therapist's professional progress. Ongoing assessment and constructive critical commentary highlight strengths and weaknesses, supporting the supervisee's evolving skills. Formative evaluation is ongoing and includes observation, feedback, and direction. Summative evaluation is formal, given in written form at established intervals. Training programs usually provide midterm and final internship evaluation forms for interns each semester. Those providing postgraduate supervision may use forms developed by the agencies where they work or develop their own tools for evaluation.

An effective evaluation is descriptive, not judgmental. It should focus on the new therapist's skill base and his or her developing knowledge, including feedback about functions and competencies, as well as acknowledging new learning. The evaluation should recognize the integration of feedback into ongoing practice. New therapists should not receive negative feedback during formal evaluation without prior warning and a reasonable amount of time to improve. Some of the ways that supervisors provide clinical observation to support internship evaluation include: coleading sessions, engaging in role-play, reading written process and progress notes, listening to audiotapes, viewing videotapes, and nonparticipatory observation. Additionally, making response art as a form of feedback is a valuable resource.

Evaluation forms should be reviewed with new therapists early in the relationship to ensure that the criteria are clear. Supervisees should participate in their own evaluation by engaging in ongoing self-assessment and providing formal input into written evaluations. The supervisor and supervisee should complete evaluations together to encourage discussion. Supervisees' defensive responses to feedback should be explored openly, when they occur, through ongoing dialogue. Supervisees should have the opportunity to respond in writing with objections to the appraisal of their performance.

It is important to have expectations for, and to evaluate the progress of, a new therapist in ways that are consistent with his or her individual learning styles and current level of training and experience. The supervisor must keep in mind that the beginning therapist is motivated, anxious, and focused on basic skills and knowledge. Early in the work, he or she may have limited self-awareness. Frequently the new supervisee does not recognize how much he or she knows. The new supervisee often looks for prescribed answers from readings or exchanges with others without truly understanding the deeper significance of the issue and the intervention. The more proficient therapist has a deeper understanding of clients and can articulate how theory supports practice. He or she is able to use varied therapeutic approaches and has learned to use his or her responses to clients clinically. The more advanced supervisee works more independently and is less defensive about feedback.

Confidentiality

The limits of confidentiality should be carefully explained early in supervision. The protection of confidentiality ends where public safety begins. Confidentiality can be broken if the client, therapist, or supervisee is a danger to himself, herself, or others; if there is evidence of abuse or neglect; or if the court orders disclosure. The supervisor and supervisee must determine if there is a serious threat to the client, the supervisee, or someone else. In each of these cases, the supervisor should guide the new therapist through the agency's reporting procedures. For example, in an instance of duty to warn, the supervisee must notify the proper authorities, the intended victim, and the parents in the case of a minor, and inform the client of the actions that have been taken. While guiding the process, the supervisor should seek counsel from his or her own supervisor and use clinical and administrative direction from the agency.

Ethical Considerations

When supervisors take on the professional oversight of new therapists, they assume ethical and legal responsibility for their work. For this reason supervisors should ensure that their malpractice insurance covers them in the event of vicarious liability. If an issue arises that holds potential liability, both the supervisor and the therapist should document their responses, including all who were notified and consulted. If the problem was identified, what were the recommendations and were they followed? Be sure to include whether or not the problem was anticipated and communicated in supervision. The supervisor should seek and document his or her own consultation.

Power, Privilege, and Agency

Culturally competent supervision supports culturally competent therapy. The supervisor should be aware of the complexities of cross-cultural supervision and cross-cultural therapy and work to sustain awareness of his or her own cultural context, power, and privilege and how these influence relationships. He or she must be sensitive to students' sociocultural backgrounds and how their contexts influence their experience. The supervisor should identify and address barriers to cultural sensitivity, engage in his or her own ongoing specialized and culturally based training, and guide the new therapist's deepening awareness and cultural competence. The chapters that follow provide examples of the use of imagery for self-exploration and communication in this fundamental aspect of supervision.

Difficult Issues

There are tough issues that must be addressed in supervision. At any point in a therapist's training or professional work, it may be necessary to counsel him or her out of the graduate program or even out of the field. This may occur if the new therapist disregards professional or ethical guidelines or does not demonstrate the emotional maturity or stability necessary to successfully provide therapy. In addition, violating professional standards or disregarding agency policy can lead to dismissal from training or employment. Examples of infractions include erratic, unreliable behavior on-site, attending work while intoxicated, and inappropriate interactions with clients. Supervisors must follow their agency's policies when addressing such issues.

Contending with serious issues should never be done in isolation. The field site supervisor addressing a problem with an intern must document information, interactions, and interventions, communicating information to the intern and within the agency. He or she must be in close contact with the faculty supervisor to ensure that the school is apprised of the situation and can provide additional support and direction. In all but the most dire situations, supervisors must try to give feedback and an opportunity to demonstrate change. During training, corrective action decisions are made collectively with the site supervisor, faculty supervisor, and other faculty members consulting about their experiences with the student.

In postgraduate work, the supervisor may be the first to know the details of a new therapist's troublesome clinical or ethical behavior. The supervisor must be careful to use his or her authority effectively. In some cases, attention to the issues and redirection can support changes in a new therapist's misguided behavior. Ongoing evaluation should document issues, changes, and improvements. When working with a problematic therapist, supervisors are advised to maintain close contact with their professional colleagues, supervisor, and agency administration to ensure the clarity of their own observations and the necessity of the chosen course of action. In the event of a serious infraction, the supervisor is required to report a licensed professional therapist to the professional credentialing body and the state board of professional regulation.

The Quality of Attention

The value of supervision rests on the quality of attention brought by both parties. New therapists are responsible for coming to supervision on time and prepared for the work with updates about prior interactions, current questions, and concerns. They should be focused on the session, without cell phones or other distractions, and be able to discuss their work. They are responsible for reliable professional behavior, including engaging with others appropriately for the setting, raising their concerns, and demonstrating the ability to receive and integrate feedback and direction. The same commitment to focused concentration is required of the supervisor.

I remember how I felt as an art therapy intern watching my supervisor doze off each week while I presented artwork from the art therapy sessions that I had with patients on an inpatient adult psychiatric unit where we worked. I was new to therapy and excited to be finally using my training. I eagerly looked forward to telling my supervisor, a psychiatrist, about art therapy by sharing patients' artwork with him. As I watched him nod off, I wondered what I was doing wrong. I was a strong, enthusiastic student, but my supervisor's behavior shook my confidence. It took me a long time to work up the nerve to bring my concerns to my supervision class at school. The support I received from my classmates helped me to challenge my supervisor and ask him to focus his attention on my work.

This experience raises a fundamental expectation. Supervisors are charged with bringing all of their resources to bear as they pay focused attention to new professionals and guide their therapeutic work. It is the supervisor's obligation to be aware of the unequal distribution of power intrinsic in these relationships, monitoring his or her own behavior while supporting the new therapist's negotiation of therapeutic relationships and systemic issues. Confused by the situation, I assumed that I had done something wrong. When I met with my fieldwork class at school, my faculty supervisor and classmates helped me to clarify that I was not at fault and that it was the site supervisor's issue. I realized that I had the right to expect his conscientious attention on my work. I felt the support of my class as I returned to my site and directly discussed my concerns with him. When I talked to my site supervisor he apologized, assuring me that he was interested in what I was doing and that he would be more attentive in the future.

Safety

Effective supervision depends on developing an environment of stability and psychological safety. Consistent, reliable meetings that focus on the supervisee's work support the development of an atmosphere conducive to deep practice. Whether supervision is provided in groups or individually, the relationship is an intentional commitment to focus on supporting and guiding the new therapist's work for the designated period of time.

Structure

Both therapy and supervisory sessions should have a clear beginning, middle, and end. The beginning helps the new therapist transition into the supervisory process. It can be a time to check-in, bring up concerns, and take care of administrative business. During the middle phase, supervisees settle into the meeting, discuss their work, problem-solve, and deepen their understanding. When it is provided in groups, the supervisor should help to develop a culture of mutuality, ensuring that each participant has ample time to discuss his or her concerns. The end provides closure and helps the therapist transition back into the world outside of the session. These are not rigid delineations; supporting these shifts can be as simple as offering a cup of tea at the start of session or scheduling the next meeting at the end. No matter how simple, I find that paying conscious attention to these components of the supervision session helps to provide predictability and structure deep work.

The use of time is an important component of supervision, as it is in therapy. Sessions that begin and end on time demonstrate mutual respect for the scheduled commitments of all of those involved. Exploring the reason for late or missed sessions may yield important information about participants' feelings related to therapy or to supervisory relationships. This attention, focused on the use of time, models how to understand and use this important factor in therapy sessions.

Boundaries

Clear boundaries are as important in supervision as they are in therapy. Although these unique relationships are often friendly and may turn into professional associations or friendships once formal supervision ends, dual relationships are ill-advised. It is important to remember that the purpose of supervision is to ensure the quality of client care and support the new therapist's professional development.

Responsible supervisors work to maintain ongoing awareness of their motivation for wanting to provide this service and the impact of their interpersonal power on those they work with. There is an inherent power differential in the relationship between senior and junior practitioners. A staff supervisor often bears administrative and evaluative responsibility over his or her protégé. Yet even in the case of independent supervision, where these responsibilities may not have direct impact on employment, an evaluative and ethical responsibility remains for the supervisor. For these reasons, professional boundaries are critical. This should inform the supervisor's level of self-disclosure with the new therapist. Supervisees are often eager to please and may take on the burden of the supervisor's issues. Personal information should be shared thoughtfully.

Clarity of purpose is obscured when the supervisor risks a friendship or some other form of dual relationship. It follows without saying that dating and sexual relationships are inappropriate in supervision. The supervisor must uphold professional standards that can require writing a critical evaluation or counseling a new therapist out of the field. In the worst-case scenario, the supervisor may feel that it is necessary to terminate the relationship or fire the new therapist because he or she is unwilling to accept direction or feedback or is inappropriate for the setting.

Clearly communicated expectations, boundaries, and ongoing feedback help ground and orient new therapists in supervision. It is essential for the supervisee to become comfortable enough to risk the vulnerability necessary to explore the personal and professional dimensions of conducting therapy. A trusting and supportive supervisory relationship is critical to work that includes investigating responses to clients based on current relationships as well as those rooted in the therapist's responses or countertransference. Therapists with strong personal resonance with their work may choose individual over group supervision to access more focused support as they sort out this challenging work.

Most graduate programs recommend that students engage in their own therapy. This experience is a valuable resource. Not only does it give student therapists personal insight as recipients of the services that they provide, but it also offers a reflection of their own issues that can help them decode personal feelings stirred in their work. Supervision can help new therapists learn to differentiate personal issues from those that are relevant to explore for the sake of their clients. Supervisees' personal issues affecting therapeutic work are important to bring to supervision. Their personal concerns, stirred by the work, are important to bring to their own therapy.

I used both supervision and therapy to support my own graduate training. I struggled with intense dread as I began my first internship in a therapeutic day school. It was more than the apprehension of a novice intern. I felt waves of anxiety that stopped me cold. After bringing my concern to supervision, I explored it in my own therapy. Together these resources help me to understand that my anxiety came from my unrecognized memories of being bullied in elementary school. Once I realized my countertransference, I was no longer thrown off balance by my past experience as a powerless child and regained my footing as an adult working with children. I went on to address my work at my internship in supervision and my personal issues from the past in therapy.

Choosing a Supervisor or Supervisee

Supervision is provided in many configurations. It may take place on- or off-site, during group or individual sessions. It is a resource for students during graduate training, for new therapists seeking credentials and licensure, and for seasoned professionals throughout their careers. There are a variety of challenges and responsibilities inherent in each of these ways of engaging in supervision. These are some of the basic considerations to inform the process of selecting this professional support.

The starting point for this potentially enriching relationship is finding someone with the expertise and theoretical philosophy to support your practice. This is followed by delineating expectations to support the work of both the supervisor and the supervisee. At its best, this is a fascinating and deeply rewarding experience. However, an unwise choice can mean extra work, frustration, and even professional embarrassment. A supervisee who is irresponsible or inappropriate can reflect poorly on the supervisor who selected the intern for training or hired the therapist. The choice of supervisor is also critical from the perspective of the supervisee. A good choice can lead to a productive, nurturing experience that facilitates the development of therapeutic skills. Choosing unwisely or in haste may leave the new therapist feeling unconstructively criticized and without support or direction.

Making a wise choice for supervision is important whether the therapist is a student or a new professional. The skills and habits therapists develop early may last their entire careers. There are many things to consider when making this decision. Whether you are interviewing a student intern or potential employee, investigating a possible internship site or looking for employment, choosing the supervisory relationship is as important as the choice of the population and the setting.

Interview Advice for the Supervisor

Self-awareness about the reasons for wanting to take on supervisory work is essential. If you are employed at an agency, why do you want to supervise interns and staff members at your site? Do you have a choice in the matter, or is procuring and overseeing the training of interns and staff part of your responsibilities? What assets and challenges might an intern potentially bring to your agency? Is supervision an opportunity for you to share your experience and contribute to the field? Will having an intern support you serving more clients, improving the value of your work? If you are not working with others from your discipline, will an intern decrease your isolation and help with your workload? What did you learn in your own supervision that might benefit an intern? Have you had experiences that taught you what not to do as a supervisor? Will having an intern increase your power and prestige in the agency?

As a supervisor interviewing potential interns or employees at your worksite, you are evaluating their possible value to clients and your agency as well as their ability to benefit from your oversight and feedback. When I meet with a potential supervisee for the first time, I look at all aspects of our interaction to determine whether his or her involvement would benefit the clients, our team, and me as the supervisor. I ask applicants for their resume, a writing sample, and examples of their artwork to determine if they have useful past experience and if communication and documentation will develop easily or will be an ongoing focus of our work. I ask the intern why he or she is interested in this site to determine the level of self-awareness and the amount of thought invested in his or her decision. I look at how the interviewee presents himself or herself and if it is consistent with my expectations for the site. I look for punctuality and appropriate attire. I notice the quality of attention and enthusiasm in the meeting. Are we communicating well in the interview? If I accept the therapist, I don't want to use supervisory time to focus on basic work habits such as timeliness and dress code. There are much more salient and interesting aspects of clinical work to address. I have learned over time to be sure to communicate workplace expectations.

Years ago I interviewed an art therapy student in her twenties for a potential internship while I was working on a long-term inpatient adolescent unit. She was on time for the meeting, wearing dress pants and a tailored shirt. She brought the written materials I requested and we had a lively discussion about her intention to help the patients understand sexual issues, particularly those related to coming out as an LGBTQ youth. We discussed the confusion often experienced by children who have endured sexual abuse and the influence it can have on their development. She was sensitive to the patients' nuanced experiences. After I reviewed her paperwork, I offered her the internship. We looked forward to working together.

The intern came to the hospital on her first day dressed casually in khaki pants, loafers, and a blue cotton shirt. She did not tuck in her shirt and left the top buttons unfastened, revealing her white tee shirt underneath. When we met later for supervision I told her that she needed to dress more professionally for the site. She listened to the feedback without saying anything. The next time I saw her she was visibly upset. She said she was going to have to leave the internship because she was not comfortable wearing a skirt to work as I did. Surprised by her interpretation of what I meant by "professional," I told her that I did not mean she should dress like me. I was referring to her casual attire. As part of the clinical staff, she needed to consider what she wore and how she could be comfortable while presenting herself professionally at the hospital. I realized that her misunderstanding was not entirely her fault. As her supervisor, I should have clearly communicated what I considered appropriate attire. As we discussed the miscommunication, I told her that if she dressed the way she did for the interview, she would be fine. With the misunderstanding resolved, she continued her placement, and clothing was never again an issue.

Interview Advice for the Supervisee

The method of selecting internships during training varies by discipline and school. Art therapy students participate in both group and individual oversight. Site supervision is usually provided individually, while small-group work is the primary mode of academic support. Field site supervision is most often provided in individual sessions by someone from the same discipline or a clinician with a master's degree from a related field. This practice affords the intern focused attention on the issues at hand with a supervisor who is currently involved with the same clients and the system serving them. Some training programs assign student interns to specific supervisors and sites, and some allow students to choose their internships based on their interest in the field and their resonance with the potential site supervisor.

Academic programs usually offer group supervision with a faculty member in a weekly class, with individual meetings scheduled as needed. In some programs, students configure the group's composition by choosing their instructor, making their decision based on what they know of the faculty member and their comfort with their peers. Some students may change classes throughout their training, sampling supervisory styles. This affords them a range of experiences, helping them to learn what to expect and to develop supervisory criteria for their postgraduate work. Others remain with a supervisor they work well with, developing a longer term working relationship. Remaining with the same supervisor has the potential to support and deepen investigation of clinical issues without spending time acclimating to a new relationship.

Many new therapists seeking postgraduate supervision find guidance from a supervisor from their own or a related discipline who is employed where they work. Because the supervisor knows the clients and coworkers, the agency policies and procedures, and the dynamics of the system from personal experience, these supervisory relationships may be a wonderful benefit of employment as well as an ideal learning experience for the new therapist. However, there are times when suitable supervision is not available on-site, leaving the new therapist to seek individual or group supervision outside of the agency where he or she works.

Supervisees should negotiate with their employer if they are not provided supervision on-site. If agencies do not have a supervisor with the required credentials on staff, some will pay for all or part of the supervisory fees that lead to licensure. When asked, agencies may give release time to cover the time spent in supervision outside of work hours. Some employers will pay for qualifying testing and licensing fees. Others will have a standard pay increase when credentials are obtained. Even if a site has not previously offered this kind of support, an informed and professional request that underscores the long-term value that professional credentialing brings to the organization may help institute such a practice. Agencies handle things differently. You will never know what they will do to assist you if you do not ask.

New professionals seek postgraduate supervision off-site when there is not a credentialed professional from the same discipline or when the access to supervision at work is not sufficient. Those looking for off-site postgraduate supervision find support in a variety of ways. Some choose supervisors with whom they have developed a relationship during their training, internship, or other professional experience. Others follow a recommendation from an instructor or colleague, or find the supervisor through his or her professional involvement, presentations, and publications. It is important to give careful consideration to the choice of supervisor. Is the supervisor knowledgeable about the setting where you are working? Is he or she easy to talk to? Does he or she understand the population you work with, their concerns, and their culture? What is the supervisor's approach to supervision? For example, I provide art-based supervision. Therapists and others who are interested in using images and imagination to deepen their understanding of their clinical work may choose to work with me.

When someone contacts me for postgraduate supervision, we meet initially to determine if we are a good fit. Before we meet I ask for a writing sample and resume. Beyond clarifying a supervisory agreement describing the parameters of supervision, as I discussed earlier in this chapter, we talk about where he or she works and if the scope of my experience is what is called for. As we talk I try to determine if the supervisee has sound training. I try to assess the new professional's willingness to seek and integrate feedback. Is he or she motivated to work on professional development? I describe art-based supervision, and I ask if my approach is consistent with the way he or she would like to work.

Whether you are interviewing for an internship or for a professional position, you are probably going to meet your potential supervisor when you interview. Remember you are making a connection with the interviewer and the agency. Be sure you are prepared for the meeting. Find out information about the site before you go. What is the agency's mission? What population does it serve? Be mindful of how you present yourself. Be on time and consider your potential role at the agency when you dress for the interview. Be sure to bring any requested written materials to the meeting, such as a resume or a writing sample. Have a list of questions to elicit information about the supervisor and the agency that will help you clarify your understanding about the learning opportunity. Be ready to talk about your interest in the site. What do you want to know about the supervisor's experience, the nature of the clients, and what your work will entail? Will you be working individually or with groups? If you will work with groups, how large will they be? Is there a designated room for the work? Is there a budget for materials? Are there opportunities for program development, co-therapy, and collaboration with other disciplines? Will there be other interns or therapists? If you are accepted, what will your schedule be?

Notice how you feel during the interview. Is the supervisor ready to meet with you and respectful of your time? Is he or she attentive to the conversation or distracted and preoccupied? Is the supervisor knowledgeable about the area of practice that interests you? Is he or she easy to talk to? Do you feel an empathic connection in the interview? Does the supervisor hold active credentials that are consistent with the requirements for your field?

After the interview, send a thank you email or written note. Be timely and responsive to all communication. Make sure you meet deadlines for requested decisions, materials, medical clearance, and training. You should be professional. Reflect on your experience with your prospective supervisor. If you have access to them, check site evaluations written by former interns. Ask teachers and colleagues for their experience with the agency and your prospective supervisor. Compare your experience to other sites you are considering before making your decision. Remember, this is the beginning of your relationship with your supervisor.

Group Supervision

Those who are beginning to work professionally must choose between group or individual supervision. This decision is often informed by the new professional's prior experience. Do you feel more able to challenge yourself in a group or in individual session? Is there a group available with the supervisor of your choice? Do the others in the group share your population and clinical concerns? Are you comfortable sharing personal concerns and countertransference in a group? Does the benefit of hearing about others' work outweigh sharing your time and focus? Is there a difference in the cost? Will your supervisor work with you on a sliding scale?

Group supervision offers different opportunities than does individual work. It provides discourse based on a rich mix of personalities, internship sites, and experiences. This way of working familiarizes new therapists with the value of peer support that can be a career-long resource. Group supervision provides limited time for direct discussion of the individual's work because the format is shared.

Distance Supervision

Some new professionals choose distance supervision for their postgraduate work. Although online resources have made distance oversight more accessible to interpersonal nuances, this form of supervision is not an acceptable mode for credentialing in all disciplines. The specific qualifications vary by discipline and location. Supervisors should be aware of and advise new therapists about the specific limitations of this kind of supervision. However, when new professionals receive supervision at work that may be used for credentialing, additional distance supervision with someone who has expertise in their area of practice may be useful, adding support and insight to their therapeutic work.

Terminating Supervision

Many postgraduate supervisory relationships evolve into professional relationships and collegial consultations. Although the boundaries of supervision are different from those of therapy, the end of formal supervision holds parallels to the termination phase of therapy. Both move from initial engagement and the establishment of trust to collaborative work on specified goals, and end with closure.

Bringing meaning to this phase of professional development is as important as creating a safe, predictable space for the beginning of supervision. Termination is an opportunity to review and affirm the work. Modeling a positive goodbye as part of closure in supervision helps new therapists appreciate the value of termination with clients.

Conclusion

Obtaining professional support is part of sound practice and is essential when engaging in the demanding work of therapy. Careful attention to the fundamentals of supervision sets the stage for this working relationship. Clearly communicated expectations within supervision reinforce appropriate structure and boundaries, facilitating deep investigation and conceptualization of therapy.

What I Need (2007) is a poem that describes what supervisees look for from their supervisors. It was written by a group of art therapy professionals reflecting on their experiences when they were interns. They presented the poem at an art therapy supervision symposium to express the supervisee's hopes for the supervisory relationship.

What I Need

I need you to be committed to my training
I need you to remember what it was like when you were an intern
I need you to be a role model
I need you to practice what you preach and make your own art
I need to trust that you will help me
I need to know what you expect from me
I need you to be honest about what you expect from me
I need you to have a good foundation of what art therapy is
I need you to make my learning a priority
I need you to let people know who I am and introduce me,
    I may be nervous about doing that myself
I need you to be on time
I need you to make me a part of the treatment team
I need you to not be condescending
I need you to be patient
I need you to know that I might be scared
I need you to know that I'm afraid I might hurt someone
I need you to ask about client artwork
I need help in learning about boundaries
I need to laugh
I need to be appreciated
I need space to grow

I need handholding sometimes
I need you to fill the silence
I need enthusiasm
I need you to take care of yourself
I need you to not burn out
I need a break sometimes
I need you to ask how I'm doing
I need you to push me when you know I can go further
I need you to help me grow
I need opportunities to try my own ideas
I need you to not take your frustrations out on me
I need you to support the work that I do
I need empathy
I need guidance
I need support
I need you to let me know I'm making a difference
I need a lunch break
I need to go home early some days
I need to be told to make my own art
I need to know that taking a day off when I'm sick is OK
I need reassurance
I need you to trust my judgment sometimes
I need no interruptions
I need independence
I need you to value my ideas and insight
I need structure
I need flexibility
I need your to realize how important you are to my experience and me
I need you.

(Heather Michel Riddle, Personal communication,
2007. Used with permission.)

Content from treatment that is processed in supervision brings personal and professional challenges for both the supervisee and supervisor. The boundaries of supervision must be clearly communicated and supported. It is important to differentiate issues relevant for supervision from those that should be taken to personal therapy. I encourage therapists to engage in supervision and in their own therapy as needed throughout their careers, supporting healthy practice and managing their personal issues. Supervisors should ground and explore their work through consultations with colleagues, their own supervision, personal therapy, and self-care in order to support the clarity of the services that they provide and their own well-being.

The use of imagery in supervision is a valuable resource that is seldom employed. Within the verbal supervisory relationship, both supervisor and supervisee combine

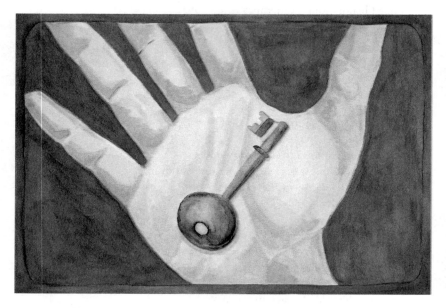

FIGURE 1.2 Key

Barbara Fish

their resources to understand and direct sound treatment for the client. Art-based supervision enlists their creative resources as well, using imagery and other expressive modalities to sort out the complexities of therapy.

My work with patients and clients has taught me the value of imagery for communication and clinical reflection. I painted *Key* (Figure 1.2) to represent the one I used to unlock the door to the art room in the state hospital where I worked for many years. In that space, patients and I ventured into our imaginations in a safe way through making and exploring imagery together. I remembered this piece as I wrote the narrative at the beginning of this chapter about the struggling supervisor and her painting of keys (Figure 1.1).

This book will delve into art-based methods for both supervisors and new therapists to understand and manage their work. The chapters that follow will discuss more art-based ways of supporting the complexities of clinical work and the challenges of the supervisory relationship. I hope these conversations will serve as keys to unlock new resources, deepening the experience, value, and efficacy of supervision.

Reference

Wilson, L., Riley, S., & Wadeson, H. (1984). Art therapy supervision. *Art Therapy: Journal of the American Art Therapy Association, 1*(3), 100–105.

2

A HISTORY OF ART-BASED SUPERVISION

Introduction

Clarity of purpose is essential to guide our use of imagery in therapy and in supervision to ensure that it is used as an effective tool and not as a dangerous distraction. As discussed in Chapter 1, it is the supervisor's task to oversee and ensure sound treatment while supporting the supervisee's professional development. Malchiodi and Riley (1996) stress the supervisor's responsibility to address clinical material that requires verbal instruction. There is a sound didactic component in art-based supervision. It consists of disseminating content, including standards of practice, ethical guidelines, informed consent, duty to warn, goal setting, and documentation.

To understand the use of imagery in supervision, let us turn from the fundamentals and look at its roots in the history of art therapy. Because of art therapy's foundation in psychological theory, the content of sessions and the supervision that supports them are similar to other forms of therapy and counseling. I offer this intellectual context for art-based supervision because the process and product of image making is at the heart of the work in art therapy. This is true whether it is used to address traditional therapeutic issues, including diagnosis, assessment, and treatment, or empowerment programs and social justice work. For this reason I am focusing on the roots of art-based supervision in art therapy.

Since the beginning of the field, art therapists have discussed the use of imagery for therapist insight and interpersonal understanding (Allen, 1995; Case, 2007b; Fish, 1989; Franklin, 1990; Henley, 1992; Henzell, 1997; Jones, 1983; Kielo, 1991; Kramer, 1971, 1979; Malchiodi & Riley, 1996; Moon, 1998; Naumburg, 1973, 1987; Robbins, 1973; Robbins & Seaver, 1976; Rubin, 1978, 1999; Wadeson, 1980; Wolf, 1990). Art therapists facilitate clients' creative expression as a way to explore and master their difficulties, supporting their strengths through metaphor.

Both the artmaking process and product are vehicles for insight and investigation. The work is accomplished within the therapeutic relationship while the therapist holds the therapeutic frame or space, finding interpersonal resonance with the client and acting as an advocate, artistic and life consultant, and witness. The image, created in session, is brought into supervision to inform the oversight of treatment. "... painting, drawing or sculpture made in therapy ... are part of the very tissue of the session; through them the event itself survives as a material object" (Henzell, 1997, p. 71).

Ulman (1961) honed a definition of art therapy, describing the essence and the image's role in this unique hybrid field.

> Therapeutic procedures are those designed to assist favorable changes in personality or in living that will outlast the session itself. ... [Image making's motivational] power comes from within the personality; it is a way of bringing order out of chaos—chaotic feelings and impulses within, the bewildering mass of impressions from without. It is a means to discover both the self and the world, and to establish a relation between the two. In the complete creative process, inner and outer realities are fused into a new entity.
>
> *(pp. 19–20)*

This description of the essential meaning-making functions at work in art therapy can be applied to the use of response art in supervision to conceptualize and guide treatment.

Other art therapists have worked to express what differentiates art therapy from other therapeutic practices. "Art is indeed the central core of art therapy. It is the only real excuse for existing as a separate discipline. Thus, art is the touchstone for determining the way transference and countertransference should be handled by art therapists" (Agell, Levick, Rhyne, Robbins, Rubin, Ulman, Wang, & Wilson, 1981, p. 6). By articulating that the use of imagery is the essential difference, these art therapists affirm art therapy's similarity to other forms of therapy as a treatment modality. The image, used as a creative response in art therapy, also holds value for supervision.

Although its initial roots are in European psychiatry and the analytic work of Freud and Jung, art therapy's scope of practice has expanded beyond the range of traditional psychotherapy. Current practice has grown to include the use of images to address psychiatric and medical issues as well as rehabilitation and personal growth, serving clients in sites that range from psychiatric treatment to community-based work (Vick, 1996).

Roots of Art Therapy

Art therapy came into being during the middle of the twentieth century, rooted in the fields of psychology and art (Rubin, 1999; Vick, 2003). Growing out of theories of psychoanalysis and art education in the United States and in Europe in the 1940s and 1950s, the field of art therapy was formalized in the United States with the establishment of the American Art Therapy Association in 1969 (Vick, 2003).

Before the development of formal art therapy training, early art therapists learned their craft as they were mentored on-site by experienced clinicians including social workers, psychologists, or psychiatrists (Case, 2007b). Since the beginning of art therapy, new therapists have brought artworks made by their clients to more experienced practitioners, seeking support and direction for their work with clients.

The American Art Therapy Association established Professional Standards of Practice as well as criteria for training. Art therapy registration (ATR), the field's postgraduate credential, was established in the early 1970s; the standardization and approval of educational training programs followed (Junge & Asawa, 1994). After that, the professional regulating bodies required that formal supervision be provided as part of academic, postgraduate training.

In the 1980s, the art therapy literature in the United States and Europe began to reflect this new attention to supervision (Calisch, 1994, 1995; Malchiodi & Riley, 1996; Moon, 1992; Robbins, 1988a, 1988b; Schaverien & Case, 2007; Wilson, Riley, & Wadeson, 1984). This emphasis on supervision became a standard ensconced in art therapy graduate training and was required for postgraduate art therapy registration (ATR).

At that time, the supervision discourse focused primarily on the exploration of client work and the investigation of the countertransference of therapists in training (Fish, 1989; Kielo, 1991; Linesch, Holmes, Morton, & Shields, 1989; Robbins, 1973, 1988a, 1988b; Wadeson, 1980; Wolf, 1990). Since then the discussion has expanded to support comprehensive issues encountered while providing therapy (Franklin, 1999; Malchiodi, 1998; Malchiodi & Riley, 1996; Moon, 1998, 2000; Schaverien & Case, 2007).

From the beginning of art therapy, therapists have brought images made by clients while in session into supervision as the foundation for discussion and case presentation of clinical process and progress. The exploration of client artwork used in this way is discussed throughout art therapy literature (Brandoff & Lombardi, 2012; Henzell, 1997; Malchiodi & Riley, 1996; Wakeman, 2013). Imagery made as part of treatment holds value and is often an underutilized resource for supervision in other disciplines.

Imagery in Training

Experiential learning is a core component of art therapy training and an integral part of supervision. It helps new therapists acquire and affirm knowledge from didactic material and engage in self-reflection (Malchiodi & Riley, 1996). Schuck and Wood (2011) considered traditional pedagogical approaches to supervision to be limited as they focus on the role of the educator or supervisor as instructor and do not consider the participatory role of adult learners. They proposed andragogy, an approach to learning that supports students' self-direction (Knowles, 1973), as opposed to pedagogy, where the teacher is in control of the content and dissemination of material. This approach calls for students to actively engage with content as they acquire and synthesize knowledge, taking ownership and responsibility for their experience. Deaver and Shiflett (2011) also included educational theory in their discussion of art-based supervision.

> Artmaking as a reflective practice results in an art product that is a metaphor for the idea and processes entailed in its creation. Furthermore, that art production is an object external to ourselves that can then become the focus of reflection (Dahlman, 2007; Eisner, 2001). This occurs when art produced by supervisees is discussed in supervision.
>
> *(p. 260)*

These approaches to therapist training and professional development support effective communication and are consistent with the intent of art-based supervision. This material is selected to encourage supervisors and supervisees to add the use of their own imagery, made in response to clinical work, to their discourse, deepening their understanding of treatment and their relationship to it.

Art therapists Case (2007a, 2007b) and Deaver and Shiflett (2011) comprehensively surveyed the history of imagery in supervision. Case focused on art psychotherapy supervision. Deaver and Shiflett reviewed the work of art therapists, counseling therapists, educators, and nurses, and its application for case conceptualization, to process countertransference and for self-care. They contended that this paradigm for art-based supervision is an effective way to view the use of media and metaphor that ". . . embraces the notion of knowledge development through engagement in the reflective process" (p. 259). I encourage you to visit their valuable work. I will highlight some of the authors they mention, adding others who have contributed their practices to the discussion of art-based supervision.

Much of the literature addressing the use of imagery in supervision focuses on its value in therapist training. New therapists' first experience of their own work is powerful and benefits from multilayered processing. Robbins and Seaver (1976) were early proponents of incorporating expressive modalities into graduate training and postgraduate supervision. They advocated for creative expression to support new therapists' reflection on clinical material and its effects on the therapist.

> In many respects, art therapy can supply a missing dimension in education and psychotherapy. Both fields of late have become increasingly pragmatic and behavior oriented in their approach. These trends are an understandable reaction to a naïve, often simplistic, application of psychodynamic theory. However, in this reaction there lies a potential danger in overlooking the positive values of an orientation concerned with development of the inner being. Symptomatic release, mastery skills and effective performance are goals that need not preclude, but may accompany, an inner search for one's

self. All too often, the worlds of performance and self-development have become compartmentalized. Clinical evidence has long indicated a firm relationship between sensory, perceptual and cognitive growth (Arnheim, 1969). Enlightened art therapy practice can address itself to these multiple areas and offer an experience that helps the patient to deal effectively with the inner as well as the outer world.

(Robbins & Seaver, 1976, p. 253)

Later, Robbins (1988a) offered a "psychoaesthetic" (p. 98) approach to therapist training, providing expressive exercises to help students conceptualize treatment and their responses to it. Robbins advocated for "countertransference education" [in supervision to] "promote the development of each therapist's unique aesthetic style in the processing of and responding to the subcurrents of treatment communications" (p. 98). Robbins (1988b) said, "The therapist's emotional connection to his or her case is in fact, the basic tool of treatment." He went on to say, "Trust your unconscious, for it can offer creative solutions that bypass the world of linear logic" (p. 11).

Lahad (2000) emphasized the utility of the analogical dream-like mechanisms of the brain's right hemisphere to help to understand the process of therapy, intervention, and support. He combined humanistic and expressive approaches, offering both a literal and a metaphoric discussion of supervision. His stories and creative exercises, used to support new therapists' work, employed dialogue and were fundamental to his supervisory practice.

Wadeson (1980, 1987, 2003) saw developing students' self-awareness as an important part of art therapy training. She advocated for the use of the students' images as a potent tool to understand personal issues and motivations related to their clinical work and to provide feedback to one another. While supporting students' involvement in personal therapy, she also believed that their artwork was an important resource for gaining self-awareness related to their practice. Wolf (1990) encouraged the use of imagery to investigate clinical material, relying primarily on the use of artwork stimulated by the therapist's responses to treatment.

. . . we continue to demonstrate the power of the non-verbal part of ourselves which is constantly reaching to the non-verbal part of our patients and ourselves. Students become highly sensitized to the power of their own imagery, and its ability to transcend secondary process defenses.

(p. 64)

Wolf (1990) urged supervisees to extend the utility of their imagery by asking therapy trainees to make spontaneous images in class to give feedback about one another's clinical presentations.

This technique demonstrated how the peer group can focus on non-verbal levels of communication offered by the presenter. The instructor structures the resulting discussion to explore images which arise in response to both the patient's and presenter's unconscious process.

(p. 64)

Carpendale (2011) described the potential of imagery used in supervision to consolidate experience by looking at its unique ability to reflect the process and content of therapy. "Art can be viewed as holding or mirroring the essence of the art therapy session and it survives the session as a material object. Images hold the possibility of simultaneity, which is impossible in discursive or verbal communication" (p. 25).

Those teaching in graduate training programs incorporate image making into art therapy coursework to facilitate experiential learning. During an informal survey of art therapists, supervisors, and clinicians, Malchiodi and Riley (1996) determined that "approximately half of the respondents indicated that art making was a method they used at some time during supervision" (p. 99). They described the role of the supervisor in supporting supervisees' imagery as a clinical and professional resource.

> Being able to witness the work with a sense of objectivity may be the most helpful, thus respecting the very tender place that many novice supervisee's [sic] are in with regard to their work with clients and their own developing identities. Often just letting the trainee tell the story of his or her art will bring up enough ideas and questions for discussion. If art therapists believe that much of the learning and growth in art therapy goes on during the art process, then a great deal of understanding will take place in a carefully chosen and defined visual assignment and sensitive witnessing of the resultant image.
>
> *(pp. 101–102)*

An early example of imagery used in the supervisory relationship to support communication is the work of Perach, Durkin, Ramseyer, and Sontag (1989). They looked at their training experiences as art therapy intern and supervisor dyads, developing a method to reflect on their practice by making art and engaging in journaling. This form of reflective listening helped them to clarify their communication. Their use of creative investigation added to their supervisory experience, helping them to reflect on their work with their clients and with one another. "As communication was enhanced significantly within the dyad, a format for a more generative relationship formed in which professional growth and learning took place" (p. 429). Case noted "as far as is known, this [example of imagery used in supervision] is unique in exploring the *supervisory relationship* with art rather than the therapist/client relationship" (Case, 2007b, p. 13).

Calisch (1994) advocated for the use of imagery as an important and underutilized tool in learning, teaching, and supervision. She contended that the use of imagery "enhances and varies the abilities in information processing allowing greater creativity and integration" (p. 34). Wilkins (1995) engaged supervisee dyads in psychodrama and drawing to explore the counselor-client relationship. He asserted that his procedure brought insight about the therapeutic relationship. This method "allow[s] a greater spontaneity and an opportunity to convey deep personal meanings in a way which other approaches may not" (p. 256).

Ireland and Weissman (1999) encouraged interns to make images after sessions to process their experiences about their encounters. Exploring their pieces in supervision led interns to increased understanding of clinical work, including their transference and countertransference reactions. Ireland and Weissman described the utility of these images.

> At first, the therapist's drawings may be only an evacuation of his or her own unbearable emotions stirred in session, but . . . even in that event the drawings can then be used by the supervisor in teaching the trainee therapist the value of holding his or her emotional reactions until they can be thought about, and then inform a clinical intervention.
>
> *(p. 83)*

Brown, Meyerowitz, and Ryde (2007) differentiate the use of images made by student therapists as part of a supervision group from those made in an experiential art group.

> What differentiates it is the focus of the understanding of all the communication in the group in terms of the clinical work. The image has been in the context of supervision; the transformed unconscious of the student can then be taken back and used in the service of therapy. . . . As Rees says, "It seems sad that the power image-making process harnessed so effectively in therapeutic situations are not more regularly exploited as part of the art therapy supervisory scenario" (Rees, 1998, p. 237). It seems so logical to use the tools of our profession in the supervisory process in order to deepen our understanding of our clinical work.
>
> *(pp. 179–180)*

Investigating the Image

Analytic art therapists advocate for the use of imaginal methods to investigate imagery in supervision to inform clinical practice.

> The Jungian theory of active imagination lends itself to the exploration of art within the therapeutic relationship (Schaverien, 2005) and, extending this idea, supervision might be considered a form of shared active imagination.

It emerges, between therapist and supervisor, as they conjure an essence of the therapist's experience of the client and the pictures.

(Schaverien, 2007, p. 45)

Case (2007b) described the work of Maclagan (1997), who explored the use of imagery and fantasy in therapy and in supervision.

What Maclagan describes is akin to Jung's (1937) "active imagination", a technique for exploring fantasy. Maclagan argues against what he sees as a "class structure of fantasy" wanting to work with all fantasy as an ally, through therapy and supervision in imaginative elaboration.

(p. 20)

Henzell (1997) explained the utility of the image as a representative from treatment. He said, "Whilst memory always runs the risk of expunging what was only said from the record, or distorting it, the image remains as the mute witness and embodiment of an intention" (p. 75). Henzell went on to differentiate diagrammatic images from embodied images, describing the difference in their uses. He said diagrammatic images are "schematic images made with simple materials which serve as prompts for conversation. Although often said to be 'spontaneously' produced, they are destined, and frequently implicitly intended, to be translated into therapy talk" (p. 75).

[Embodied images] possess the power to sort, discriminate and combine perceptions from apparently disparate realms of experience with extraordinary speed and force—just because they avoid lexicale structures. The essence of the image, particularly the invited image, is that it directly *presents* rather than indirectly *describes* its concerns.

(p. 76)

Schaverien (1992) described this differentiation concisely. "Whilst the diagrammatic picture stays within known territory, the embodied image transcends what is consciously known" (p. 87).

These art therapists and others recommended that student therapists create artwork about their clients as part of their training. I agree with Allen (1995), Robbins (1988a, 1988b), Wadeson (1980), and Wolf (1990), who took this practice further by making images as a part of their roles as teachers and supervisors. Moon (2000) believed that the supervisor had an important opportunity to mentor supervisees by making images alongside them to help develop empathy in their relationship, provide an expressive outlet for feelings, and serve as a starting point for supervisory dialogue.

Robbins, an art therapist and educator who focused on the use of expressive modalities in supervision, said, "Supervision is an art form taking place within a professional relationship" (2007, p. 153). Calisch (1995) defined metatherapy as supervision focusing on the relationship's transactional process that mirrors that of the therapist and client. Describing supervision as "a therapy of therapy," she shifts the focus of supervision "from an exclusive emphasis on client pathology and therapist technique to a wider concern with the therapist–client relationship" (p. 127). She advocated for the use of imagery in this process to access a fuller observation of the therapeutic relationship.

Response Art

Art therapy literature explores some of the ways that art therapists use imagery in their work. These include making response art in session to reflect and communicate the therapist's understanding of the client's experience, provide client feedback in session, and empathize with the client's experience during or after session. Image making is useful outside of therapy as well, supporting the therapist's understanding of the work. Images used for the therapist's clarity of purpose bring clinical and personal insights, supporting sound work (Fish, 1989, 2008, 2012; Franklin, 1990, 1999; Lachman-Chapin, 1983; Malchiodi & Riley, 1996; Miller, 2007; Moon, 1998, 2007; C. Moon, 2001; Robbins, 1988b; Wadeson, 2003; Wolf, 1985).

Art-based supervision uses images and image making as a forum for the exploration of internship issues and professional material (Deaver & Shiflett, 2011; Fish, 2008; Wadeson, 1987, 2003). The heart of art-based supervision is response art that is made by both supervisees and supervisors before, during, and after sessions. Many have discussed the use of response art in art therapy (Fish, 1989, 2006, 2012; Franklin, 1999; Havsteen-Franklin, 2014; Kielo, 1991; Miller, 2007; Moon, 1998; Wadeson, 2003). Response art refers to imagery made about the therapist's work to hold experiences, investigate them, and communicate them to others (Fish, 2012). The use of response art in supervision provides a method to hold experiences while engaging in empathic resonance. It presents a forum for conceptualizing treatment and investigating interpersonal dynamics including transference and countertransference. Further, it supports therapists' effective work by facilitating the communication of challenging and nuanced content.

By engaging in this use of imagery, the supervisor leads by example, demonstrating the use of response art to explore clinical issues as well as his or her own personal concerns. Response art can hold an empathic response, investigate the content of treatment, and facilitate communication within therapeutic and supervisory relationships. This method frames our discussion of this history of art-based supervision.

Empathy

Empathy is the ability to understand and share the feelings of another person. Supervision supports therapy by clarifying and helping to remove impediments to the therapist's compassionate engagement with the client. In a parallel manner, the supervisor's empathic understanding of the therapist and his or her work is the foundation for their supervisory alliance. Clark (2007), relating the history of empathy, said that the concept was first used in the field of aesthetics to describe a felt response to nature. Seen in this light, it follows that images might help us understand and align with the feeling states of others. Making and processing imagery can shore up and deepen empathy, supporting this necessary interaction.

Tolstoy (1899) contended that the function of art is to recollect emotions and make them conscious, eliciting empathy in the viewer. His ideas can help us to appreciate the role of images in supervision.

> To evoke in oneself a feeling one has once experienced, and having evoked it in oneself, then, by means of movements, lines, colours, sounds, or forms expressed in words, so to transmit that feeling that others may experience the same feeling this is the activity of art.
>
> *(p. 50)*

Imagery used in supervision supports both the supervisee's and supervisor's resonance with therapeutic material. Response art can help both parties work with content from session, externalizing it and offering a conduit for empathy.

Many authors have explored the use of images to cultivate empathy in their work. Kramer (1971), an art therapy pioneer, discussed the potential intensity of the therapeutic relationship and its challenge for the therapist.

> In the therapeutic interchange the psychotherapist maintains a state of openness toward the patient's communications, allowing them to find an echo in his own inner life. The precision and subtlety of his responses depend equally on his knowledge and training and on his capacity for empathy.
>
> *(p. 89)*

Other art therapists advocated for the use of the therapist's art to attain deeper understanding and empathy for the client (Fish, 1989, 2012; Franklin, 1990, 1999, 2010; Kielo, 1991; Lachman-Chapin, 1983; Miller, 2007; Ramseyer, 1990; Rubin, 2001; Wadeson, 1987, 2003). Ramseyer (1990) described how she used her own images, made after sessions, to understand difficult feelings aroused by clients. She contended that using her images to explore her clinical relationships helped her establish "visual empathy" (p. 118). Franklin examined empathy through his own clinical practice as he made art in sessions with his clients. He referred to this interactive process as his "visual empathic response" (1990, p. 44). He contended that, "The active expression of this information through the use of art materials allows us to share that which we have formed. The viewer sets in motion the self-object relationships of the empathic cycle" (p. 46). Later, Franklin

(2010) described the utility of his "visual art responses" (p. 160). He spoke about the value of this use of the therapist's images. "With careful attunement, art therapists can develop unique, aesthetic forms of empathic resonance that will help clients feel deeply seen and develop empathy for themselves and compassion for others" (p. 160).

Some art therapists make imagery alongside their clients within session, finding it useful to cultivate empathy (Fish, 1989, 2012; Franklin, 1990, 1999, 2010; Lachman-Chapin, 1983; Rubin, 2001). In Allen's words, "Making art together breaks down barriers between people, creating compassion and empathy" (1995, p. 163). Art therapist Moon (1998) agreed, "... whenever art therapists make art in direct response to patients or their images, they open up the possibility for [the] deepening of relationships" (pp. 61–62).

Art therapist Lachman-Chapin (1979) looked at the function of the image as part of the mirroring transference during session. She proposed that the image served as a self-object for the therapist to attend to with empathy and vicarious introspection. Lachman-Chapin said that she made art in session along with the client "using my own art as a kind of mirroring response" (p. 8).

Rubin (2001), an art therapist and analyst, discussed making images along with clients to create empathy. She engaged in a parallel process where she and the client made art side by side and discussed the images when they were finished. Rubin focused intensely on the client's issues as she worked. She understood the role of the art pieces in session from Kohut's theoretical perspective, seeing the images as "self objects" for the client and therapist to explore together.

Sustaining empathy requires self-care. Finding ways to attend to ourselves during and after session makes it possible for us to sustain our focus on the client. By making imagery we can physically handle media as we work with the content of session. This sensory response can help us remain open to the work and find empathic resonance. Making response art is a way to hold our reactions, allowing us the time and space to reflect on them, bringing closure to our work and the freedom to move on.

Many therapists support their ability to participate empathically with clients by making images to self-soothe and contain difficult experiences during and after sessions. Wolf (1990) advocated for the use of personal imagery to manage the effects of engaging in clinical work in order to sustain it.

> I have become increasingly aware of the importance of my artwork in facilitating an important avenue of discharge of these feelings. At times when I am struggling with how to deal with a particularly difficult patient I seek the organizing effect of the sculpting process. Other times I may just need a more general experience of seeing some concrete change effected by my energy to counterbalance the painfully slow and imperceptible changes in certain patients, which tend to build up as frustrations within me.
>
> *(p. 69)*

Art therapist Lavery (1994) worked with youth who were primarily wards of the state at his internship at a psychiatric hospital.

> The detailed descriptions of abuse, violence, and death related in group therapy by these inner city adolescents left me in a state of shock. My emotions were stirred during these sessions, and I felt an intense need to make art.
>
> *(p. 14)*

Lavery developed a three-part image making process that he engaged in outside of session and processed on his own during supervision. His practice helped him to hold the content and manage all that he felt after he listened to the youth describe their intense experiences. Lavery's image making was a resource for managing the difficult material he encountered in therapy as well as sustaining his empathy for the patients.

Gasman, an art therapy intern at a pediatric medical hospital, worked with her own images outside of session to cope with her responses to the dire circumstances that she witnessed there. She made and reflected on her artwork while working with a boy with leukemia in order to unravel her reactions to his disease. "Gasman realized that the picture shows how transfixed she was on how poor Billy's prognosis could be and how traumatized she felt by this possibility" (Wadeson, 2000, p. 140). Gasman's artwork was a resource for reflection and self-care, supporting her empathic response to her patient and helping her find relief from it.

The therapist's sustained attachment to the client is critical to treatment (Schaverien, 1995). He or she may be more able to maintain investment in work with challenging clients, or those that stir countertransference, when an empathic connection is established. Maintaining responsiveness may be difficult when those we work with reenact interpersonal impediments from the past or activate our own countertransference. Image making as part of supervision can help to shore up empathy. Because images can express emotions that may be difficult to articulate with words, they may be used as an important resource for maintaining the investment necessary for treatment.

Managing empathy, and other difficult affects, is an ongoing challenge for those providing both treatment and supervision. Witnessing the work of clients can expose therapists to disturbing content. Our own empathic responses to traumatic and painful stories can be hard to manage. Without a way to hold and cope with what we feel, we may leave sessions filled with the emotions of another. The focused attention and intimacy of therapeutic work must be balanced with healthy boundaries, realistic perspectives, and self-awareness in order to preserve the therapist's equilibrium.

Rogers (1961), the founder of humanistic psychology, discussed the personal challenge that the therapist faces when holding him or herself open in an empathic exchange. He encouraged therapists to be brave in their communication, relinquishing judgments as they focused on the client. He cautioned that this openness to empathy has an impact on the therapist.

> If you really understand another person in this way, if you are willing to enter his private world and see the way life appears to him, without any attempt to make evaluative judgments you run the risk of being changed yourself. You might see it his way, you might find yourself influenced in your attitudes or your personality. This risk of being changed is one of the most frightening prospects most of us face.
>
> *(p. 333)*

Both therapists and supervisors should heed Rogers's warning. Empathic connections established in treatment can open us to the experiences of clients and supervisees in ways that affect us deeply, leaving us changed in ways that may take work to understand. This is a fundamental reason for the use of imagery in supervision. This resource can hold toxic material encountered in therapy and supervision while helping us excavate and examine its meaning professionally and personally (Fish, 2014).

Robbins (1988b) also warned therapists of the challenges that accompany empathic resonance.

> Being a psychoanalytic therapist creates an ongoing and grueling emotional balancing act. In order to be effective therapists we must maintain an appropriate objective emotional distance from our patients while, at the same time, we transmit an essence of humanity as we touch our patient's raw emotional nerves. We also try to be openly receptive to our patient's communications, offering ourselves as "containers" for such intensely powerful affects as abandonment, rage, loss, and love. This state of containment requires an emotional centering of ourselves, and demands that we put aside the stresses of our personal daily lives when we enter the office and confine our patient's confidential struggle to a very private section of our psyche.
>
> *(p. 13)*

Robbins's caution reminds us of the necessity for resources to manage the intensity of our practice. The use of the therapist's imagery in supervision is a powerful tool that must be employed mindfully. To ensure the positive use of images in supervision and in therapy, it is critical to be attentive to the potential for their misuse. Employed without intention, image making can distract us from important material or soothe us into inaction. With that caution, I support Robbins's (1973) contention that the creativity of art therapists should be applied to their work, using it as needed to create understanding personally, interpersonally, and in the communities where they work. This applies to art therapy educators and supervisors as well as those from other disciplines who are engaged in clinical practice.

The course of therapy is affected by the internal states of the client, therapist, and supervisor. Supervision supports the therapist's sustained investment in clients. Many clients come to treatment with interpersonal and behavioral barriers developed in response to negative experiences from the past. Just as the therapist is challenged when the client discusses past trauma vividly in therapy, so is the supervisor as the therapist relates his or her experience of it. I join Deaver and Shiflett (2011), Franklin (2010), Moon (2000), Robbins (1988a, 2007), and Schaverien and Case (2007) in recommending that we extend the utility of the therapist's imagery into supervision, allowing it to guide those who provide therapy as well as support those who supervise them.

Response art, created as part of art-based supervision, provides a vehicle for engaging material that is interpersonally distancing or difficult to witness, or that resonates with the therapist's or supervisor's own issues. Imagery offers a way to engage and hold challenging material while the therapist explores it in order to understand its significance. When imagery is engaged as a supervisory resource, it affords the supervisee and supervisor the opportunity to share their process, demonstrating their attention to one another's experience.

Response art holds the potential to support the therapist's efforts to maintain his or her emotional health while sustaining difficult work. However, image making may not always be the best recourse. Imagery used this way can pull the therapist's focus from looking at difficult material that has implications for his or her own well-being. I have made images about interactions or work conditions to calm and soothe myself. Looking back at the images, I can see that I turned away from the issues that eventually caused me to resign from the job. A frank supervisory discussion might have helped me to clarify my resolve to look at my situation realistically. Sensory involvement with media may calm our brains, but it does not inform our action unless we engage it with that clarity of purpose. Having a distinct intention for the work is critical when using response art or any other tool for self-care.

Our empathic responses to clients often resonate with our own experiences. Imagery created and made for use in supervision is a way to process this content and reflect on our relationship to it. London, an artist and art educator, said, "The creative process has the potential to wake us up to the vast unexplored domain of our own nature" (1989, p. 46). Used in this way, art-based supervision leads us to a discussion of countertransference and the use of imagery to untangle this complex response to treatment.

Countertransference

Supervision is a forum for therapists' introspection, often challenging us to grow personally as we work to manage the practical aspects of treatment. Psychoanalytic and depth psychologists contributed the concept of the unconscious to psychological theory. They contend that the unconscious of both the client and the therapist are stirred in treatment; the therapist's response is referred to as countertransference. A classic definition of countertransference is the unconscious response of the therapist to the client. A later definition (Corey, Corey, & Callanan, 2011) extended the perspective to encompass all of the responses the therapist has to the client, whether or not they are unconscious. The supervisor may also have personal issues that are stirred by the work of those that he or she supervises. These are based on the supervisor's prior relationships and experiences as well as his or her current involvement with the supervisee and his or her clients.

Countertransference may be investigated and understood by making art (Fish, 1989; Kielo, 1991; Lachman-Chapin, 1983; McNiff, 1989; Miller, 2007; Moon, 1998; Wolf, 1985, 1990). Image making often helps to clarify the therapist's view of the client, alleviating confusion stemming from the therapist's personal issues stirred by clinical work. The therapist may use imagery to address issues related to the therapeutic relationship in supervision. This personal work supports the therapist's ability to maintain his or her focus on the client. Any intense reaction felt by the clinician or supervisor can be a cue to make response art to sort out feelings about the work. I turn to images when I feel irritation, dislike, disappointment, frustration, disinterest in the work, or lack of clarity. I also make imagery when I have overly positive reactions to address positive countertransference as well.

Images made during or brought to supervision can form the foundation for investigating reactions to clients and the content that they bring to session. The therapist's artwork may convey the first inkling of countertransference helping to inform treatment. Supervision functions within a relationship, as does therapy. Our responses to one another hold valuable information that, if ignored, can be an impediment or, if investigated and understood, can support therapy.

I saw an art therapist for the supervision of her clinical practice at a residential agency for children and her work as a beginning supervisor. As therapists in the early years of their practice become new supervisors, they often seek the guidance of a more experienced professional to help them navigate the challenges. She painted *Tank* (Figure 2.1) as we discussed her supervisory relationship in order to help her understand her work with her supervisee. Reflecting on the piece, she said that the intern was "sort of running her own thing and maybe trying to just take over." Her painting depicts her arms outstretched trying to hold the tank, representing the intern, at bay. She painted blood on the ground around the tank that she said represented the level of violence present at the agency at the time. She said that she knew that the intern was overwhelmed and upset by the trauma that she witnessed there.

> It felt like she was charging at me almost like a bull or a tank, like she was going to run me down or gun me down. When I did this painting with you, I realized that the tank was so armored and protected that no bullets could get through to it. It's the ultimate ground war vehicle. The tank represented how vulnerable and guarded she was. Maybe her wanting to take over was

FIGURE 2.1 Tank

Anonymous

> her need to feel safe and in control of the situation. The painting helped me
> to realize that that is a big piece of her too. Maybe this was more a part of it
> than feeling like she was trying to run me down that I hadn't quite grasped.
> I knew it but seeing it in the image was really different.
>
> *(Anonymous, Personal communication, May 22, 2015)*

Painting and reflecting on this image helped the new supervisor realize how to work more effectively with her intern without feeling intimidated by her. The painting, created in the supervisor's own supervision, helped her to see the intern's vulnerability. This provided her with insight into a different way to approach, understand, and provide supervisory support for the intern.

Robbins (1988b) explored the dynamics of countertransference in relationship to art therapy from a psychoanalytic perspective. He believed that the therapist's use of self, cued by a visceral response to the patient, is an important resource to address countertransference issues. "Defended patients transmit nonverbally their symbolic material and the therapist becomes a receptacle for this material which will in turn demand some type of inner exploration" (p. 41). As "receptacles," therapists need ways to move that material out of themselves for their own well-being. Art-based supervision offers unique resources for conceptualizing counter-transference and supporting the healthy investigation of this content.

In my own work (Fish, 1989), I investigated the use of image making to address countertransference, exploring my work with hospitalized adult psychiatric patients. During that inquiry, I made images after sessions when relationships with patients felt unclear or problematic. The images helped me to understand the relationships and processes that unfolded in treatment, sometimes learning that the issues were rooted in interpersonal dynamics within the session. Other times the lack of clarity came from my unresolved personal issues stirred by interactions that I had with patients.

Allen (1995), an art therapist and educator, recommended the use of imagery to explore relationships in therapy as they involve unequal power. She warned that those that we work with might not recognize when we, as their therapists or supervisors, may be responding to our own unrelated issues. It is our responsibility to be vigilant in our efforts to deal responsibly with our use of power, allowing us to respond with clarity and focus to our patients' concerns.

Allen (1995) recalled a troublesome relationship with a supervisee whom she worked with in graduate fieldwork supervision. She turned to her own imagery to explore the irritation she felt about the intern's unconditional acceptance of the authority of experts. Allen's artwork helped her shift her focus from her supervisee to the personal issues that the interaction aroused in her. Allen became aware that the intern's experience brought up her own feelings about allowing her own common sense to be overridden in deference to established theory. This helped Allen understand her personal issue stirred in supervision while detoxifying a potentially harmful reaction to her student.

> You may find your irritation or idealization shift or disappear once you place your conflict in the realm of the image. This frees you to relate to the person in simpler and less charged terms. Most important, it lets you know what qualities in yourself require your attention.
>
> *(p. 173)*

Wadeson (1990), an art therapist and educator, made images to investigate her own countertransference issues, exploring why she was fascinated with her clients' dark side. She made masks outside of session, formed on her own face, to explore and connect to her clients' painful material. This was her personal work, created outside of session, to gain self-awareness. "The mask is a metaphor, an image that tells me of my fascination with the underside, the dark side" (pp. 108–109). Reflecting on the importance of the therapist's awareness to avoid mining the clients' issues out of her own repressed need for excitement, Wadeson said, "The key to working with patients in an emotionally non-exploitive, clinically responsible way is self-awareness" (p. 110). Imagery used to explore countertransference in supervision supports this work toward insight.

It is important to be mindful of the boundary between training experiences and therapy when we are addressing countertransference in supervision.

Malchiodi and Riley (1996) warn supervisors to avoid unwarranted focus on the supervisee's personal issues, ensuring that the focus of supervision remains on the client's treatment. "It may become a delicate balance when art making, which can quickly bring emotional content to the surface, is relied upon for a large part of the supervisory experience" (p. 111).

Images made in supervision can reveal intensely personal issues. The supervisor must understand when the image leads to material that is important to explore to clear the way for responsible treatment and when it is necessary to refer the student to his or her own therapy. The supervisor must also be aware of his or her own power in this relationship. Our images are an open door. It takes the supervisor's self-awareness and clarity of intention to explore the images responsibly.

Communication

London (1989) said, "art can be said to be—and can be used as—the externalized map of our interior self" (p. 34). Because therapy is rooted in nuanced communication within the therapeutic relationship, as well as the supervisory one, it makes sense to utilize all available resources to support and clarify personal and interpersonal understanding. Imagery used as a part of supervision can communicate treatment and interpersonal issues by manifesting them externally, adding to the verbal discourse.

Deaver and Shiflett (2011) viewed art-based supervision from a constructivist perspective, describing it as experiential learning. In that light, imagery used in supervision offers opportunities to make meaning by reworking past experiences, in the context of new information, through active engagement with the material. Working with imagery is a way to handle the content by engaging media and metaphor to communicate and deepen understanding.

There are many ways to configure the use of art in supervision. Some supervisees bring art to supervision from session while others make imagery outside of supervision and bring it to help to conceptualize the work. Still others make art as part of supervision to ground themselves during discussions, helping them to more fully explore the content. Art-based supervision employs response art in all of these ways. How it is employed depends on the learning styles and needs of the participants. Both supervisees and supervisors are encouraged to make and explore imagery in response to their clinical work to expand their understanding and to communicate effectively with one another.

Franklin (2010) explained how the therapist's imagery supports the communication of affect in session.

> Art therapists are in a unique position to build on intersubjective understanding by mindfully utilizing empathic art to receive, consolidate, and

offer back expressions of deflected affect to their clients. In doing so, potentially disorganized emotions can be responded to with art and skillful verbal and visual listening.

(p. 166)

Creating and exploring imagery is a valuable resource for experiential learning and communication in supervision. Images made by clients, therapy students in training, and new professionals and supervisors, and then investigated individually and in groups, offer unique opportunities to access issues and concepts reflecting them back to the individual from new perspectives.

For art therapists, the use of our own images to investigate and communicate our work parallels the way we work with clients. . . . It is a form of active listening that uses imagery as well as words. As supervisors using images to communicate with art therapy interns, we lead by example.

(Fish, 2008, p. 76)

Participants in art-based supervision regularly work with materials, engaging in nonobjective sensory activity as well as making more formed images during sessions. This engagement with media calms the nervous system, grounding participants and making them more receptive to verbal discussions of traumatic or other difficult material (Perry & Szalaviz, 2006; van der Kolk, McFarlane, & Weisaeth, 1996).

The image making process and product may be the focus or backdrop for the unfolding discourse. Response art includes spontaneous uncensored images, stimulated by unconscious material roused in session, as well as carefully planned and articulated pieces that are made over time and considered in the realm of conscious thoughts and attitudes. Creating imagery that holds, investigates, and communicates clinical content orients and supports discussion and multifaceted understanding, leading to insight and the clear transmission of supervisory content. Making and investigating images can transcend defenses or help to shore them up. This work should be carefully incorporated into verbal discussions so that it supports the work of supervision and does not distract from it.

Research

Examples of research supporting the use of imagery in supervision include the work of Fish (2008), Kielo (1991), and Deaver and McAuliffe (2009). In her qualitative study, Kielo interviewed art therapists about their postsession imagery used to reflect on their work. The therapists reported varied levels of involvement, and several indicated that they found value in the process, gaining insight and clarifying countertransference issues. In my own research (Fish, 2008), I investigated the use of response art in art-based supervision during art therapy training as a formative evaluation. My study indicated that students found response art valuable; their comments stressed the importance of a foundation of trust and safety in supervision. They also discussed the importance of a careful balance between art-based investigation and more direct verbal instruction disseminating practical, didactic information in supervision.

> [My research reinforced that] making art in supervision is a tool, not a panacea. Art-based supervision is not innately good and response art does not remedy all difficulties. As educators [and supervisors], we have limited time in which to train art therapists. Balancing the effective use of response art in supervision with verbal problem solving is critical to our success.
>
> *(Fish, 2008, p. 76)*

Deaver and McAuliffe (2009) engaged in a qualitative, multiple-case study that investigated the combination of visual journaling, image making, and verbal reflection in supervision to support art therapists and counselors in training. "The imagery depicted emotional reactions to internship, complex and confusing situations, and imagined solutions to problems, and was an effective catalyst for in-depth discussions. . . . The journals themselves became catalysts for reflection" (p. 630).

Deaver and Shiflett (2011) discussed three related articles written in the late 1980s that explored the use of imagery in supervision. Amundson (1988) discussed the use of drawings and collage, made to explore treatment metaphorically, to focus case discussion and to support the synthesis of clinical material. Ishiyama (1988) provided guidelines for a "visual case processing method" (p. 154), a process for creating images for case conceptualization in supervision, elaborating on the work of Amundson (1988). This standardized approach was intended to make the process predictable, facilitating its use for clinical practice and research. Stone and Amundson (1989) wrote about their research to determine the effectiveness of what they called "metaphoric case drawing" (p. 362). They implemented their procedure during group supervision provided to counselor trainees working within a crisis intervention agency. Participating counselors processed their work after crisis interventions through verbal processing or metaphoric case drawings. Stone and Amundson implemented a questionnaire assessing counselors' experiences of these two methods. In the drawing method, trainees "translate the thought-metaphor into a representative case drawing, which would then be the central feature of the trainee-directed case debriefing" (p. 363). Stone and Amundson concluded that the metaphoric case drawings "demonstrated a concise, visual framework which played a pivotal role for integrating trainees' thoughts, feelings, and experience" (p. 369).

In recent years, those engaging in art-based research have explored the value of art-based ways of acquiring knowledge and understanding. Beyond the use of response art to address personal or countertransference issues, making and investigating imagery can be a method used for art-based research. Images can be employed in narrative, heuristic, and phenomenological investigation (Allen, 1995; Fish, 2006, 2013; McNiff, 1998, 2013). The discussion of art-based research is beyond the scope of this work. However, it is important to note that many of the methods that researchers use for finding and communicating understanding are consistent with the use of imagery in supervision. I encourage you to investigate these resources to bolster your own ideas for creative means of investigation.

Ethical Considerations

Deaver and Shiflett (2011) raised ethical considerations and advised practitioners of art-based supervision to work within the area of their professional training and competency. They stressed the importance of providing clearly articulated informed consent for supervisees specifying the supervisor's art-based methods and his or her training in their use. They also said that imagery made in supervision should be treated with the same consideration as that made in therapy, including ensuring confidentiality and obtaining informed consent for presentation, publication, and exhibition. Providers of art-based supervision are ethically obligated to obtain ongoing training in the use of media in therapy. Our familiarity with a range of materials makes it possible for us to effectively support the art-based work of others. "Only when supervisors are knowledgeable and comfortable with the arts can they ease the trepidation of their supervisees and promote the effectiveness of art-based techniques" (p. 269).

The use of imagery in supervision rests on the expertise of the supervisor, who must be knowledgeable about its application in order to clarify clinical issues and bring insight to those he or she supervises. The supervisor's ability to assess supervisees' most effective mode of conceptualizing and understanding the complex material they experience in therapy informs the use of art-based supervision. The most effective supervisors are well versed in a range of approaches to treatment. There are times when a straightforward verbal approach to the work is most effective.

It is critical to be cognizant of supervisees' strengths, limitations, and learning styles, choosing the most effective methods to support their development. Discussing the work of Guiffrida, Jordan, Saiz, and Barnes (2007), Deaver and Shiflett (2011) advocated for the use of metaphor to deepen understanding in supervision. "Effective use of metaphor in supervision is likely dependent on the supervisee's ability to think abstractly and creatively as well as the supervisor's level of skill and comfort with developing appropriate ways of incorporating these techniques" (Deaver & Shiflett, 2011, p. 262).

These authors indicate that making and investigating imagery may be a useful resource in supervision. But turning to our images is not always the answer. Making art in times of crisis may potentially distract us from the work necessary to deal with the situation needing our attention. For example, practical information about reporting child abuse must be conveyed before making response art to explore the multifaceted components of that issue. There are times when supervision must focus on reviewing policy or act to ensure safety before turning to personal and interpersonal reflection.

Distance Supervision

There are new challenges for the supervisor as he or she works to support supervisees' practice and professional development. Distance supervision, and the use of imagery in it, warrants our thoughtful attention and further investigation. Orr (2010) offered a useful protocol of best practices for distance supervision, exploring three domains; crossing borders, confidentiality, and relationship building.

Therapists seek distance supervision for a variety of reasons. Often students from other countries return home after training and seek credentials from organizations in the United States. Some therapists working in remote areas do not have access to a local supervisor. There are also times when new therapists do not have an available on-site supervisor with the training or skills to support their practice. Still others look for the expertise of a familiar supervisor, continuing an ongoing relationship from their training.

The eligibility of supervised hours for the credential sought by the new therapist should be clearly specified within the supervisory agreement at the start of supervision. This clarity is even more critical when providing distance supervision because of the complexity of licensing in different locations. In addition, supervisors must be sure to clarify professional licensing specifications and laws and regulations for distance supervision and communicate them clearly to the supervisee. Some professions, including counseling, require supervisors to be licensed in the state or province where the supervisee provides services. Those practicing supervision with professions that are nationally credentialed may have more flexibility with distance supervision. Orr (2010) said if a therapist in the United States is working exclusively toward art therapy registration (ATR) in supervision, then working across state lines may not be an issue. This is also the case for international art therapists seeking supervision for their ATR. "This credential offered by the ATCB [Art Therapy Credentials Board] is a national credential and can be obtained by international art therapists after a course-by-course review of their education is conducted" (p. 109). Supervisors should also be aware of the limits of their malpractice insurance and ensure that they perform within state and federal law, the professional standards of their practice, and the limitations of their licensure.

Brandoff and Lombardi (2012) offered their work as an example of the challenges and resources available through distance supervision. They emphasized the value of images brought into supervision, as well as those made during it, and offered technological suggestions to facilitate visual communication. They stressed the importance of a supervisory agreement delineating liability, the limits of professional oversight, and confidentiality. Brandoff and Lombardi cautioned "supervisors and supervisees must strive to reap benefits from the assets of technology without succumbing to the liabilities. The information shared during distance supervision must be encrypted to protect privacy and confidentiality" (p. 95). Client information must be protected to ensure confidentiality and not shared or stored in ways that may be breached, lost, or hacked. The use of supervisory material, including response art, should be discussed. Any use for educational or other purposes would require the informed consent of the supervisee.

The response art of the supervisor and supervisee, when used in video conferencing, can contribute important perspectives, deepening the discourse about clinical work. When engaged carefully and responsibly, distance art-based supervision can provide a valuable resource for new therapists seeking support and direction for their work.

Conclusion

Art-based supervision utilizes the metaphoric representations of both supervisees and supervisors to facilitate therapy, challenging participants to venture into uncertain territory and to clarify sensitive issues. Those engaged in art-based supervision use response art as a tool for multifaceted reflection. Response art can be used for supporting the communication of concerns, the examination and conceptualization of case material, and the investigation of problematic relationships. It offers a way to navigate the challenges of therapy by providing resources for contemplation, exploration, and feedback. Response art, used this way, is a form of reflective listening that employs imagery as well as words.

The engagement of imagery in supervision is a powerful resource that must be used mindfully. As with any intervention, response art should be considered in the light of the supervisory relationship and its implications for productive discourse and learning. There is always the potential for boundaries between supervision and therapy to blur. The supervisor must be careful to redirect supervisees to personal therapy in the event that they bring unresolved issues through the image making process and the ensuing discussion that are not pertinent to their work. In addition, the supervisor must be aware of his or her own power in the relationship when asking students to explore unconscious material in such an uncensored forum as supervision.

With this caveat, I believe that the creativity of the therapist should be used liberally and I advocate for its engagement by educators and supervisors as well as those providing direct clinical services. My work strives to cultivate the use of therapists' and supervisors' imagery in their discourse, recognizing its potential as a powerful resource to reflect on and clarify their work. Provided during training, this way of working affords student therapists the opportunity to begin a practice that incorporates the use of their own artwork for reflection and insight.

Engaging in this approach early in their careers provides students and new professionals a useful skill that may become an ongoing professional resource.

When the supervisor makes artwork about the practice of the supervisee, he or she may gain a deeper appreciation for the new therapist's efforts as well as a better understanding of his or her role in supporting the supervisory relationship. This artwork gives the supervisee a concrete example of the supervisor's response to his or her work. We have reviewed the practice of therapists who make art during therapy sessions to communicate understanding to their clients and afterward to reflect on their work. We have looked at therapists' use of their own imagery to cultivate and sustain empathy and communicate effectively with clients. We have examined the work of those using imagery to understand countertransference, as well as those employing imagery for research. Deaver and Shiflett (2011) summed up the value of working this way. "In short, art-based supervision techniques are inherently experience based and meaning making, increasing supervisee learning and enhancing supervision" (p. 272).

This chapter has reviewed a history of art-based supervision and provided a foundation for its use from the literature of art therapy and other social service fields. Next we will turn our attention to practical examples of how imagery is used in supervision. Chapters 3 and 4 present ways to create space for making imagery during supervision and discuss methods for engaging imagery in art-based supervision.

References

Agell, G., Levick, M. F., Rhyne, J. L., Robbins, A., Rubin, J. A., Ulman, E., Wang, C. W., & Wilson, L. (1981). Transference and countertransference in art therapy. *American Journal of Art Therapy, 21*(1), 3–23.

Allen, P. B. (1995). *Art is a way of knowing*. Boston, MA: Shambhala.

Amundson, N. E. (1988). The use of metaphor and drawings in case conceptualization. *Journal of Counseling & Development, 66*(8), 391–393.

Arnheim, R. (1969). *Visual thinking*. Berkeley, CA: University of California.

Brandoff, R., & Lombardi, R. (2012). Miles apart: Two art therapists' experience of distance supervision. *Art Therapy: Journal of the American Art Therapy Association, 29*(4), 93–96.

Brown, C., Meyerowitz, J., & Ryde, J. (2007). Thinking with image-making: Supervising student therapists. In J. Schaverien, & C. Case (Eds.), *Supervision of art psychotherapy: A theoretical and practical handbook* (pp. 167–181). New York, NY: Routledge.

Calisch, A. (1994). The use of imagery in teaching, learning and supervision. *Canadian Art Therapy Association Journal, 8*(1), 30–35.

Calisch, A. (1995). The metatherapy of supervision using art with transference/countertransference phenomena. *The Clinical Supervisor, 12*(2), 119–127.

Carpendale, M. (2011). *A traveler's guide to art therapy supervision*. Bloomington, IN: Tafford.

Case, C. (2007a). Imagery in supervision: The nonverbal narrative of knowing. In J. Schaverien, & C. Case (Eds.), *Supervision of art psychotherapy: A theoretical and practical handbook* (pp. 95–115). New York, NY: Routledge.

Case, C. (2007b). Review of the literature on art therapy supervision. In J. Schaverien & C. Case (Eds.), *Supervision of art psychotherapy: A theoretical and practical handbook* (pp. 11–27). New York, NY: Routledge.

Clark, A. J. (2007). *Empathy in counseling and psychotherapy: Perspectives and practices.* Mahwah, NJ: Laurence Erlbaum Associates.

Corey, G., Corey, M., & Callanan, P. (2011). *Issues and ethics in the helping professions* (8th Ed.). Belmont, CA: Brooks/Cole, Cengage Learning.

Dahlman, Y. (2007). Towards a theory that links experience in the arts with acquisition of knowledge. *International Journal of Art and Design Education, 26*(3), 274–284.

Deaver, S. P., & McAuliffe, G. (2009). Reflective visual journaling during art therapy and counseling internships: A qualitative study. *Reflective Practice, 10*(5), 615–632.

Deaver, S. P., & Shiflett, C. (2011). Art-based supervision techniques. *The Clinical Supervisor, 30*(2), 257–276.

Eisner, E. (2001). *The role of the arts in the transformation of consciousness.* Paper presented at the 10th Occasional Seminar in Art Education, College of Fine Art, University of South Wales, Sidney, Australia.

Fish, B. J. (1989). Addressing countertransference through image making. In H. Wadeson, J. Durkin, & D. Perach (Eds.), *Advances in art therapy* (pp. 376–389). New York, NY: John Wiley & Sons.

Fish, B. J. (2006). *Image-based narrative inquiry of response art in art therapy.* (Doctoral dissertation). Retrieved from Dissertations & Theses database. (UMI no. AAT 3228081).

Fish, B. J. (2008). Formative evaluation of art-based supervision in art therapy training. *Art Therapy: Journal of the American Art Therapy Association, 25*(2), 70–77.

Fish, B. J. (2012). Response art: The art of the art therapist. *Art Therapy: Journal of the American Art Therapy Association, 29*(3), 138–143.

Fish, B. J. (2013). Painting research: Challenges and opportunities of intimacy and depth. In S. McNiff (Ed.), *Art as research: Opportunities and challenges* (pp. 209–219). Chicago, IL: University of Chicago Press.

Fish, B. J. (2014). *Harm's touch: The gifts and cost of what we witness* [Abstract]. Proceedings of the American Art Therapy Association, USA, Published CD. Alexandria, VA.

Franklin, M. (1990). The esthetic attitude and empathy: A point of convergence. *The American Journal of Art Therapy, 29*(2), 42–47.

Franklin, M. (1999). Becoming a student of oneself: Activating the witness in meditation, art, and super-vision. *American Journal of Art Therapy, 38*(1), 2–13.

Franklin, M. (2010). Affect regulation, mirror neurons, and the third hand: Formulating mindful empathic art interventions. *Art Therapy: Journal of the American Art Therapy Association, 27*(4), 160–167.

Guiffrida, D. A., Jordan, R., Saiz, S., & Barnes, K. L. (2007). The use of metaphor in clinical supervision. *Journal of Counseling & Development, 85*(4), 393–400.

Havsteen-Franklin, D. (2014). Consensus for using an arts-based response in art therapy. *International Journal of Art Therapy, 19*(3), 107–113.

Henley, D. (1992). *Exceptional children: Exceptional art.* Worchester, MA: Davis Publications.

Henzell, J. (1997). The image's supervision. In G. Shipton (Ed.), *Supervision of psychotherapy and counselling* (pp. 71–79). Buckinham: Open University Press.

Ireland, M. S., & Weissman, M. A. (1999). Visions of transference and counter-transference: The use of drawings in the clinical supervision of psychoanalytic practitioners. *American Journal of Art Therapy, 37*(3), 74–83.

Ishiyama, F. (1988). A model of visual case processing using metaphors and drawings. *Counselor Education and Supervision, 28*(2), 153–161.

Jones, D. L. (1983). An art therapist's personal record. *Art Therapy: Journal of the American Art Therapy Association, 1*(1), 22–25.

Jung, C. G. (1937). *Analytical psychology.* London: Ark.

Junge, M. B., & Asawa, P. P. (1994). *A history of art therapy in the United States*. Mundelein, IL: American Art Therapy Association.

Kielo, J. (1991). Art therapist's countertransference and post session imagery. *Art Therapy: Journal of the American Art Therapy Association, 8*(2), 14–19.

Knowles, M. (1973). *The adult learner: A neglected species*. Houston, TX: Gulf Publishing.

Kramer, E. (1971). *Art as therapy with children*. New York, NY: Schocken Books.

Kramer, E. (1979). *Childhood and art therapy*. New York, NY: Schocken Books.

Lachman-Chapin, M. (1979). Kohut's theories on narcissism: Implications for art therapy. *The American Journal of Art Therapy, 19*(3), 3–8.

Lachman-Chapin, M. (1983). The artist as clinician: An interactive technique in art therapy. *American Journal of Art Therapy, 23*(1), 13–25.

Lahad, M. (2000). *Creative supervision: The use of expressive arts methods in supervision and self-supervision*. Philadelphia, PA: Jessica Kingsley.

Lavery, T. P. (1994). Culture shock: Adventuring into the inner city through post-session imagery. *American Journal of Art Therapy, 33*(1), 14–20.

Linesch, D. G., Holmes, J., Morton, M., & Shields, S. S. (1989). Post-graduate group supervision for art therapists. *Art Therapy: Journal of the American Art Therapy Association, 6*(2), 71–75.

London, P. (1989). *No more second hand art*. Boston, MA: Shambhala.

Maclagan, D. (1997). Fantasy, play and the image in supervision. In G. Shipton (Ed.), *Supervision of psychotherapy and counseling* (pp. 61–70). Buckingham: Open University Press.

Malchiodi, C. (1998). *The art therapy sourcebook*. Los Angeles, CA. Lowell House.

Malchiodi, C. A., & Riley, S. (1996). *Supervision and related issues: A handbook for professionals*. Chicago, IL: Magnolia Street.

McNiff, S. (1989). *Depth psychology of art*. Springfield, IL: Charles C Thomas.

McNiff, S. (1998). *Art-based research*. Philadelphia, PA: Jessica Kingsley.

McNiff, S. (Ed.). (2013). *Art as research: Opportunities and challenges*. Chicago, IL: University of Chicago Press.

Miller, R. B. (2007). The role of response art in the case of an adolescent survivor of developmental trauma. *Art Therapy: Journal of the American Art Therapy Association, 24*(4), 184–190.

Moon, B. L. (1992). *Essentials of art therapy training and practice*. Springfield, IL: Charles C Thomas.

Moon, B. L. (1998). *The dynamics of art as therapy with adolescents*. Springfield, IL: Charles C Thomas.

Moon, B. L. (2000). *Ethical issues in art therapy*. Springfield, IL: Charles C Thomas.

Moon, B. L. (2007). *The role of metaphor in art therapy: Theory, method, and experience*. Springfield, IL: Charles C Thomas.

Moon, C. H. (2001). *Studio art therapy*. Philadelphia, PA: Jessica Kingsley.

Naumburg, M. (1973). *An introduction to art therapy*. New York, NY: Teachers College Press.

Naumburg, M. (1987). *Dynamically oriented art therapy: Its principals and practice*. Chicago, IL: Magnolia Street Publications.

Orr, P. P. (2010). Distance supervision: Research, findings, and considerations for art therapy. *The Arts in Psychotherapy, 37*(2), 106–111.

Perach, D., Durkin, J., Ramseyer, J., & Sontag, E. (1989). A model for art therapy supervision enhanced through art making and journal writing. In H. Wadeson, J. Durkin, & D. Perch (Eds.), *Advances in art therapy* (pp. 376–389). New York, NY: John Wiley.

Perry, B., & Szalaviz, M. (2006). *The boy who was raised as a dog and other stories from a child psychiatrist's notebook*. New York, NY: Basic Books.

Ramseyer, J. (1990). Through the looking glass: III. Exploring the dark side through post session artwork. *Art Therapy: Journal of the American Art Therapy Association, 7*(3), 114–118.

Rees, M. (1998). *Drawing on difference: Art therapy with people who have learning difficulties.* London: Routledge.

Robbins, A. (1973). The art therapist's imagery as a response to a therapeutic dialogue. *Art Psychotherapy, 1,* 181–184.

Robbins, A. (1988a). A psychoaesthetic perspective on creative arts therapy and training. *The Arts in Psychotherapy, 15,* 95–100.

Robbins, A. (Ed.). (1988b). *Between therapists: The processing of transference/countertransference material.* New York, NY: Human Science Press.

Robbins, A. (2007). The art of supervision. In J. Schaverien, & C. Case (Eds.), *Supervision of art psychotherapy: A theoretical and practical handbook* (pp. 153–166). New York, NY: Routledge.

Robbins, A., & Seaver, L. (1976). *Creative art therapy.* Brooklyn, NY: Pratt Institute.

Rogers, C. R. (1961). *On becoming a person.* Boston, MA: Houghton Mifflin.

Rubin, J. A. (1978). *Child art therapy: Understanding and helping children through art.* New York, NY: Van Norstrand Reinhold.

Rubin, J. A. (1999). *Art therapy: An introduction.* New York, NY: Routledge.

Rubin, J. A. (Ed.). (2001). *Approaches to art therapy: Theory and technique.* New York, NY: Routledge.

Schaverien, J. (1992). *The revealing image: Analytical art psychotherapy in theory and practice.* New York, NY: Routledge.

Schaverien, J. (1995). *Desire and the female therapist: Engendered gases in psychotherapy and art therapy.* New York, NY: Routledge.

Schaverien, J. (2005). Art and active imagination: Reflections on transference and the image. *Inscape, 10*(2), 39–53.

Schaverien, J. (2007). Framing enchantment: Countertransference in analytic art psychotherapy supervision. In J. Schaverien, & C. Case (Eds.), *Supervision of art psychotherapy: A theoretical and practical handbook* (pp. 45–63). New York, NY: Routledge.

Schaverien, J., & Case, C. (Eds.). (2007). *Supervision of art psychotherapy: A theoretical and practical handbook.* New York, NY: Routledge.

Schuck, C., & Wood, J. (2011). *Inspiring creative supervision.* Philadelphia, PA: Jessica Kingsley.

Stone, D., & Amundson, N. (1989). Counsellor supervision: An exploratory study of the metaphoric case drawing method of case presentation in a clinical setting. *Canadian Journal of Counselling and Psychotherapy/Revue canadienne de counseling et de psychothérapie, 23*(4), 360–371.

Tolstoy, L. (1899). *What is art?* (Trans. Aylmer Maude). London: W. Scott.

Ulman, E. (1961). Art therapy: Problems of definition. *Bulletin of Art Therapy, 1*(2), 19–20.

van der Kolk, B. A., McFarlane, A., & Weisaeth, L. (1996). *Traumatic stress: The effects of overwhelming experience on mind, body and society.* New York, NY: Guilford Press.

Vick, R. M. (1996). The dimensions of service: An elemental model for the application of art therapy. *Art Therapy: Journal of the American Art Therapy Association, 13*(2), 96–101.

Vick, R. M. (2003). A brief history of art therapy. In C. Malchiodi (Ed.), *The clinical handbook of art therapy* (pp. 5–15). New York, NY: The Guilford Press.

Wadeson, H. (1980). *Art psychotherapy.* New York, NY: John Wiley & Sons.

Wadeson, H. (1987). *The dynamics of art psychotherapy.* New York, NY: John Wiley.

Wadeson, H. (1990). Through the looking glass: I. When clients' tragic images illuminate the therapist's dark side. *Art Therapy: Journal of the American Art Therapy Association, 7*(3), 107–110.

Wadeson, H. (2000). *Art therapy practice: Innovative approaches with diverse populations.* New York, NY: John Wiley.

Wadeson, H. (2003). Making art for professional processing. *Art Therapy: Journal of the American Art Therapy Association, 20*(4), 208–218.

Wakeman, C. (2013). Building imaginative bridges: Creative arts supervision and therapeutic work with children. In A. Chesner, & L. Zografou (Eds.), *Creative supervision across modalities: Theory and applications for therapists, counsellors and other helping professionals* (pp. 109–126). Philadelphia, PA: Jessica Kingsley.

Wilkins, P. (1995). A creative therapies model for the group supervision of counsellors. *British Journal of Guidance and Counselling, 23*(2), 245–257.

Wilson, L., Riley, S., & Wadeson, H. (1984). Art therapy supervision. *Art Therapy: Journal of the American Art Therapy Association, 1*(3), 100–105.

Wolf, R. (1985). Image induction in the countertransference: A revision of the totalistic view. *Art Therapy: Journal of the American Art Therapy Association, 2*(3), 120–133.

Wolf, R. (1990). Visceral learning: The integration of aesthetic and creative process in education and psychotherapy. *Art Therapy: Journal of the American Art Therapy Association, 7*(2), 60–69.

3

CREATING A SPACE FOR IMAGE MAKING

I walk into the supervision class that I teach at least a half an hour early to set up the room. I clean off tables and chairs, reconfiguring them into an arrangement and setting a small colorful bowl filled with dark chocolate in the center. I get water for tea and set up the coffeemaker on a table along one wall. The smell of coffee fills the room as I arrange handouts, graded papers, and journal entries with my written responses to return to the students when they arrive. I sit, take a deep breath, and anticipate the beginning of class.

This chapter describes why it is helpful to make images during both group and individual supervision to create a supportive environment for novice therapists to share their work. The supervisory milieu is facilitated by the quality of attention that is given to consistent and predictable space, careful consideration of time, and the use of rituals. In addition to these components, the use of materials for investigation and communication of clinical work can serve to ground participants, providing sensory involvement that supports deep reflection on therapeutic work. Student therapists come to class with all of their internship experiences, thoughts, and questions in tow. The supervisee's ability to communicate sensitive and often difficult material is critical to successful supervision.

The experiences of new therapists come quickly, filling each with seemingly endless incidences to unpack and examine. With managed care, the expectation for the size of therapists' caseloads has increased. Often, before a clinician can begin to process an interaction at work, the next one calls for his or her attention. It is important to have time to plan, attend to, and reflect on treatment as well as communicate interactions through written notes, staffings, and consultation.

Supervision is a time that is set aside to review the work of therapy with the guidance of a more experienced practitioner. Art-based supervision utilizes verbal discourse while bringing additional image-based resources to bear. Those engaged in art-based supervision are encouraged to use the creative process and product to steady themselves while reflecting and problem solving about treatment issues, just as their clients do in art therapy. Engaging in sensory work with materials can help therapists settle in for the discussion of their experiences, allowing them to be accessible to witness and support their peers' interactions. Imagery produced in supervision fosters the consideration of therapeutic encounters from new perspectives. This way of working holds a space for both bold and tentative exploration. It facilitates communication about content supporting insightful practice.

Supervisor's Intentional Practice

The supervisor's intentional focus supports new therapists' engagement in supervision. In the same way that therapists help to hold the psychological space in session by concentrating their attention on the client, supervisors can intentionally create a calm, focused environment and foster creative exploration, setting the stage for deep reflection. Whether providing group or individual supervision, the consideration of space, time, and the image-making process and product help to create a sense of psychological safety that is necessary for new therapists to discuss their work.

The ability to provide dedicated attention is the most important quality of both the therapist and the supervisor. The foundation of the supervisory alliance is the senior therapist's intentional commitment to concentrate on the work of the therapist in training, facilitating sound services for clients, and supporting the therapist's professional understanding and development. The way in which the supervisor sets the environment for supervision is an example of this intentional focus, introducing the new therapist to the supervisor's attention to the process. In doing so, the supervisor models the quality of care that the therapist should strive for with the client.

Holding the Space

My conscious effort to create a warm and comfortable environment helps new therapists feel welcomed into the space and the relationships that form there. When I make an effort to come to class early enough to set up the room in the same configuration each week, I create a predictable forum to support our work together. Arranging the room also grounds and prepares me for the content to come. Student therapists, anticipating that I will be there, often come to class early to join in setting up the room or to relax, eat their lunch, and chat before the group begins. When they join in putting away art supplies and cleaning up coffee and tea at the end of the class, they actively participate in the supervision group's closure. Materials are our tools. The way we care for them, as well as how we handle, store, and communicate about the imagery that we make, conveys their importance to us.

When the supervision class meets for the first time, I tell the new therapists about my expectations. I explain why I think so carefully about holding the space for supervision as it provides support for those processing the work of therapy. Beginning clinicians, engaging with the intense experience of others for the first time, are challenged by these novel experiences that are often painful and traumatic. Supervision is a place where new therapists develop skills that are necessary to explore and process the material from their sessions.

A predictable setting can bolster students, helping them shift their attention from what they were doing before class to the powerful, and often personally challenging, material shared in supervision. After having an initial discussion with supervisees, they understand what to expect. In subsequent sessions, student therapists come into the room, get a drink, and gather around the table, settling in for the work to come.

Intentional and nuanced ways of holding a space in supervision have implications for therapy as well. Many have discussed the importance of space and materials in art therapy (Allen, 1995, 2005; Ault, 1989; Cane, 1983; Case & Dalley, 1992; Henley, 1992, 1995; Hinz, 2009; McGraw, 1995; McNiff, 1995; B. Moon, 1998; C. Moon, 2002, 2010; Rubin, 1999; Wadeson, 1980). However, I have found little attention given to the use of space in supervision.

Clinicians theorize that a predictable environment, as well as sensory stimulation, helps to settle the brains of those exposed to traumatic events (Barton, Gonzalez, & Tomlinson, 2012; Bloom, 1997; Perry & Szalaviz, 2006; van der Kolk, 2014; van der Kolk, McFarlane, & Weisaeth, 1996). When supervisees are able to anticipate a welcoming environment with art materials to work with, they are more equipped to contend with the experiences of their clients. This can help to ground them in the same way that it supports clients who have endured trauma.

This purposeful reflection on the use of space encourages new therapists to think about how they approach their sessions with clients. The conscious use of space can contribute to physical and psychological safety. Therapy is provided in endless configurations and settings. Often therapists work in places that are not dedicated to therapy or that are shared with other disciplines—in day rooms with others milling around, outdoors, in homes, in medical hospital patient rooms, and so on.

This shift in attention to the environment does not have to be elaborate. Small acts that support art-based supervision, such as bringing materials into the room and arranging furniture consistently, can change the space and impact the session. As a supervisor, working with the space helps me to hone my expectations for what is to come. I find that when I ground myself by physically and psychologically attending to the space, both clients and new therapists feel my attention and are more able to mirror the same focus.

When we work to create a space that supports art-based supervision in a shared area, it is important to consider the impact that changing the environment has on the group and those who use the same space. Supervisors who have their own spaces may be able to make more autonomous decisions about how to set up their rooms. Those of us who teach in graduate therapy programs share areas with others who have varied agendas and curricula. This requires us to be flexible and creative as we think about our impact on the space.

Changing a shared environment in any permanent way is not possible. The modifications we make must be easily set up each week and temporary so as not to interfere with another's use of the room. Images put up on walls for viewing need to be removed at the end of supervision to make room for experiences in other classes. Unfinished projects must be put away or taken home.

Attending to the space can have a significant influence on how people feel welcomed into supervision. A cloth for the table, a colorful bowl with pretzels or candy to share or other sensory items can be useful in helping people shift their attention from what came before to the present. Setting up the room helps me to transition as well. It supports my ability to leave the last moments before class behind and focus on supervision. When I am truly present, others sense it and feel invited to join me.

Time

I share my expectations about punctuality during the first supervision session. I start and end sessions on time. My intention for stressing this boundary is to communicate the value of the gathering and emphasize the importance of mutual respect for everyone's time. During group supervision, we come together to hold the space. There are instances when a participant may have to arrive late or leave early. These events become less frequent when those involved are mindful of the impact of their disruptions on others. Bringing the discussion of interruptions into the supervisory group discussion can raise awareness of the impact of disruptions, helping new therapists problem-solve about how to address similar distractions in their clinical work.

Time in supervision is valuable and it should be used in ways that bring deeper understanding of treatment and related issues. I ask students to make response art as a weekly assignment to reflect on their work and bring it to supervision as the foundation of their discussion. Artworks that are created this way can support focused attention and contribute to forming group cohesion just as they can when working in group therapy.

Ritual

Patterns of behavior orient our lives. A ritual is an intentional series of actions taken in a prescribed manner to bring our attention to and recognize the significance of an event. It is a way to acknowledge importance and bring deeper meaning. Creating a ritual to intentionally shift our focus can help us value and fully take advantage of supervision. Readying my home for company, or the classroom for supervision, can entail purposeful, meaningful preparation. Saying goodbye to guests or ending a session may similarly have consistent, thoughtfully constructed components for closure.

There are parallels between the effective structure of group supervision and group therapy as well as between the structure of individual supervision and individual treatment. As in therapy, supervision has a beginning, middle, and end. I help student therapists in group supervision transition mindfully into their work and support their closure at the end by developing unique rituals that incorporate their ideas.

During our initial supervision session, each class creates a unique ritual used for opening and closing supervision. My current class developed a ritual that starts our gathering with each of us stating our own intention for what we hope to accomplish during the supervision class. For instance, I might say, "I hold this space for deep investigation" or "I understand how to be helpful." Each of us takes a turn performing a physical gesture, which is mirrored by the group. Finally I ring a chime and light a candle. After the work of session, we repeat the ritual in reverse order, ending with blowing out the candle. We repeat the sequence each week. These rituals can be as simple as beginning the class with each of us offering a one-word check-in and ending with each of us contributing a one-word checkout. Regardless of how simple or complex the ritual, the purpose is to shift and focus our attention. Coming together to decide on the ritual's components gives supervisees a sense of ownership in the evolving group process and sets the stage for ongoing collaboration.

I have developed an opening and closing ritual for individual supervision as well. It consists of greeting the therapist, gathering art materials or setting up an ongoing project, and settling down at the table with coffee or tea. By transitioning from what I was doing before the session and shifting my attention onto supervision, I intentionally bring my consciousness to this work. The practice welcomes participants and allows me to transition between meetings.

These examples are offered as intentional ways to start and end supervision and inspire supervisors to find ways to hold spaces that are consistent with their styles of working. Establishing opening and closing rituals, such as breathing and centering exercises, a one-word check-in, or lighting a candle, can be rich sensory experiences that provide grounding and shift our attention to supervision. Working together to create and incorporate rituals into supervision can facilitate the development of a supportive group that engages in profound work.

Using Media During Supervision

Once we clarify expectations, talk about our intensions, and establish our ritual for opening and closing our sessions, I invite students to make art during both group and individual supervision. This work with media does not necessarily result in a formed expression. Sensory engagement with the materials themselves can be the rationale for the experience. Many supervisees find working with media soothing, allowing them to concentrate on the discussion of clinical work. This can be accomplished with the manipulation of simple materials as well as skillful articulation by more experienced artists. Doodling with a fine-tip marker or colored pencils (Figure 3.1) can be grounding. Collage, drawing, painting, or working with yarn, fabric, embroidery, or clay can provide tactile, sensory experiences while new therapists recall their work and witness their peers' stories.

Supervisees' artistic skill levels vary. There are some who are familiar with art materials and others who pick them up cautiously as unfamiliar tools. In supervision as in therapy, the process of engaging in making images is as important as the product. Tentative and unskilled use of media can be as useful to ground us and clarify communication as are bold and skilled efforts. My intention is to provide media that others feel comfortable with, supporting reflection, exploration, and insight into therapeutic work.

The use of materials during supervision does more than provide a pleasurable activity. It can help to strengthen new therapists as they contend with content from treatment that is often beyond their own experience and challenges their worldview. It is one thing to learn about methods for addressing trauma. It is quite another to sit with a child as he or she describes the details of a traumatic or

FIGURE 3.1 Drawing During Supervision

Heather Vernon

violent event from personal experience. New therapists need ways to cope with the onslaught of real material that they contend with in their work with clients. Art materials are consistent. Their intrinsic nature does not change. The reliable, sensory qualities of media can help to steady supervisees' work.

As supervision class begins each week, students select materials from the supply closet, bring them into the classroom, and spread them onto the table (Figure 3.2). As I teach in an art school, this closet is stocked with two- and three-dimensional, traditional and nontraditional art supplies including found and recycled objects. It is important to have media with qualities that range from those that are easily controlled such as pencils and markers to those that are more stimulating like paint and clay. This allows participants to choose media they are comfortable with. The ability to select materials that feel familiar and technically accessible facilitates grounding and offers opportunities for enhanced communication.

When I provide postgraduate supervision in my own space, those I work with choose from a wide variety of materials that I have collected and stored in bins. At the beginning of each session, I ask what he or she would like to use, find the supplies, and set them up as we begin to work. The images that supervisees make range from two-dimensional drawings and watercolor paintings to collage, clay, and painted tape and aluminum foil sculptures. *Moving On* (Figure 3.3, Plate 1) is a

FIGURE 3.2 Supervision Table

Barbara Fish

FIGURE 3.3 (PLATE 1) Moving On

Sangeetha Ravichandran

pastel chalk drawing made by Sangeetha Ravichandran as she discussed her work in a domestic violence shelter.

It is important to consider the nature of the materials that we offer. Others have discussed the qualities intrinsic in media, explaining the importance of having a range of materials available for use in therapy (Allen, 1995; Case & Dalley, 1992; Hinz, 2009; C. Moon, 2010; Seiden, 2001; Seiden & Davis, 2013). This discourse informs the selection of media offered for supervision. I encourage you to investigate these sources to support your art-based practice.

Those providing group and individual supervision in more traditional academic settings should offer as many choices of supplies as possible. This facilitates the exploration of those with less formal art experience as they venture into the use of unfamiliar media and modes of expression. I strongly recommend that supervisors provide only materials that they themselves are familiar with and comfortable using. Encouraging others to engage supplies with qualities that require an intense learning curve is not useful to support a collaborative environment that facilitates a critical focus on clinical issues. Basic instruction is fine, but it is important to remember that the intention is to work with media to support the oversight of clinical work.

It is important to have a clear intention when asking supervisees to make art to respond to a specific conversation or topic during supervision. Making quick images can be an effective way to explore ideas and reactions. There are occasions that these beginning images can lead to deeper work. There are also risks. Time constraints can limit the development of the image and the supervisee's reflection on it. Quick responses that are not valued and given time and recognition in class can leave students feeling that this way of working is art-on-demand, a superficial and obligatory way of processing.

There are many ways to facilitate image making in supervision beyond using media to ground supervisees, supporting supervisory discussion, and exploring response pieces made during class. We will discuss examples of these art-based assignments in depth in Chapter 7. The following are some of the ways that I hold the space for imagery in supervision during both therapist training and postgraduate work.

Skill-Sharing

Skill-sharing is a part of fieldwork supervision class that I offer to provide students a forum to introduce media-based experiences to one another. In addition to providing an opportunity for student therapists to serve as instructors and guides while they introduce new media or processes, this experiential learning provides a backdrop and grounding for supervisees during group discussion of clinical issues.

Each supervision group is different, coming to the work with unique needs and expectations. Each establishes its own tone, rituals, and effective use of time to address the needs of the participants. Students in some fieldwork classes decide to share their skills with each other to serve the dual purpose of adding to their materials repertoire and providing a sensory platform to help ground their discussion. When the group decides to incorporate skill-sharing into our work together, the students and I each sign up to act as the leader for a week. Then, during the first five to ten minutes of each class, we take turns teaching our skill with a specific medium or project. After the initial instruction, students may choose to continue to work with the new skill, select another media, or engage in the discourse without the use of materials.

We have taught each other a wide range of skills, including making wrap dolls out of cloth and yarn, finger knitting (Figure 3.4), creating sock animals (Figure 3.5, Plate 2), needle felting (Figure 3.6), making wish sticks, fashioning glass amulets, forming intention beads, sewing and embroidery, printmaking, and beading. After initial instruction these crafting techniques are straightforward and repetitive. They quickly become automatic, allowing our hands to operate while leaving our minds free to concentrate on the classroom discussion. Rhythmic, tactile tasks foster an ability to focus our attention rather than distract us from the intensity of our supervisory mission.

Sangeetha Ravichandran's skill-share is an example of how we engage in this kind of image making during supervision. She taught us how to finger knit, a skill she learned from one of the women she worked with as an intern at a domestic violence shelter serving immigrant women. Finger knitting is a way of knitting yarn by using fingers instead of knitting needles (Figure 3.4). This way of working

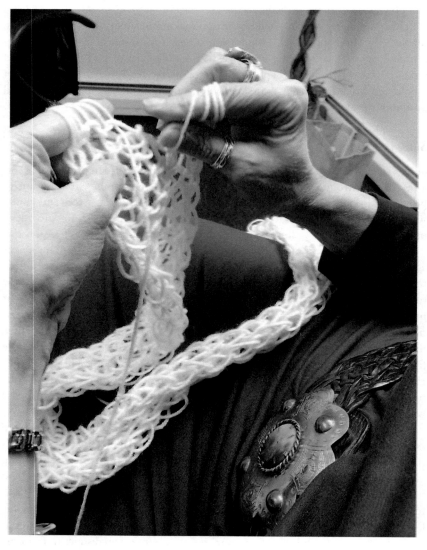

FIGURE 3.4 Finger Knitting

Barbara Fish

FIGURE 3.5 (PLATE 2) Sock Animals

Emily Allbery, Barbara Fish, Julie Krause, Leigh Ann Lichty, Ashley Melendez, Kelly Riddle

FIGURE 3.6 Needle Felting

Emily Allbery, Barbara Fish, Julie Krause, Leigh Ann Lichty, Ashley Melendez, Kelly Riddle

with yarn is not complicated; we picked it up easily when she demonstrated it at the beginning of the class. Many of us continued to knit throughout supervision as we engaged in clinically focused discussion. Some of the students finger knitted for weeks, making scarf after scarf. Sangeetha told the woman at the shelter that she had taught finger knitting to our class and that we enjoyed the process. The woman was thrilled that her therapist's class appreciated what she had thought of as a simple skill.

In another session Ashley Melendez taught us how to make sock animals (Figure 3.5, Plate 2). She planned the experience, bringing polyester fiberfill, sewing needles, thread, and buttons to class while we brought our own socks. She showed us a sample sock animal and a pattern. After her instruction, we cut and stitched the socks, making them into stuffed animals as we talked about each intern's experiences in therapy that week. Julie Krause, an intern working in a substance use program serving adolescent boys, taught us how to needle felt (Figure 3.6). This process transforms wool roving (unspun wool) into shapes and designs by poking it repeatedly with a felting needle.

Other techniques that we taught to one another included making affirmation amulets out of glass beads, making wrap dolls out of cloth and yarn scraps with intentions nestled inside, and making simple books for use as handmade journals. The possibilities for exploring materials are endless. The point is to share varied experiences with media and try out a range of materials.

This use of media provides patterned, sensory involvement during the intense discussions in supervision. By teaching one another new ways to work with materials, we add to our inventory of media-based ways to engage clients while grounding our discussion with the same sensory activity that we offer them. Although this process is pleasurable, it also serves as an important support for our work. It is a backdrop for the serious focus of supervision, providing sensory involvement and relief as we explore issues that are often painful and challenging to discuss. In this way, our engagement with materials helps to support the quality of client care.

Treatment of Imagery

The way that we attend to artwork in supervision models how to care for imagery in therapy. How we hold a space, facilitate engagement with materials, and attend to images that are made in or come into supervision determine their utility. Valuing the image's presence and making it the focus of multifaceted investigation and mutual support demonstrates respect and appreciation for the work and the concerns that it expresses. As in therapy, it is critical to see the person who makes the image as the authority over its content.

It is not our role as supervisors to use imagery to pry open new therapists' concerns and personal material. I agree with Schaverien's approach to working with the image in therapy (Steinhardt, 1998) and apply it to my work with those I supervise.

> Working with the transference, the art can become the assistant, the hand-maiden of psychotherapy, but I'm not interested in that. I'm interested in allowing it [the image] to be central and having it's [sic] space—not to be spoken of too soon, not to be intruded upon, or abused by the premature use of the word.
>
> *(p. 109)*

There are times when a supervisor may think that an image made by a new thera-pist has personal meaning. The wise supervisor does not delve into the super-visee's issues unless it is pertinent to the clinical work being discussed. As with clients, supervisees often take time to realize the implicit meaning of their work or may be reticent to share concerns in supervision. Engaging imagery gently, with the intention of supporting the supervisory relationship, fosters the develop-ment of trust and interpersonal safety.

Clean-Up as Closure

Whether we use materials in supervision during graduate or postgraduate train-ing, or in a group or individual format, clean-up is a significant part of ending the session. Cleaning up materials can become part of the ritual performed at the end of supervision, supporting successful closure. Supervisees use clean-up as an important way to transition out of session to what is next, just as clients come to the surface after deep discussion. As new therapists gather fabric, put oil pastels back into boxes, or wash paintbrushes, they put themselves back in order. Reflect-ing on this process with supervisees is an opportunity to talk about the value of clean-up as a significant part of session for clients.

Conclusion

The intentional use of materials in art-based supervision supports the deep engagement of new therapists in reflection and critical discourse about their clini-cal work. Whether supervision takes place in the classroom, office, or studio, how we think about and use the environment is important. The thoughtful use of space is as significant as the use of didactic material. How we create places for this challenging work reflects similarities in the therapeutic relationship.

We have explored the importance of thoughtfully establishing a space for art-based work that is both flexible and consistent. Each week new therapists come to supervision filled with fresh experiences that may be difficult to articulate and share. Creating a space that helps them settle and focus supports the supervisory process.

The way in which the supervisor presents him or herself can contribute to the sense of safety and predictability of the space. During the early years of my work, children in residential care noticed that I had a purple plastic briefcase. They used this information as a social lubricant, assuming that purple was my favorite color. The children teased me, giving me nicknames like Petunia and Violet. They wrote poems about purple and drew images about me in a purple world. This was often the way the children entered our relationship, engaging with me in a safe and playful way. Purple remains my signature color. Even now the fact that I wear purple is a topic of conversation with those I supervise and work with that is superficial yet personal, allowing them to engage easily.

There are simple ways to warm the environment for creative work in art-based supervision. Designing rituals that shift and intensify our focus onto the experience helps to bring it value. Bringing food, coffee, or tea to share, along with a candle and a chime are small but powerful interventions that I use to help establish a comfortable space. Supervisors' styles and the needs of those they supervise may differ. Nevertheless, establishing a consistent, familiar, inviting environment that has the ability to ground and focus those who come to engage in supervision supports sound work.

The supervisor's intention for the use of the space is critical for the development and process of art-based supervision. How he or she transforms the environment facilitates the effective use of art for profound work and collaboration. Just as therapists create a safe place to hold sensitive issues in session, supervisors must do the same to contain the material that new therapists bring to supervision.

This chapter has discussed and given examples of some ways to support and make imagery during art-based supervision. We have looked at the supervisor's intentional use of space, time, and materials to support engagement in the work as well as closure. Now we will turn our discussion to working with imagery created independently and brought in supervision to support the understanding of clinical work. The chapters that follow will present examples of the use of response art to explore and support insight as an integral part of art-based supervision.

References

Allen, P. B. (1995). *Art is a way of knowing*. Boston, MA: Shambhala.

Allen, P. B. (2005). *Art is a spiritual path*. Boston, MA: Shambhala.

Ault, R. E. (1989). Art therapy with the unidentified patient. In H. Wadeson, J. Durkin, & D. Perach (Eds.), *Advances in art therapy* (pp. 222–239). New York, NY: John Wiley & Sons.

Barton, S., Gonzalez, R., & Tomlinson, P. (2012). *Therapeutic residential care for children and young people: An attachment and trauma-informed model for practice*. Philadelphia, PA: Jessica Kingsley.

Bloom, S. (1997). *Creating sanctuary: Toward the evolution of sane societies*. New York, NY: Routledge.

Cane, F. (1983). *The artist in each of us* (Rev. Ed.). Craftsbury Common, VT: Art Therapy Publications.

Case, C., & Dalley, T. (1992). *The handbook of art therapy.* New York, NY: Routledge.

Henley, D. (1992). *Exceptional children: Exceptional art.* Worchester, MA: Davis Publications.

Henley, D. (1995). A consideration of the studio as a therapeutic intervention. *Art Therapy: Journal of the American Art Therapy Association, 12*(3), 188–190.

Hinz, L. D. (2009). *Expressive therapy continuum: A framework for using art in therapy.* New York, NY: Taylor and Francis.

McGraw, M. K. (1995). The art studio: A studio-based art therapy program. *Art Therapy: Journal of the American Art Therapy Association, 12*(3), 167–174.

McNiff, S. (1995). Keeping the studio. *Art Therapy: Journal of the American Art Therapy Association, 12*(3), 179–183.

Moon, B. L. (1998). *The dynamics of art as therapy with adolescents.* Springfield, IL: Charles C Thomas.

Moon, C. H. (2002). *Studio art therapy: Cultivating the artist identity in the art therapist.* Philadelphia, PA: Jessica Kingsley.

Moon, C. H. (Ed.). (2010). *Materials and media in art therapy: Critical understandings of diverse artistic vocabularies.* New York, NY: Routledge.

Perry, B., & Szalaviz, M. (2006). *The boy who was raised as a dog and other stories from a child psychiatrist's notebook.* New York, NY: Basic Books.

Rubin, J. A. (1999). *Art therapy: An introduction.* Philadelphia, PA: Brunner/Mazel.

Seiden, D. (2001). *Mind over matter: The uses of materials in art, education and therapy.* Chicago, IL: Magnolia Street Publishers.

Seiden, D., & Davis, A. (2013). *Art works: How making art illuminates your life.* Chicago, IL: Ganesha Books.

Steinhardt, L. (1998). Interview with Joy Schaverien, PhD, London. *American Journal of Art Therapy, 36*(4), 109–114.

van der Kolk, B. (2014). *The body keeps the score: Brain, mind, and body in the healing of trauma.* New York, NY: Penguin.

van der Kolk, B. A., McFarlane, A., & Weisaeth, L. (1996). *Traumatic stress: The effects of overwhelming experience on mind, body and society.* New York, NY: Guilford Press.

Wadeson, H. (1980). *Art psychotherapy.* New York, NY: John Wiley & Sons.

4

ENGAGING IMAGES
IN ART-BASED SUPERVISION

New therapists bring their work into supervision through verbal description, transcripts, process and progress notes, and formal case presentations. Additionally, as a supervisor, I have a firsthand view of new therapists' work through site visits, consultation, and evaluations from their site supervisors. It is standard practice for art therapists, with their clients' consent, to view and talk about clients' images that they bring into supervision to add to the clinical picture. These pieces may be original images that clients made in session, facsimiles, or digital representations. When therapist and supervisor view the image as a representative from session, it supports a keener understanding of the therapeutic content. This use of imagery brings discourse containing nuanced information from therapy. In addition, I advocate that both supervisors and therapists engage their own imagery, using their imaginations and the creative process to foster therapeutic insight. Anyone providing counseling, therapy, or other social services can use imagery and metaphor to investigate their work.

The oversight of the new therapist's practice is effectively supported when the supervisor is well versed in a wide range of options. In Chapter 3 we discussed ways to create a space that facilitates making imagery during supervision. We talked about how to create a predictable setting and ways to use media to ground verbal discourse while addressing challenging material. Now we will look at ways to engage images that are made independently and brought to supervision to help guide our practice. I will offer suggestions and caveats for how to participate in this work.

Response art is the therapist's imagery about his or her work. It can be created inside or outside of therapy as well as supervision. Following a general discussion of intention and response art, I will describe some of the ways to work with imagery that is brought into art-based supervision.

I will discuss how to work with images to address supervisory content, differentiating personal material that is valuable for supervision from that belonging in personal therapy. We will continue by talking about projects including a weekly response art assignment, imagery for case presentation feedback, a fairy tale assignment, and the use of active imagination with new therapists during postgraduate work and for supervisory reflection. We will end this chapter with reflection on the supervisor's imagery, its use, and my rationale for sharing it.

Although written or art-based assignments help to structure and orient supervision during training, they never take precedence over clinically urgent discussion. The way we interact with images in supervision is determined by the course of treatment, the new therapist's concerns, and his or her strengths and challenges. There are times when response art is the most effective way to support investigation and ground discussion and other times when verbal discourse and didactic information is more appropriate.

Intention

To be used as an effective lens, art-based supervision must be intentionally oriented. An intention may be as simple as "I am present and open to feedback." Or, it can be more complex: "I learn why my client makes me feel so angry." When we take the time to think about and articulate what we hope to gain or accomplish with our efforts, we are more likely to see the results we are working for. This focus brings openness to the subtleties of treatment, which can help us understand issues ranging from beginner's anxiety to countertransference. Creating and using a rote intention elicits in-kind information. The use of a carefully crafted intention for our work brings all our faculties to bear, making us more present and available to take in nuanced information.

Supervision is a critical opportunity, and the time invested in it should be spent productively. Not all discussion is valuable, and not all artmaking is useful. Choosing to use imagery in supervision should support the dual purpose of ensuring the quality of care for clients and furthering new therapists' professional growth.

Taking supervision seriously does not mean that it has to be dull and without levity. The process may be stimulating, interesting, and even fun. Working with images has the dual capacity to be pleasurable and to support intensely challenging work. Imagery used in supervision holds the content of our practice—the trauma, fears, and anxiety that clients share and hope to find mastery over as well as the therapist's feelings about it. When we bring imagery into supervision, it is not a frivolous use of time but an endeavor to handle the content of therapy and our responses to it.

Response Art

Since my earliest experiences as a therapist, I have used imagery to understand my practice. I made and investigated my artwork after session to explore countertransference, bringing clarity to therapeutic relationships (Fish, 1989). I continue working with images as a fundamental resource (Fish, 2006, 2008, 2012, 2013).

This has led to my working understanding of response art as the art of therapists that is used to contain, explore, and communicate about their work.

I make response art when an incident strikes me powerfully, when I feel overwhelmed or confused, or when I have a reaction that seems overly intense or does not make sense for the situation. Working with imagery makes it possible for me to take the event and give it form so that I can look at it outside of myself. Creating and reflecting on response art slows me down and allows me to consider things deeply, helping me to gain understanding and avoid being reactive. It gives me the time and space to pause and consider options as I sort out my experiences and choose how to respond, facilitating my effective communication to others. As they say, a picture is worth a thousand words.

I ask students to engage in response art as a primary resource in supervision during both training and postgraduate practice because I have found it so valuable in my own work. By making and processing their own imagery, new therapists quiet themselves, allowing careful consideration of their practice. Imagery can bring insight. It can help to increase personal and interpersonal understanding, leading to a greater capacity for empathy and the ability to sustain their work. Response art is useful for clarifying communication with clients, clinical team members, and supervision participants. It can help therapists to untangle countertransference and other personal responses to treatment, including those that arise in the supervisory relationship.

Working With Images

Images used in art-based supervision, witnessed and supported by the supervisor and new therapists, provide a vehicle for profound work. Response art can be made during supervision or independently and brought into session. Imagery that is completed before supervision should be given our time and focus as a valuable resource. It can be created to investigate the implications of a situation, to reflect on an interaction, or to give feedback. Overlooking or not taking time to fully engage artworks is a lost opportunity. All of these images should be welcomed as important resources and investigated intentionally. As discussed in Chapter 3, creating a space to make imagery and the process of working with materials provide grounding and support multifaceted exploration.

When provided in a group format, art-based supervision offers a rich range of imagery from many perspectives. During fieldwork we engage artwork as a foundation for discussion of clinical concerns, helping us to hone in on issues. In order to ensure all participants have time to engage with their work, discourse must be more limited. Images help us move quickly to the heart of the matter, supporting tentative discussion and giving us all increased opportunities for interpersonal resonance and empathy.

Assignments to create artworks about clinical experiences bring a steady flow of imagery from the outside into supervision. These support and orient the group discussion as we process issues. Beyond the benefit that the new therapist gains while creating the piece, it is a rich resource for the individual and his or her peers as well as the supervisor when shared within the group.

Personal Work

Cultivating therapeutic insight requires attention, patience, and a belief in the innate knowledge available to the supervisee through the creative process. This way of reflecting on therapy is guided by the supervisor to ensure client care, but it is still the individual therapist's creative journey, rooted in his or her relationship with the image. Insights and realizations come when we are ready to accept them. As in art therapy, the maker of the image is the authority of its meaning. Projections and interpretations by others are just that. They represent the commenter's perspective and may distract the new therapist from finding his or her own understanding of the image.

As we discussed in earlier chapters, there are similarities between the material addressed in therapy and the material explored in supervision. The tools used in each are often the same. It is essential to clearly differentiate between the two (Corey, Corey, & Callanan, 2011). Therapists and supervisors may resonate with the content of session, feeling it echo with their own experiences. Effective work challenges the supervisee to engage in deep reflection and introspection, as does therapy. The essential difference is that supervisory material supports clinical work. Personal material that is not related to the service provided for others is the work of private therapy. Making and investigating imagery can help to differentiate issues that are related to treatment from those that are private and belong in the clinician's own therapy. There are times when issues overlap, affecting the supervisee's personal and professional life. In those instances, both supervision and private therapy are indicated.

Weekly Response Art Assignment

When I provide art-based supervision for students during graduate training, I ask them to make response art each week. They reflect on some aspect of their internship through their imagery and bring it to the following class. I have adopted this assignment as a consistent foundation during therapist training to help new therapists learn to appreciate this use of imagery. These works are created outside of supervision to allow students to have a free choice of media and unlimited time and space for their process. The pieces support the discussion whether the supervisee decides to focus on the image or verbally relates his or her issues. The artwork directs our attention, supporting multifaceted discourse.

Kelly Riddle drew *First Day* (Figure 4.1, Plate 3) after starting her internship at a public elementary school and brought it to fieldwork supervision class. On her first day, she spent time being introduced to students and teachers and visiting

FIGURE 4.1 (PLATE 3) First Day

Kelly Riddle

classrooms, trying to learn the students' behavioral program and the school's culture. Her drawing represents how the cacophony of experiences excited and overwhelmed her. She created a trail of white sewing machine stiches weaving around the composition. "The whole day was a mesh of color, sound, excitement, and new faces. The stitching represents my presence in this mix, trying to take it all in and find a place for myself" (Kelly Riddle, Personal communication, January 22, 2015). When sharing her work she said that making the drawing helped her organize the experiences and find focus.

There is a rhythm created that opens the discourse in supervision as each student takes a turn presenting his or her response art. We focus our attention on problem solving and witnessing the clinical work as we provide feedback and support. Moving to the next student's image, we repeat the process.

Allison Ancel displayed her assemblage *Boundaries* (Figure 4.2) in front of her supervision class as she described the challenges that she faced working in a sexual assault prevention program designed to empower adolescent girls. As a young therapist, the intern questioned the interpersonal boundaries that she was expected to follow with high school girls and the potential benefits and intrinsic complications of self-disclosure. She worked to reconcile the mandate to adhere to professional standards for therapy with the more intimate and less clinical environment in the school where the program was implemented.

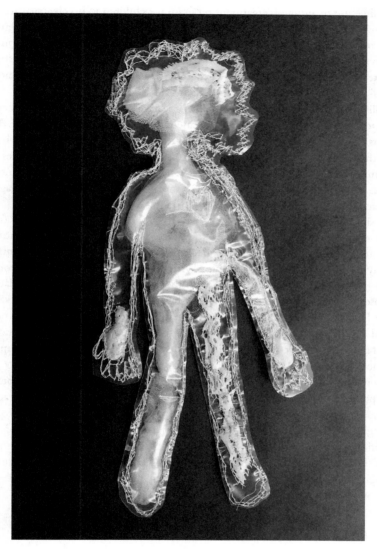

FIGURE 4.2 Boundaries

Allison Ancel

Her image is a self-portrait, depicting her as a transparent plastic figure, stitched around the edges, with all that is twisted and tangled inside clearly visible. How could she keep the personal resonance that she felt to herself when working with these girls? What was in their best interest? What was in hers?

Allison's work stirred a group discussion about boundaries in vastly different settings, including a medical hospital, a residential program for adolescent boys in substance use treatment, a treatment program for children in psychiatric care, and an assisted care facility for the elderly. We explored the reasons for agency guidelines and shared thoughts about the impact of disclosure on clients and on the supervisees. Together, we discussed how important it is to unpack and investigate countertransference that is stirred in therapy when considering the implications of self-disclosure, supporting effective therapeutic boundaries.

Allison and the others in the group returned to their internships having reflected deeply on the importance of carefully considering self-disclosure. After discussing some of the ramifications of sharing personal material with their clients, they appreciated both the potential value of their personal experiences and the importance of careful consideration when deciding to share them. Instead of rote compliance with the rules, Allison's imagery helped the group engage in nuanced decision-making about this important aspect of therapy.

Leslie Garb brought her drawing *Fragility of Familiarity* (Figure 4.3) to fieldwork class as her response to her experience as an intern in a day treatment program for adults with dementia. She described a session that she had with an elderly mother and her adult daughter. With the drawing on the table in front of her, Leslie talked about how she sat with the women and listened as the daughter discussed the impact of dementia and her mother's diminishing abilities. The piece helped Leslie to reflect on and resonate with the sadness that the woman talked about as well as communicate the fragile connection the family yearned to maintain. The group contributed to a discussion of the importance of empathy and how personally challenging it can be to sustain.

This consistent response art assignment offers the opportunity to approach therapeutic work through a creative lens, using media and imagination to access art-based ways of exploring and understanding. Students have the chance to sort through their feelings and reactions to find out what is going on in session. My intention is to introduce new therapists to response art as a tool to support their work. After using it consistently throughout their training, students are familiar enough with response art to reach for it when they need it as they move into more independent professional work.

Case Presentation Feedback

In fieldwork supervision class, student therapists give a formal presentation of their work with clients each semester. Their presentations follow a format that includes the client's age and demographics, the presenting problem, the reason for and source of the referral, the client's previous experience of therapy, the diagnosis and strengths, and the duration, goals, and course of treatment. The student presents an overview of a session, concluding with questions that he or she poses to the supervision group. After observing the presentation and participating in discussion, the other supervisees and I consider the work and create a piece of response art outside of class to give the presenter feedback the following week.

FIGURE 4.3   Fragility of Familiarity

Leslie Garb

When class reconvenes, we begin by putting all of the imagery made to give feedback on a table by the side of the room. As the students and I arrange our pieces, we begin to look at the work together. We have developed a ritual where each student presenter views all of the images and then asks each of us in turn to reflect on our work. Each discusses his or her image and its relationship to the case presentation, highlighting striking aspects of the work and its relevance to treatment. Many of us also share personal insights that making the response art brought to light as we created the image to reflect on the work of another. This practice provides valuable opportunities for witness, feedback, and collaboration.

Sze-Chin Lee, an art therapy intern, digitally created "*Help!?*" (Figure 4.4) at home and brought it into supervision class as his response to a peer's presentation. The peer had described her session with a patient at a behavioral health hospital serving adults with psychiatric disorders. The therapist had explained how the

FIGURE 4.4 "Help!?"

Sze-Chin Lee

staff didn't seem to listen to the patient because she cycled in and out of the hospital over the years. Sze-Chin responded to the patient's statement, *"I push people away with my behavior"* by drawing the presenter's patient drifting at sea, shouting and waving at a passing ship. The boat continued sailing and the crew ignored her pleas to be rescued.

Sze-Chin provided feedback for his peer's work by responding to her view of her patient as someone who was left behind without help. His response art demonstrated the quality of his attention to the presentation and its effectiveness in conveying the therapist's feelings about her patient's situation. We look at our encounters through the lens of our own experience. Moved by the story of the abandoned patient, Sze-Chin represented her in the most frightening situation he could think of, flailing in deep water. Sze-Chin is from Singapore. When he described how he represented his peer's patient struggling in the ocean, he shared his own fear of deep water and the panic that it brought up for him.

This is a generous and powerful way to witness. Those in supervision refine their intentions, making a commitment to find resonance with each other's work and express it through their response art. The images bring valuable feedback that can zero in on issues and demonstrate empathy and support. Those involved in this assignment frequently describe feeling profoundly understood. In addition to demonstrating critical feedback and empathy, this use of response art gives us a chance to resonate with the concerns presented from our own perspective.

Listening to a presentation, knowing that we will make art in response to it, requires intense attention on a cognitive, affective, and creative level. When we witness with our imaginations open, we gather material to meld into creative responses. This assignment directs the focus of the supervision group. It fosters a parallel quality to that of the therapist's attention to the therapeutic relationship described by Kramer (1971): "In the therapeutic interchange the psychotherapist maintains a state of openness toward the patient's communications, allowing them to find an echo in his own inner life" (p. 89).

Fairy Tale Assignment

To infuse supervisees' clinical work with creative potential, I developed an assignment that offers an imaginal view of the client. I ask students to write and create imagery for a fairy tale featuring one of their clients as the protagonist. My intention is to give therapists in training the opportunity to shift their view of their clients to a more aphoristic one that identifies strengths and resilience in the face of challenges. Just as we ask clients to work toward creative problem solving, we can look to our own imagery to guide our work with them.

In these stories a depressed and bullied client can find magical powers within himself to overcome insurmountable obstacles. A client who is hearing voices can fly to faraway planets, finding enchanted mentors that help her stand up to the

ead. A child without a family can be transformed into a bird
ne with rabbits in a land far away.
ercise to expand students' consciousness and to awaken them
ts of stereotyping patients with labels and diagnoses. Watch-
ronic mental illness is often painful. New therapists are filled
hope for their clients. They come to their work with clear
pointing experiences of entrenched psychopathology, limited
resources, and lack of agency support. For that reason they are often able to make
profound connections with clients with whom others have given up. Clients who
seem resistant or unable to take advantage of treatment are often engaged by the
hope and unjaded attitudes of these novice therapists.

Supervisees do not share these tales with their clients. These are intended for
their own reflection, reminding them of their clients' strengths as they help them
to discover their hidden potential. At first glance, this may sound far from clinical
exploration. However, looking at real resources through metaphor can help new
therapists learn that there is more to treatment then problem lists and treatment
plans. Of course those clinical tools are necessary to guide sound work, but without poetry and creativity the work can become deadened and repetitive. The use
of stories and imagery can help supervisees learn to think about clients with fresh
eyes, appreciating their strengths and potential.

I usually give the fairy tale assignment once during graduate training. Initially
students are sometimes resistant, not understanding its usefulness. Once they have
engaged in this way of thinking about their clients, most reflect on the assignment
as one that helped to shift their thinking and deepen their practice. We discuss the
fairy tale assignment in more depth in Chapter 7.

Active Imagination, Imaginal Dialogue, and Witness Writing

Accessing imaginal resources is another way to bring understanding and direction
to clinical work. McNiff (1989) referred to the unconscious as an operational
term describing an absence of awareness. By making a space for information that
resides just outside of our awareness, we can become cognizant of tacit understanding and operationalize visceral reactions and unconsidered resources to use
in treatment.

One way to engage imagery is through witness writing as used in the Open
Studio Process (Allen, 2005). This practice is rooted in Jung's work with active
imagination (1959, 1963, 2009) and McNiff's work with imaginal dialogue (1989).
These methods are ways to access information from our personal and collective
unconscious that has not yet reached our conscious thought. This work can bring
deeply personal and universal ways of understanding that may be applied to clinical practice.

According to Chodorow (1997), Jung conceived of the process of active imagination as consisting of two parts: "First, *letting the unconscious come up*; and second,

coming to terms with the unconscious. As I understand Jung, it is a natural sequence that may go on over many years" (p. 10). Hannah (1981) described Jung's methods for engaging the unconscious. "As a rule, the first step in active imagination is to learn, so to speak, to see or hear the dream while awake" (p. 17). These manifestations of the unconscious can take many forms.

> For many people, it is easiest to write them down; others visualize them, and others again draw or paint them with or without visualization. If there is a high degree of conscious cramp, often only the hands are capable of fantasy; they model or draw figures that are sometimes quite foreign to the conscious mind.
>
> *(Jung, 1968, pp. 21–23)*

Witness writing, developed as a part of the Open Studio Process (Allen, 2005), is a specific way of engaging in active imagination. It taps into our personal and collective resources, using the creative process as a window into the imaginal encounter. This process involves specific steps. Each participant begins by clearly articulating an intention that states what he or she hopes to learn or accomplish by engaging the work. The intention may be straightforward or multifaceted and should be written in the present tense, as if it has already happened. Consider your goal as you write your intention. It is important to be as specific as possible each time you begin this process.

Next, each participant focuses on an image, becoming open to the imaginal information, including dialogue, and transcribes on paper whatever thoughts or conversations come. This includes describing the piece and noticing feelings, resistance, and anything else that surfaces during the artmaking experience and while writing the witness. This process continues until it feels complete.

When finished writing, those who choose can read their written material aloud as others witness it without commenting. This allows the interaction between the new therapist and the image to be expressed and resonate within the group without interference from the projections of others.

Each person has the opportunity to reflect internally from his or her own perspective, holding the space for the one reading and taking what he or she can from the experience. Suspending discussion allows both the reader and the witnesses to connect with the work, engaging in their own critical thoughts and judgments, which they note without expressing them aloud. Both the reader and the witnesses can access their own internal imaginal resources and the creative solutions stimulated by their own work and the work of another. This is not to say that there is no interactive critical engagement with supervisory material. Critical discourse and problem solving follow the witness writing process.

We engage witness writing on many levels as part of supervision. Supervisees may write detailed verbal observations about their piece, engage the work in imaginal dialogue, read their witness writing to the group, or sit silently and witness others as they read. It is important to have a supervisory agreement that specifies the philosophy and methods of supervision employed by the supervisor. When offering this resource it is critical to be responsive to the interest and tone of the group. To be a useful support for therapists to gain insight into their work, it must feel psychologically safe for all.

During supervision, I facilitate supervisees' engagement in imaginal inquiry when there appears to be rich material to unpack and when there is time and interest in engaging in the process. When we participate in witness writing, we may interact with our own or someone else's imagery, choosing any piece that calls for our attention. This way of working can require considerable time and focus, and time is short during fieldwork supervision class. For that reason, I engage in it less during therapist training. I use active imagination and witness writing more in postgraduate supervision to support clinical introspection and to access my own supervisory insight.

Supervisors who facilitate witness writing and work with active imagination or other ways of engaging imaginal material must be personally familiar with the process. There is no method of inquiry that is appropriate for everyone in all situations. There are times that the material brought into supervision requires direct verbal intervention and pointed problem solving; other times more imaginal resources are useful.

The following vignette recalls my witness writing with a piece that I made for supervision class, speaking to how imaginal work can give clinical guidance to both supervisee and supervisor. Response art helps me to unpack and understand my work. Active imagination and witness writing are the tools that I use to move this process deeper, accessing material that lies outside of my conscious thought.

I drew *Response Art* (Figure 4.5) to respond to a supervisee's presentation of her work with a woman with dementia at an assisted care facility serving elderly clients. The image shows the intern and resident sitting side by side next to the client's drawing of an aerial view of her childhood home on a farm in Ireland. I wrote my intention to focus my interaction with the image: I am open to what my image has to bring about art-based supervision and the student's relationship with her client as well as mine with the student.

The student sits with the resident, paying attention to all that she has to say. The resident is the authority, sitting confidently and pointing.

I said:	Will anyone speak?
The student said:	I'm listening carefully so that I won't miss anything. I am careful and respectful.
The resident said:	I have a lot to say and it doesn't come easy. I want to show you this, not tell it.
I said:	What do you mean?
The resident said:	Pictures go to the heart of it. This is a bird's eye view of the fields I love. I remember the sight and smell of it, black dirt in my hands, green plants and the sun.

FIGURE 4.5 Response Art

Barbara Fish

The student said:	How can I help?
The resident said:	Witness me as I am. Don't look for whole memories. I have valuable snapshots of my experience.
I said:	How is this helpful for my work with the student?
The resident said:	It's all the same. Each encounter offers a snapshot. Value the depth of experience. Each offers material to build on.
I said:	You are being abstract. Can you be more clear?
The resident said:	That's the point. I can't be more clear than I am. I have dementia. It is your job and the student's to sit with the snapshots and make meaning of them. This is true of your work together as well.
I said:	Thank you.

In this instance, working with the image through witness writing helped me hone in on an effective supervisory direction. The goal was not to help the resident retrieve memories that were no longer accessible. The focus of treatment was to help the client engage in the moment, sharing interpersonal experiences, enriching her life, and decreasing her feelings of frustration, loss, and isolation. By engaging my image I clarified my role in supporting the new therapist in understanding and addressing her client's treatment goals.

Supervisors' Imagery

In order to facilitate the use of these imaginal resources, supervisors must be familiar with a range of materials and engage in image-based investigation. Supervisors help to identify the content to explore, find supplies that support safe and productive engagement, and facilitate the interaction with the imagery that is produced.

Whether I am serving as a supervisor or as a therapist, the more I engage in my own creative process, the more able I am to cultivate others' creative work. I demonstrate my commitment to this practice through the use of my own imagery. I make response art to reflect clinical concerns to students, demonstrate how I conceptualize case material and explore relationships. I help others to recognize the value and potential pitfalls of making and sharing response art by showing them how I navigate its use in my own practice. Although I advocate for this use of imagery in the service of the supervisee, creative self-reflection benefits the supervisor as well. I gain supervisory and personal insight when I make response art to explore the practice of new therapists.

As supervisors, the way that we engage our own images, as well as how we work with the imagery of others, guides new therapists as they learn to use their artwork effectively in their own practices. There are times that I make images outside of supervision to reflect on the work, keeping my images and process to myself. There are other times when I find it useful to bring artwork into supervision to share it with those with whom I work. The supervisor's response art can be a powerful example for those in training, demonstrating art-based investigation.

Supervisors should consider their motives carefully before sharing the response art that they create outside of supervision to ensure that it benefits the new therapist. This decision should be considered in the light of the relationship with the supervisee and the implications for productive discourse and learning. These pieces are made as personal work and may not be valuable or may even be harmful if shared with the client or supervisee. For example, to clear my issues from the supervisory relationship, I may make a piece to untangle countertransference toward a student who reminds me of my sister. That image is important work for my practice, but it is not relevant or appropriate to show to the student. I might retrieve the piece at a later date and show it to other supervisees as an example of imagery that I created and used to gain clarity.

I thought carefully before bringing my painting *Tornado* (Figure 4.6, Plate 4) to fieldwork supervision class. I painted the piece to express how I felt after witnessing a violent outburst. At the time I was consulting to a residential facility for

FIGURE 4.6 (PLATE 4) Tornado

Barbara Fish

adolescents with behavioral and emotional problems; the agency was dysfunctional and would eventually close. The adolescents' aggressive behavior was stirred by years of systemic problems at the agency.

I painted this image after observing girls rioting, roaming the grounds, and attacking numerous staff. The assaults resulted in several arrests. When I talked with the girls about the incident, they complained about not feeling safe. They reported that the fight was retribution for the staff's violent behavior during a restraint the prior day. As I painted the image, I considered the agency's cycle of violence. My painting depicts the girls being torn apart by the chaos, stirred by the program's turmoil and their responses to it.

I painted *Tornado* (Figure 4.6, Plate 4) to hold how I felt as the youth milled around in aggressive cohorts. Painting the piece helped me endure thinking about the incident as I worked to understand it. As I handled the painting, I recognized how clients' behavior often parallels the dynamics of the staff on all levels of the agency. When staff feel unsafe and without support, clients are often experiencing the same trepidation. Aggression, rooted in familiar responses to trauma, often follows in these circumstances. The painting helped me to remember that the behavior of both clients and staff has meaning.

I made this piece to manage and explore my reaction to this frightening event. Soon after, I began to see its value in demonstrating the use of response art to those I supervise. At the time, the image helped me clearly communicate my concerns to staff, clinicians, and administrators at the agency. Since then I have used it to help new therapists understand this dynamic.

Honest reflection on real practice is important for supervisees to witness. New therapists are eager to take on their work. Although some may be reticent or even fearful, the risk for new therapists is not that they will withdraw from the intensity, but that they may steel themselves and unquestioningly become used to it. When therapists maintain their pace after an incident without taking time for reflection, it can lead to bad habits, subverting sound treatment and having implications for the therapists' well-being.

I have had several interns come to class days after being attacked by clients only to say that it was not a big deal and that everyone gets assaulted at their site. As the supervisor, I am responsible for listening to the therapist, processing the incident, and problem-solving the situation. I help the therapist discuss feelings related to the situation and identify resources and responsibilities for communicating the incident. Most of all I help the therapist realize that his or her own personal safety is critical to the work. Expectation for personal and interpersonal safety is important. Its erosion is dangerous for all concerned.

I considered many things before showing this piece to my class. Why would I share personal imagery with students and new therapists? Would it be useful for supervisees to know that I was afraid at my work? How would this help them? I was careful to present this piece in a way that protected the confidentiality of the agency, clients, and staff. Not all programs are dysfunctional and dangerous. Nevertheless, many therapists work with clients who are removed from the community because of psychiatric issues leading to interpersonal strife. Agencies themselves can be unsupportive and unrealistic in their expectations. It is essential that students and new therapists gain a realistic understanding of the challenges that they may face.

It is critical to have a clear intention when sharing response art made beyond session. In addition to the images that I create to give supervisory feedback, I make response art outside of session about supervision and therapy to explore the work. These pieces may include personal responses and content that has no place in the supervision that I provide for others. I take these to my own supervision or therapy. There are also images that I make to process supervision, or my own practice as a therapist, that have immense value as examples in supervision.

In addition to understanding our reasons for sharing our artwork, as supervisors we must be mindful of our use of power as we decide on the direction the class will take. Supervisory disclosure affects boundaries. It can encourage or inhibit supervisees' participation. It is important to carefully assess the ability of the supervisee to understand and integrate disclosed material before sharing it in the supervisory relationship. Some students may understand supervisory images as models for their own introspection, the unraveling of countertransference, and their self-care, seeing them as authentic efforts to demonstrate real work. Others may be confused or intimidated by the images that are shared, feeling disoriented by the disclosure or worrying about the supervisor, thus taking on a burden that is not their responsibility.

As supervisors, we must be sure to consider the ways that we present and explain our response art. We are demonstrating a method for the therapist's use of his or her own imagery with clients. To ensure the psychological safety of the class, the supervisor must support the group in a way that does not overchallenge the most vulnerable. Imagery and discussion that is too intense for one student creates a lack of safety for all. Supervisors must be mindful that their imagery brought into supervision has the potential to encourage students to engage their imaginations or to overwhelm them. After carefully considering what I hoped to accomplish by sharing this image and others, I developed the following guidelines.

Reasons to Share the Supervisor's Imagery

- Is the work made specifically to communicate a point, to reflect on the supervisee's practice, or to give feedback?
- Does the piece demonstrate personal commitment to art-based practice?
- Will sharing the artwork offer a realistic example of challenges supervisees might encounter at work?
- Does it demonstrate the use of response art to support effective communication with coworkers?
- Does it communicate a specific point that needs to be raised as a supervisory issue?
- Does it demonstrate self-care?

Reasons Not to Share the Supervisor's Imagery

- The supervisee's material from therapy should take precedence over the supervisor's planned discourse.
- The supervisor has not carefully examined the image beforehand. This can lead to the group feeling responsible for helping the supervisor process the work. This is not the supervisees' responsibility.
- The supervisor is still too involved in unpacking the work to fully attend to the supervisees' processing and understanding of it.
- The work does not relate to the new therapists' work.
- The content that the piece addresses may not be safe for one or more of the supervision group members. In this case it is important to consider a way that relevant issues that are sensitive may be addressed so that supervisees are able to tolerate the conversation without shutting down.

Tornado (Figure 4.6, Plate 4) continues to be a useful springboard for discussion in supervision. New therapists find permission to express their fears when they see my feelings processed in my imagery. By demonstrating how I manage intense interactions that occur while providing therapy, students and new therapists can come to believe that they can handle their own.

Conclusion

We have discussed some of the ways that response art may be used in art-based supervision. There are many more. They are as unlimited as our imaginations and our ability to engage them in clinical work. Art-based supervision provides opportunities to hold difficult material, exploring it from new vantage points and engaging it through personal reflection, interpersonal communication, and imaginal work. Supervision is a forum to explore internal issues and external concerns stirred by treatment. Response art can help us look at treatment issues, investigate countertransference, and establish realistic expectations for our work, as well as understand and communicate systemic and practical concerns.

The following section presents the challenges and opportunities of art-based supervision. This work is divided into two chapters. Chapter 5, "Understanding Power in Supervision," discusses the use of imagery to clarify interpersonal communication and serves as a resource for reflexivity, supporting awareness of supervisory power. Chapter 6, "Harm's Touch: How We Are Affected by What We Witness," moves deeply into a discussion of the use of imagery to manage and learn from the traumatic and painful content that we witness in therapy and in supervision. In both chapters we will explore the use of response art to sustain and support healthy practice.

References

Allen, P. B. (2005). *Art is a spiritual path*. Boston, MA: Shambhala.

Chodorow, J. (1997). Introduction. In J. Chodorow (Ed.), *Encountering Jung: Jung on active imagination* (pp. 1–20). Princeton, NJ: Princeton.

Corey, G., Corey, M. S., & Callanan, P. (2011). *Issues and ethics in the helping professions* (8th Ed.). Belmont, CA: Brooks/Cole, Cengage Learning.

Fish, B. J. (1989). Addressing countertransference through image making. In H. Wadeson, J. Durkin, & D. Perach (Eds.), *Advances in art therapy* (pp. 376–389). New York, NY: John Wiley & Sons.

Fish, B. J. (2006). *Image-based narrative inquiry of response art in art therapy.* (Doctoral dissertation). Retrieved from Dissertations & Theses database. (UMI no. AAT 3228081).

Fish, B. J. (2008). Formative evaluation of art-based supervision in art therapy training. *Art Therapy: Journal of the American Art Therapy Association, 25*(2), 70–77.

Fish, B. J. (2012). Response art: The art of the art therapist. *Art Therapy: Journal of the American Art Therapy Association, 29*(3), 138–143.

Fish, B. J. (2013). Painting research: Challenges and opportunities of intimacy and depth. In S. McNiff (Ed.), *Art as research: Opportunities and challenges* (pp. 209–219). Chicago, IL: University of Chicago Press.

Hannah, B. (1981). *Encounters with the soul: Active imagination as developed by C. G. Jung.* Boston, MA: Sigo Press.

Jung, C. G. (1959). *The basic writings of C. G. Jung*. New York, NY: Random House.

Jung, C. G. (1963). *Memories dreams and reflections*. New York, NY: Vintage Books.

Jung, C. G. (1968). *Alchemical studies vol. 13, collected works*. Princeton, NJ: Princeton University Press.

Jung, C. G. (2009). *The red book: Liber novus* (S. Shamdasani, Ed.) (M. Kyburz, J. Peck, & S. Shamdasani, Trans.). New York and London: WW Norton.

Kramer, E. (1971). *Art as therapy with children*. New York, NY: Schocken Books.

McNiff, S. (1989). *Depth psychology of art*. Springfield, IL: Charles C Thomas.

5

UNDERSTANDING POWER IN SUPERVISION

Cultural Competence

Responsible supervision requires reflexivity and an awareness of the use of power. This chapter demonstrates the use of imagery to understand intersectionality and its implications for power in both the supervisory and therapeutic relationships. I advocate for the use of response art. It is a tool that supports the efforts of the supervisor and supervisee in their ongoing work to gain the awareness necessary for sound practice with others with varied experiences, contexts, and perspectives. The examples presented here demonstrate the value of art-based work, supporting insight into personal and sociocultural contexts and bolstering comprehension of nuanced communication and interpersonal understanding.

Culturally informed work is as critical to sound supervision as it is to therapy. Those in supervisory relationships differ from one another in contexts that may include race, class, gender, age, religion, sexuality, and physical, emotional, and intellectual agency, all of which are influenced by historical and current events. Because these are the roots of values, personal perspectives, and worldviews, without vigilant reflexivity these differences often lead to interpersonal misunderstanding and the misuse of power and privilege in supervision and in therapy. Whether these contexts are obvious or nuanced, approaching practice with attention to these varied perspectives is critical. Supervision is a practice that calls for supervisors and new therapists to reflect on their own intersectionality as well as that of those they work with. Talwar (2010) described the comprehensive nature of intersectionality.

> The systems comprising social hierarchy are interconnected and embedded in a society's institutions. As individuals, we each experience our lives through culturally defined categories; through them we may occupy

positions of dominance or subordination, and sometimes both simultaneously. Thus identity is not a fixed category but rather a complex set of intersections that shift and change.

(p. 15)

Cultural competence is a requirement in therapy just as it is in other mental health professions; it is as critical to supervision as it is to therapy. To begin to understand the interpersonal nuances of working and supervising cross-culturally takes dedication, study, and deep personal reflection. Making art about supervision can aid in the supervisor's self-reflexive investigation of his or her own cultural context as well as the cultural contexts of clients and supervisees. Creating and exploring response art offers opportunities to look at what lies below our consciousness that may drive the behavior or expectations of both those we work with and ourselves. Ter Maat (2011) describes four areas required for culturally competent practice that are equally important for culturally competent supervision:

(a) Awareness of self, (b) awareness and knowledge of other cultures' beliefs and behaviors, (c) awareness and knowledge of cultural dynamics and interactions that exist between the art therapist and the client, and (d) skills and interventions that are ethical and appropriate for clients with cultural backgrounds that differ from the art therapist's.

(p. 9)

Many educators have engaged in discourse about the importance of a reflexive approach to intersectionality in training, practice, and supervision to support competent work (Calisch, 2003; George, Greene, & Blackwell, 2005; Hiscox & Calisch, 1998; Howie, Prasad, & Kristel, 2013; Talwar, 2010; ter Maat, 2011). I encourage you to investigate these resources and others to support your understanding.

As a supervisor I engage my artwork to investigate many manifestations of power, including those present in interpersonal relationships and in systemic work. Maintaining our awareness of our own cultural context as we engage others in these layered interactions is challenging. It is critical to be mindful of culturally rooted perspectives and learning styles when we engage in supervision. It takes ongoing vigilance and integrity to avoid promoting our own biases at the expense of those we supervise.

Supervisors hold the responsibility and power of evaluation. Although graduate training with students and postgraduate work with new professionals may be cocreated and collegial, they are not equal. This discrepancy in power can impede effective work. Because supervision rests on the supervisees' ability to accurately describe what goes on in treatment, those who feel interpersonally misunderstood may be unable to bring sensitive issues to supervision. Supervisors are challenged to provide a relationship that supports the safe investigation of material that is sensitive to cultural perceptions, styles of learning, and nuanced interpersonal and systemic responses. By striving to be conscious of our use of power and privilege in our supervisory relationships, we can raise the insight and clarity of purpose of those we supervise and support their effective work with others.

I am a White, Jewish, upper middle-class, United States citizen with advanced educational degrees and several decades of experience as an art therapist. I work hard to understand my power and privilege as I strive to help supervisees feel safe and heard in supervision instead of presenting my experience and context as a formidable obstacle.

Misunderstandings are prevalent when supervising cross-culturally. When discussing clinical work, the best intentions of the supervisor and supervisee may lead to an impasse rooted in differing cultural perspectives, leaving the supervisee feeling disempowered and the clinical situation unaddressed. Listening carefully is not enough. The supervisor must be alert when assessing responses to feedback and seek additional resources when supervising those from diverse contexts. Cross-cultural work brings ever-shifting and deepening complexities that require personal stamina for introspection, reflection, and training.

I provide supervision to emerging professionals from a wide range of cultural and socioeconomic circumstances. I recognize the multiple intersections and disconnections between those I supervise and myself. I have worked with student therapists and new professionals from the United States and international locations. They ranged in age from their mid-twenties to their early sixties and bring a variety of life experiences rooted in their race, class, gender, age, religion, sexuality, and physical, emotional, and intellectual agency. Helping new therapists recognize and address their own contexts is critical to ethically sound practice.

Although I will never fully understand the experiences of those I work with who come from contexts differing from my own, I work to take responsibility to awaken and reawaken my awareness of power and privilege in these relationships. This includes working to appreciate my use of power and recognizing when I cannot be helpful. Supervisors should be mindful of their responsibilities to support those they work with in their professional development, modeling involvement and facilitating networking opportunities. In these situations and others, I help students and new therapists make connections with others who may offer different resources that are beyond the scope of my experience and abilities.

I am fortunate to teach in a school that serves many international students. It is not unusual to have several students in my fieldwork supervision class who come from outside of the United States, many of whom speak English as a second language. This adds to the richness and complexity of the discourse and provides important insights and resources for those serving clients from diverse backgrounds.

Self-awareness is critical when providing both supervision and therapy. Cultivating self-awareness requires work. It calls for looking at the legacies, contexts, and experiences that inform our worldview, biases, and preconceived ideas. I spent the first fifteen years of my career working with African American children in hospital and residential care. I thought that I was aware of the importance of cultural competence and tried to pay attention to my own power in relationships with others and in the systems where I worked. When I started to intentionally investigate my own heritage I began to understand the challenge and the value that identity holds for us all.

My deliberate work to understand my identity began when I accompanied my mother on a heritage trip to Eastern Europe led by Chaim Potok, a rabbi and Jewish scholar. Although I knew I was Jewish by heritage, prior to that experience I did not think of myself as Jewish. I was not interested in Jewish history and avoided information about the Holocaust. I prepared for the trip by reading *Man's Search for Meaning* (Frankl, 1985) and painting *Self Portrait* (Figure 5.1).

As I walked the streets that my family had walked in Poland and Lithuania and listened to the history of their lives before the Holocaust and their fate during it,

FIGURE 5.1 Self Portrait

Barbara Fish

I began to understand the importance of my own roots. It was only after I returned that I recognized that the self-portrait that I painted was a Jewish woman.

During the trip, I walked the streets and visited the only remaining synagogue in Vilna, Lithuania, a vital center for Jewish culture and religious study before the war. In the late 1800s, my mother's paternal grandmother fled pogroms in Lithuania. I painted *Gone* (Figure 5.2, Plate 5) after visiting the Ponar Forest in Vilna, a site of mass murder of Lithuanian Jewish people by the Nazis.

FIGURE 5.2 (PLATE 5)   Gone

Barbara Fish

My heritage trip continued through Poland and the Czech Republic, bringing more visceral experiences. I stopped painting and instead photographed what I saw, capturing my feelings digitally to unpack later. Since my return I have spent more than a decade studying, painting, and writing to understand the experience, trying to comprehend the influence of my family's history on who I am. I painted *Legacy* (Figure 5.3) to express the importance of the past. The watercolor image

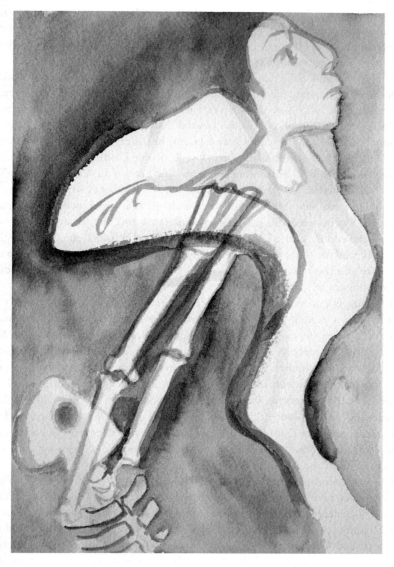

FIGURE 5.3 Legacy

Barbara Fish

depicts me pulling forward as I try to move beyond a skeleton that drags heavily on my arm, representing the legacy of my Jewish culture and the accompanying intergenerational trauma.

Beyond the importance of this inquiry to me personally, it has helped to deepen my awareness of and appreciation for the influence of history and heritage for others. That does not mean that the new awareness of my heritage gives me the right to say that I understand the history, contexts, and challenges of others. Removing my blindfold about my own identity and history helped me appreciate its importance to me as well as to those I work with. What I learned helped me to resonate with the legacy of others' trauma because I began to understand the influence of intergenerational trauma in my own life.

I began to think differently about the distrust I encountered when I worked with African American children and their families and the meaning of their resistance to therapy and to systems of care. I thought about experiments performed on African American people in the United States without their knowledge or consent and those performed on Jewish people in concentration camps. I remembered visiting ghettos in Europe where Jewish people lived and died and thought about the plight of African Americans in the ghettos in Chicago. I recalled how I felt in desecrated Jewish cemeteries where headstones were smashed and removed to make sidewalks for people to walk on as a way of dehumanizing my ancestors. I considered the past and current racist and abusive acts that weave through the culture of the United States. My work on self-awareness was a beginning. It helped me to see that I have much more work to do. This has added to my sensitivity as a therapist and supervisor, helping me gain a visceral understanding of the influence of identity.

The imagery made by those I supervise serves as a resource for their cultural reflection as well. Lisa Thomas, an art therapist I see for postgraduate work, brought *Breathing In and Breathing Out* (Figure 5.4, Plate 6) to supervision. She talked about the piece as she discussed her work in an elementary school with African American children from families that were socioeconomically challenged. As a therapist who identifies herself as Black, Lisa struggled with her feelings of fondness and sadness for the children she worked with as she navigated their complex and layered contexts. She said that taking in their distress stirred her love and sadness for these children as she saw the impact of their struggles with personal, family, economic, systemic, and social challenges. She wished she could just "scoop them up and carry them away" with her.

Lisa went on to say that she realized this yearning to rescue the children had hardened her to the complex challenges of their families. This was significant because she understood how important it was for her to engage the parents in their children's care. Giving examples of situations that aroused her mixed feelings, Lisa described her frustration with one boy's mother who, after taking her child for a psychiatric evaluation, refused to give him the prescribed medication. She told me about another child who referred to himself as black and ugly, repeating what she referred to as "color struck" values that he heard at home about

FIGURE 5.4 (PLATE 6)   Breathing In and Breathing Out

Lisa Thomas

the appeal of lighter skin. Lisa described the term as a bias that sometimes exists within African American families based on internalized racism.

We talked about what might cause her clients' mothers to behave in these ways. Why would one mother resist giving her child medication? Why would another mother tell her child that he was dark and ugly? Together we discussed her countertransference and her rescue fantasy about the children. We explored the differences between her clients' families' beliefs and values and those of her own, which were influenced by those held by her family.

Lisa understood the roots of these behaviors far better than I did. She described feelings about the stigma of medication and distrust of medical systems that one mother may be experiencing and the internalized racism that might cause the other mother to react to her child's skin tone. Referring to her drawing, she said that her work was like breathing in and out—breathing in to resonate with the children and breathing out to reach and understand the parents.

Discussing Lisa's image in supervision allowed her to explore these complex relationships and helped me to deepen my appreciation for the layers of cross-cultural work. In this situation, both the therapist and clients were African American. However, there were vast differences between them related to power, privilege, socioeconomic status, and education. As a White supervisor, I tried to be mindful of my own power and privilege while I supported Lisa's authority and agency in the situation and encouraged her to be self-reflective and open to investigating the personal responses that were stirred in her.

Personal Space

Space and time are important components in therapy that, if misunderstood, may become problematic in treatment. Interpersonal values, cultural norms, and effective communication are critical to understanding these aspects. Supporting reflection on a diverse perspective of the use of space and time is an important part of supervision.

Sandie Yi was a Taiwanese art therapy intern in her early twenties when I supervised her graduate training at a center for adults with developmental disabilities. During supervision class, Sandie told me that one of her clients, an older man, leaned his body close as he talked and spit saliva on her. I suggested that she ask him to give her more personal space. I thought the advice would set an example of more appropriate social interaction for the client and provide a way for her to define her own boundaries. Sandie accepted the feedback in class. She came back to supervision, periodically reporting the same issue with the man. Each time, I supported her dealing with the problem by redirecting the man and establishing a boundary to support a more appropriate exchange.

At the end of the semester, Sandie revealed to me that the situation persisted because she felt culturally prohibited from confronting a man who was older than she. Although she understood my advice, she could not figure out how she could ask him to step away while maintaining the respectful behavior that she felt his age and status required. To compound her lack of agency, she felt that her inability to follow my direction disappointed me. Because of the cross-cultural misunderstanding, she felt unheard, unsupported, and unable to address this ongoing issue from therapy in supervision. Once she shared her perspective, I was able to support her as she found her own way to establish space with the client. At the end of the semester she was able to "gather her guts" and ask the man to give her some personal space, ending "the shower of saliva" that occurred when she had conversations with him.

Time

I worked with a Japanese student therapist in her twenties, who was an intern at a psychiatric hospital treating children. Each week she turned in her hours log, indicating many more hours of work than were required by the graduate training program. I was concerned that, in her enthusiasm for her work, she might be extending her time beyond what was required and sustainable. When the overage of hours continued, we talked about how she should cut back to the required amount of time to maintain appropriate boundaries and establish practical work habits. Our conversations seemed to go well and she appeared grateful for the feedback, saying she could use the time for the rest of her schoolwork. However, the next time she turned in her report, her hours were still far above the program's requirements.

After several exchanges in which we discussed the issue and she assured me she would cut back on her hours, I initiated a deeper conversation. I asked the student therapist if there might be a culturally based reason for her excessive hours. Her eyes widened with surprise, and then she seemed relieved. She told me that in Japan, workers are considered to be disrespectful if they leave their job before their supervisor. The intern began work at 8:00 a.m., but her supervisor arrived at work at 11:00 a.m. and left after 7:00 p.m. Yet she felt unable to leave even though this extended her hours far beyond those required by the school. Once the student and I realized the cultural underpinnings of the issue, she was able to resolve the issue by decreasing her hours in a way that felt comfortable to her, helping her to reevaluate her time and establish healthy boundaries at her site.

Stigma

Culturally rooted attitudes toward illness, disability, and medical interventions are important factors in the course of treatment. Exploring these influences on therapy supports effective interventions. In addition to the intersectionality of the therapist and the client, the same factors must be looked at between the supervisee and the supervisor. These complex and nuanced perspectives must be considered to facilitate sound work.

Jung-Eun Jeanne Park, a Korean art therapist who had attended high school, college, and graduate school in the United States, returned to Korea and began to provide art therapy services for children. During distance art therapy supervision, she explored her work with a young girl diagnosed on the autism spectrum. Jung-Eun's drawing, *The Boxed Child* (Figure 5.5) depicts a girl contained within a box inside of another box with a padlocked door and only a small ladder for access.

We looked at the drawing together as we met on Skype for supervision. Jung-Eun said that when she met with the child in her home, she became aware of the parents' attitude toward the young client's psychiatric condition. Jung-Eun told me that Koreans value homogeneity and are reluctant to expose those with psychological disorders to others. Their ideas of perfection and beauty are intertwined with their idea of "normal," and those who deviate from it are not easily accepted. She told me that the girl's parents did not ask when their daughter would be "better." They asked when she would be "normal."

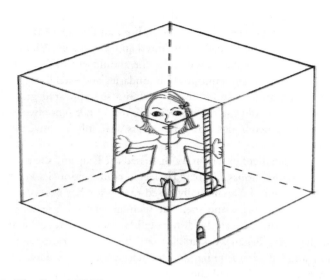

FIGURE 5.5 The Boxed Child

Jung-Eun Jeanne Park

Jung-Eun described how she felt that the girl was locked away by cultural biases, stereotypes, and her parents' attitudes. The girl's parents were ashamed of her differences and only exposed her to a narrow circle of people, including those at her special school and those who worked with her therapeutically. Her access to the world beyond that was controlled, limiting the client's ability to grow. Having been educated outside of Korea, Jung-Eun struggled with the conflict between her own beliefs rooted in her Korean culture, Western concepts of mental illness, and the more traditional Korean attitudes toward it. She worked to find a way to be respectful of the values of the girl and her parents while simultaneously supporting the child's growth as a Western-educated, Korean-born therapist.

In this instance my supervisory role was that of a sounding board and witness to the earnest work of a new therapist. Jung-Eun's drawing helped me to understand her dilemma so that I could support her as she worked to find her way to provide therapy as the authority of her own cultural experience.

Silence

One of the most difficult things to understand in supervision is silence. In both supervision and therapy it is often misunderstood as resistance. Silence can bring up feelings of powerlessness and frustration in the supervisor, which are often counterproductive to understanding the issue. When I am confronted with silence in supervision, I work to understand its meaning. It is useful to look beyond the intrapersonal and interpersonal roots of the silence to consider it in the context of culture, privilege, and agency.

There are times when silence comes from a reserved interactive style, deference to authority, or cultural expectations for interactions in an educational setting. A student from China told me that in her educational experience, students were expected to formulate their ideas before speaking. This approach to discussion can contrast dramatically with other students who contribute to the discourse by talking their way to the point they want to make. The Chinese student said that by the time she clarified what she wanted to contribute, the discussion had moved on. This left her looking like she was not participating when she was truly very thoughtful and engaged with the material. This challenges the supervisor to hold the space for varied paces and approaches to learning and styles of engagement in supervision.

Faith

Clients come to therapy because of interpsychic and interpersonal disruptions that shake their worldview. Belief in someone or something can provide a valuable resource for clients as well as for the therapists who work with them. But discussions about religion and spirituality as part of treatment can raise complicated issues. These nuanced conversations benefit from sensitivity and a high level of clinical skill. There are times when supervisors, believing that those in their charge are not equipped to handle such complex discussions, may tell new therapists that religion is a subject that should not be discussed. This was the case with Erin Gasim, a student therapist working at a community mental health program that served adults with chronic illness. As Erin found her own faith to be an important resource for her work, she struggled to understand when her site supervisor told her not to talk about spirituality with her clients. Erin felt torn between adhering to her site supervisor's directive and carrying out her responsibility to attend to the religious content that her clients brought into sessions.

Erin brought her conflict into fieldwork supervision class. She tried to reconcile the agency's mission to offer services tailored to the diversity of its clients with the supervisor's lack of openness to include spirituality in treatment. Because she felt silenced and disappointed, I suggested that she make imagery to explore how she felt about the limit set by her site supervisor. This helped her to clarify the importance of the issue to her and bridged communication with her peers. Reflecting on her experience, Erin said:

> In the context of my supervision class and other classes, I was encouraged to use my faith for guidance and to continue to make art about my

questions or concerns. I experienced a sense of being heard and valued. In supervision, I was encouraged to speak up and assured that my voice was important too.

(Erin Gasim, Personal communication, April 7, 2015)

Erin created a body of work that she discussed in supervision at school. *Self Portrait* (Figure 5.6) is a piece that represents her made speechless by a bandage that binds her mouth. She shared this image to explore the silence she felt had been imposed on her and others. It helped her explain to me, her peers, and other faculty members how she felt when silenced about her spiritual values. Processing this piece helped her to gain valuable insight into her concerns. Erin's challenge to find her public voice related to spirituality continued throughout her training. Her image making became an essential resource that supported her work and growth as a therapist. Summarizing her use of her imagery, she said:

I believe a connection was made with the help of the art. My art played an important role in helping me regain my voice and it served as a bridge to talk about uncomfortable and or difficult issues. Creating helped me to further understand my role as an art therapist, in terms of modeling how to use my artwork to express myself.

(Erin Gasim, Personal communication, April 7, 2015)

FIGURE 5.6 Self Portrait

Erin Gasim

Beyond the value that Erin's exploration held for her, I found her work useful to me on several levels. As her faculty supervisor, her heartfelt visual expressions helped me to understand her struggle to comprehend the prohibition of the discussion of religion and its impact on her. Erin's imagery helped me look at the complexity of diverse values in supervision. Her artworks, and her explanation of them, reinforced the importance of the supervisor's responsibility to support the safe and respectful expression of differing core values.

As a Jewish woman, I often find myself silent in faith-based discussions and unwilling to be assertive when my religious practices are not considered in academic and work schedules. Erin's work helped me to look at my own defensiveness about sharing my faith in professional settings. Even as I write this, I have twinges telling me that this is not a safe part of my life to disclose. As supervisors, engaging in self-reflexive work facilitates our increasing awareness of those we supervise, supporting their effective practice. Art-based supervision provides imagery as an additional resource to strengthen comprehension and communication of these issues.

Mandated Reporting

Supervisors and therapists are mandated to report abuse and neglect of children, the elderly, and those with disabilities. Misunderstanding between the client and therapist is prevalent when working cross culturally and can easily lead to ineffective or inappropriate interventions when intersectionality is not considered. The supervisor's role is pivotal in guiding those they supervise when they report abuse and neglect. Lack of clarity in addressing these important and sensitive interactions is compounded by issues of power and privilege intrinsic in social service agencies and the child welfare system in the United States.

In a supervisory discussion of mandated reporting that explored how clients describe discipline, a student therapist from Singapore told me that in the Chinese language, the word for "discipline" is the same as the word for "beat." When an English-speaking therapist is told by a Chinese child that his parent "beat" him, does it require a hotline report to protective services?

Language and culturally rooted attitudes are nuanced and deeply ingrained. It is important to understand the language describing behaviors. The use of terminology to describe individuals based on race, gender, age, religion, sexuality, and physical, emotional, and intellectual agency require vigilance as they change over time. Inquiring about preferred terminology demonstrates respect and supports agency.

Therapists and supervisors must use all of the resources available to them to understand situations and take appropriate action. I provided training with an African American colleague for a primarily African American childcare staff working in residential care. We asked how many of them had, as children, been disciplined by being hit with objects. Almost everyone in the room raised his or her hand. When we asked how many of them felt that they were abused, no one indicated that they were. The training helped us all to think about the potential for miscommunication rooted in cross-cultural communication.

Self-reflexive practice is most critical when supervisors guide new therapists' work reporting abuse and neglect. Actions motivated by unexamined power and privilege can be most harmful when taking action can have lifelong consequences for those we treat. Mandated reporting raises issues that require supervisory oversight. How are incidents of abuse communicated, first to the therapist and then to the site supervisor? What are the facility's policies for reporting abuse? Did the therapist seek clarification about the incident, asking the client for information that might reveal nuanced facts to consider before making the report? Was the client informed before making the call to protective services or involved in the process of reporting? Participating in the report can help the client to feel agency in his or her life's course. Was there a safety plan developed in case the parent or caregiver was angered by the investigation? Were efforts made to find support outside of the immediate family to help the client cope with parents' or caregivers' reactions? These questions, as well as immigration status, socioeconomic stressors, substance use, and other contributors to domestic violence support complex understanding, facilitating responsible and effective interventions that may include reporting the incident to protective services.

Run Away (Figure 5.7) is a drawing that I made outside of fieldwork supervision and brought into class to share my response to a student's conflicted feelings about reporting abuse. It helped to stimulate a conversation about culture, class, privilege, and agency. We explored the validity of historically rooted cultural distrust of the child welfare system, discussing the potential of unintended consequences of reporting abuse and neglect and how to function within a broken child welfare system. We went on to talk about how to support the clients we work with while advocating for systemic change.

Understanding the dynamics of our interpersonal roles as supervisor and supervisee is a never-ending challenge. In addition to gender, race, class, age, religion, sexuality, and physical, emotional, and intellectual agency, as well as our diverse and complex cultural contexts, there is power intrinsic in the evaluative nature of supervision. There are also differences between the power, privilege, and agency held by the new therapist and by the client. Although we cannot be investigators and probe into abuse allegations, it is critical to be clear about what we are reporting. Once the report is made, new therapists, as well as seasoned professionals, often feel little agency to shape the course of events that follow. There are times when abuse and neglect are clear and procedures are followed, but the system does not respond in a way that is helpful. It is the supervisor's responsibility to help new therapists navigate these failures while advocating for their clients, caring for themselves, and working for systemic change.

FIGURE 5.7 Run Away

Barbara Fish

Countertransference

Interpersonal dynamics become even more complicated when countertransference is aroused in supervision. Effective supervision is supported by the supervisor's self-reflective practice, including working to understand personal responses stirred in the supervisory relationship. Working with countertransference in a way that is culturally sensitive requires that we recognize our deeply imbedded perspectives, attitudes, and beliefs aroused by the content of the supervisee's work as well as the supervisory relationship.

Talwar (2010) asserts that the reflective nature of intersectionality has a precedent in the concept of countertransference. Here the term countertransference is expanded from the original Freudian concept of the projection of unconscious material (Kahn, 2002) to all of the responses of the therapist to the client (Corey,

Corey, & Callanan, 2011) or, in this case, to the supervisee. Working to understand countertransference in supervision supports the self-reflective stance necessary to be cognizant of and to support intersectional awareness in therapy.

I used my imagery to explore my countertransference and deepen my appreciation of the complexity of this interpersonal work. There are times when I make images about a supervisee outside of supervision to try to understand a relational dynamic that is unclear to me. *African Cloth* (Figure 5.8) demonstrates my art-based struggle to understand the difficulty that I had in communicating with a supervisee. I painted this image as self-reflective work to understand my perspective and the interpersonal dynamics in this supervisory relationship. In this instance, as it was for my own learning and I did not see how it would benefit the supervisee, I did not share my imagery with her.

I decided to paint *African Cloth* (Figure 5.8) as I struggled to support a student in my fieldwork supervision class. I felt she was holding back when we investigated the content of her work. I thought about our relationship, trying to check myself to see how I was contributing to the situation. Then I made an image to further explore the dynamics. Because she was African American, I decided to paint a piece of African cloth. The deeper I went into making the piece, the more I realized that the investigation did not make sense. There are many reasons why this work was incongruous to investigating the relationship. I did not know

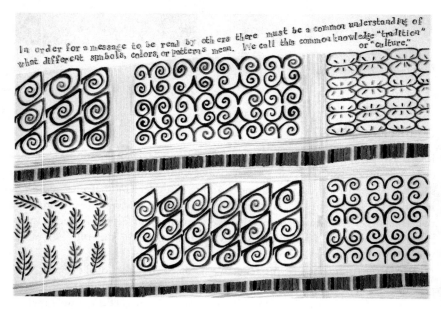

FIGURE 5.8 African Cloth

Barbara Fish

anything about the student's background, including whether or not she identified herself as having African heritage.

As I started to paint, I realized that I did not know what "African cloth" looked like. I went online to look it up and was reminded that there are many countries and cultures in Africa and seemingly endless uses, motifs, and meanings imbued in African cloth. I printed out an image as a beginning point and started to paint. As I looked closely at the cloth, I realized how specific the colors and patterns were. I began to paint the symbols that were stamped on the cloth and became aware that I was painting symbols that I did not understand. As my awareness of the superficial nature of my understanding unfolded, I looked up the symbols and found out that I was painting an image of Adinkra cloth made by the Asante people in Ghana. I read about the way the Asante made textiles and the meaning of the symbols present in the photograph that I worked from. I learned the cloth that I copied was used as a traditional ceremonial mourning cloth.

As I explored the painting, I realized first that it had nothing to do with the supervisee in fieldwork class. I was humbled as I recognized that my assumptions led me to look more at the method that I used to try to understand the student rather than the dynamics at work between us. Although I thought that my investigation was intentional, I had assumed that there was a general fund of knowledge that I could dip into to understand a specific individual. I had mistakenly thought that this investigation would help me learn about her history and her multifaceted contexts and provide valuable insight that would help me to support her. Coming from a privileged perspective, I thought I could figure out the issues without the student's input. I realized that I could not learn about the intricacies of culture and its impact from generalized investigation but must see the individual as the authority of his or her experience and ask for feedback and direction about the situation. Painting and working with the image, as well as exploring it in my own consultation and supervision, brought information about how to explore intersectionality and increased my appreciation for the complexity of cross-cultural understanding.

Conclusion

As supervisors we must model dedication to self-reflexive work and commitment to ongoing efforts to improve our awareness and skills. Ter Maat (2011) described the work necessary for culturally competent practice.

> Acquiring and mastering these competencies requires more than simply supplementing what the art therapist already knows. It requires internalizing these concepts into personal and professional realms. It requires honest commitment and effort to reflect, numerous supervised trials and errors, knowing right from wrong, exercising good judgment, and possessing a great deal of humility and integrity. It requires an intensive search for

techniques proven to be effective in working with different cultural groups and their individual members. It is an exhilarating and life-long journey on which each art therapist is encouraged to embark.

(p. 9)

Art-based supervision supports this practice. Image-based modes of expression can clarify layered communication and are especially useful when working cross-culturally. They add the imagery of the therapist and supervisor to the resources that support sound work. This use of response art can help us appreciate the contexts and perspectives of those we work with, supporting their agency while reflecting on our use of power and privilege. Making and investigating images adds to our ability to support awareness and competent work in supervision as well as in therapy.

It is the supervisor's responsibility to engage in reflexive, culturally competent practice and to oversee the same professional standards in those they supervise. Appreciation for the contexts of supervisees, and those of their clients, must begin with an awareness of our own context, power, and privilege, personally, professionally, and as supervisors. Our intersectionality, as well as the evaluative component that supervision brings, creates a power differential. Without conscious and responsible reflection, effective supervision is often impeded.

References

Calisch, A. (2003). Multicultural training in art therapy: Past, present and future. *Art Therapy: Journal of the American Art Therapy Association, 20*(1), 11–15.

Corey, G., Corey, M., & Callanan, P. (2011). *Issues and ethics in the helping professions* (8th Ed.). Belmont, CA: Brooks/Cole, Cengage Learning.

Frankl, V. E. (1985). *Man's search for meaning*. New York, NY: Simon and Schuster.

George, J., Greene, B. D., & Blackwell, M. (2005). Three voices on multiculturalism in the art therapy classroom. *Art Therapy: Journal of the American Art Therapy Association, 22*(3), 132–138.

Hiscox, A. R., & Calisch, A. C. (Eds.). (1998). *Tapestry of cultural issues in art therapy*. Philadelphia, PA: Jessica Kingsley.

Howie, P., Prasad, S., & Kristel, J. (Eds.). (2013). *Using art therapy with diverse populations: Crossing cultures and abilities*. Philadelphia, PA: Jessica Kingsley.

Kahn, M. (2002). *Basic Freud: Psychoanalysis for the 21st century*. New York, NY: Basic Books.

Talwar, S. (2010). An intersectional framework for race, class, gender, and sexuality in art therapy. *Art Therapy: Journal of the American Art Therapy Association, 27*(1), 11–17.

ter Maat, M. B. (2011). Developing and assessing multicultural competence with a focus on culture and ethnicity. *Art Therapy: Journal of the American Art Therapy Association, 28*(1), 4–10.

6

HARM'S TOUCH

How We Are Affected by What We Witness

As we work with people who are in pain, we may take on the emotional impact of the stories that we hear and the images that we see, leaving us feeling brittle, inflexible, and numb, with little room for anything else. *Harm's Touch* is an original concept describing how we are affected by what we witness (Fish, 2006). This is a framework for understanding the impact and value of our experiences with others. Response art is a tool to hold this content, explore it, and communicate about it to others.

It is not uncommon for those working with survivors of trauma to develop their own trauma reactions as a result of their exposure to the material (Trippany, Kress, & Wilcoxon, 2004). These effects are often addressed in discussions of vicarious trauma (Pearlman & Caringi, 2009; Pearlman & Saakvitne, 1995), secondary trauma (Figley, 1995), and burnout (Baker, 2003). Harm's touch, vicarious trauma, and secondary trauma can affect us both inside and outside of session. All of them can be detrimental to the therapist and can impede his or her work, leading to burnout.

Harm's touch differs from vicarious trauma and secondary trauma in that it holds value as well as risk. This concept does not imply an exclusively pathological response to what we witness. It offers an opportunity to engage in a way that is rich with potential for personal growth, awakening us to deeper levels of involvement and empathy. Without careful attention, being touched by harm can lead us down the same path as vicarious trauma and secondary trauma, limiting our ability to engage fully in our lives and in our work. Reframing our encounters with traumatic material in this way offers a relational perspective instead of describing them in distancing and pathologizing clinical terms.

Harm's touch is unavoidable and cumulative for those who experience their work deeply. It occurs as we listen to clients and coworkers, and as we provide supervision. We can be affected by witnessing traumatic incidents directly, seeing homeless people in the street, or watching images of war on the news. It may manifest itself as intrusive thoughts and ruminations, creeping into our dreams and affecting our personal relationships.

This material is challenging to new therapists and supervisors as they explore their practice during supervision. Beyond supporting supervisees as they strive to understand their work, supervisors must contend with their own responses to supervisory content. Without a practice for managing and learning from this material, it can build up over time and become toxic. The concept of harm's touch acknowledges the risks, as well as the benefits, of witnessing profound work and provides a model for managing these experiences.

Response Art

I began to use response art to manage harm's touch early in my career as my creative answer to the intensity of therapy. As an artist-therapist, I turned to my images for many years without a clearly articulated reason because I had always used them to manage intense feelings in my life.

During my own internship, I was flooded with feelings when I saw my patient's frail body lying in a hospital bed, her hands bandaged and leather belts securing her arms and legs. After a weekend off, I was returning to my internship at a hospital that treated adults with acute psychiatric disorders. I found the young woman I worked with in art therapy the week before in mechanical restraints when I arrived at the unit. When I left Friday afternoon she was lucid, sitting quietly in the dayroom, although she was rigidly unwilling to eat and preoccupied with romantic fantasies about the priest from her church. When I returned Monday morning she was terrified and incoherent, having experienced the onset of her first schizophrenic episode. Horrified by her hallucinations, she tried to pull her own eyes out. I was overwhelmed as I watched her lie on her bed, secured by four-point mechanical restraints, her hands bandaged for her own protection.

My mind was spinning. The sight of her in this condition frightened and confused me. I considered leaving the hospital and going home. I worried that if I stayed, I might burst into tears. I was afraid that I missed something during our work the week before. Feeling powerless, I wondered if I should have been able to see the onset of the disorder coming. I was most disturbed by her attack on herself and the use of leather restraints to keep her safe. She remained in restraints for several days as her doctor worked to find effective medication.

I was shaken by the use of restraints, even though I could see that they were keeping her from attacking herself. The use of mechanical restraints disturbed me. I had seen people in restraints before, but this was the first time I saw someone comforted by the containment that they provided. As I watched her over the days that followed, I saw how the young woman was overcome with terror when she was released from restraints. When the nurse periodically removed the leather cuffs, one limb at a time, to ensure circulation and range of motion, the young woman became more agitated and started to scream. She was only relaxed when the leather straps were back in place and she was secured again. The restraints comforted her until the medication helped to stabilize her mind. I began to think about the profound impact of mental illness and the use of medical and mechanical interventions to ensure safety.

I drew *Restraint* (Figure 6.1) at home to hold all that I felt about what I saw. I knew that I needed to unpack my personal reaction to the experience before I would be able to explore it with others. I didn't know where else to turn, so I drew this piece. I worked with colored pencils because I knew that the control and predictability they provided would comfort me. The image helped me to hold my feelings while I tried to comprehend them. I worked to understand the rapid deterioration of the woman's condition, her self-destructive behavior, and how she appeared to be comforted by the containment the restraints offered. I also worked to understand my own responses to all that I had witnessed.

As I worked with the image I realized that part of my reaction had to do with my own struggle with my health. Before I began graduate school a sudden physical illness required me to be hospitalized. The swift onset of my own disease, and the impact it had on my life, shook me. I quit my job and asked my parents

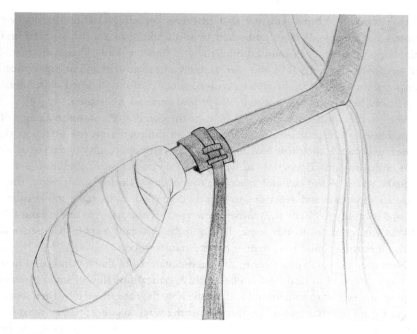

FIGURE 6.1 Restraint

Barbara Fish

for help. This changed my life's course, eventually leading me to graduate school. These issues and others were stirred as I watched the young woman struggle to regain control of her life.

Restraint (Figure 6.1) was my response to the first time I witnessed the onset and impact of schizophrenia. I was horrified at how quickly and profoundly this young woman's mind transformed from one that functioned to one that tormented her. Although her situation was entirely different from mine, her circumstances resonated with my own. Supervision provided me an opportunity to engage with this content and grow from the experience. I took the drawing to supervision at my internship site and to my supervision class at school, where it helped me to describe what happened, work to understand my reactions, and receive support.

For years I made response art in this way, to manage and deepen my understanding. Over time, I began to see the value of what I witnessed beyond clarifying my practice with clients, recognizing that the experiences were having an effect on me as well. I began to look at the varied uses of response art. As I investigated this practice in depth, looking closely at my images and the artwork of others (Fish, 2006), I realized that I was using my artwork in this way to understand and manage what I came to refer to as harm's touch.

Response Art Used in Supervision

Harm's touch is a broad concept that describes the effects of trauma that we witness at any time. It is an embodied sense of taking in another's ordeal and offers opportunities for profound empathy and understanding. Traumatic material originates in clients' lives and is encountered in treatment and in supervision. Response art, used in art-based supervision, is a powerful tool. Used with intention, it can help us find the value in the painful material we witness.

Veteran therapists and supervisors manage the content of sessions in a range of ways. Some assume professional distance, taking a clinical perspective on the work. Others experience their role as witness and ally as an opportunity to deepen their own empathy and connection to others. As supervisees and supervisors strive to make sense of the difficult material from therapy during supervision, their personal responses and reactions to treatment provide important information. Beyond its utility to clarify the course of therapy, it is important to understand and address our responses to our work. Traditionally, clinicians refer to this personal work supporting sound treatment as countertransference.

New therapists are vulnerable to the intense material of therapy and need support and direction to deal with it effectively. A critical function of supervision is helping supervisees to understand and handle how they are affected by their work. In this forum supervisees find resources, learning ways to conceptualize what has happened and care for themselves. It is an opportunity for new therapists to be guided as they explore ways to handle their work.

Supervisors have an important role in demonstrating the value of processing personal responses to content to support healthy practice. Art-based supervision employs response art as a primary resource to address harm's touch. Because new therapists are often overwhelmed by what they see, the supervisor has an opportunity to serve as an example, offering firsthand instances of managing what he or she witnesses. When the supervisor makes response art to explore an issue in supervision, the supervisee has a real-life chance to witness deep attention and reflection about providing therapy shared on his or her behalf. Supervisors are also affected by the content of supervision. I use my own imagery and encourage other supervisors to use theirs as well to navigate our own experience of harm's touch.

The following images and narratives are examples from art-based supervision. They demonstrate some of the ways that I have seen response art used to address harm's touch. I was sometimes the object of the rage of patients when I worked in a state psychiatric hospital providing long-term care for adolescents. I drew *Fear* (Figure 6.2) at the hospital, right after an incident with an adolescent boy. He walked into the dayroom where I was sitting with a group of patients, cursing under his breath and aggressively shoving chairs. When I asked him to go to his room until he could behave appropriately, he turned his anger on me, balling up his fists and screaming threats. The situation escalated into a fight when one of the staff members stepped in, resulting in the boy being put into mechanical restraints. Afterward, for what seemed like hours, I could hear him shouting threats from the room where he was restrained.

All I could think of was running away. I made the drawing to contain my fear and tell others about how shaken I was by the experience. It helped me ask for

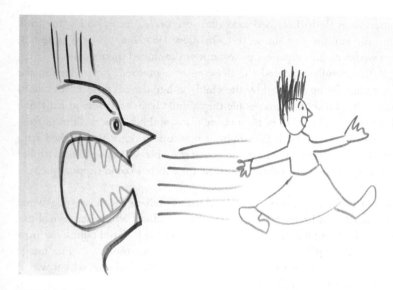

FIGURE 6.2 Fear

Barbara Fish

support from my supervisor and colleagues, including having someone accompany me when I talked to the patient about what happened. When we finally met we were able to talk about the unrelated incident that enraged him to begin with, repair our relationship, and resume treatment.

My drawing helped me to manage and communicate my feelings at the time of the incident. Later I used it to explore the personal issues it stirred for me. We are attracted to the work we do for our own complex reasons. As therapists, it is important to have an understanding of our motivation as we enter the work to ensure that we don't act out unresolved or unconscious issues with our clients. The practice of therapy offers opportunities to explore our personal responses to our work with others.

My investigation of this image helped me to realize that my practice is a way of healing wounds from my past. As an adult who was bullied as a child, I have opportunities to create safe places for those struggling with their aggression. This awareness continues to help me understand and manage my reactions to aggression, my need for control, and how to use my skills to support therapeutic work.

I drew *Fear* (Figure 6.2) to work with harm's touch before I understood the concept. Response art can be made at any time before, during, or after the encounter. The intensity of the experience can be productively revisited years later by working with the image with a revised intention, in the same way that I did with this drawing. The piece may be a highly developed art piece or a fast, chaotic expression of a situation that needs containment. The ability of our imagery to help us as we are touched by harm depends on the clarity of our intention for its use.

Beth Enterkin was a young professional I saw for postgraduate supervision while she worked with children in an outpatient domestic violence program. During supervision Beth described case after case of violent episodes that took place within the families that she served. She drew *Witnessing Abuse* (Figure 6.3) over several weeks during supervisory sessions as she shared their stories.

While Beth carefully rendered the drawing of a mother's eye reflecting the image of her child being attacked by the child's father, she told me about clients who endured physical abuse from people they should have been able to trust. She described her young clients' fears, their safety plans, and her own feelings of frustration and powerlessness. Beth talked about how one mother she worked with dissociated whenever Beth tried to discuss what she observed in sessions with her children, what their behavior meant, and how the mother could support them.

> I drew it because I was trying to understand where she was going when she dissociated as I tried to talk to her. She could talk about her own abuse, what her husband was doing to her. But as soon as I started telling her how this was affecting her kids, she wasn't with me anymore. . . . The image helped me explore on a visceral level not an intellectual one, why it was so hard for her to stay with me when I was talking about those things. That helped me be less frustrated and more compassionate with her.
>
> (Beth Enterkin, Personal communication, April 21, 2015)

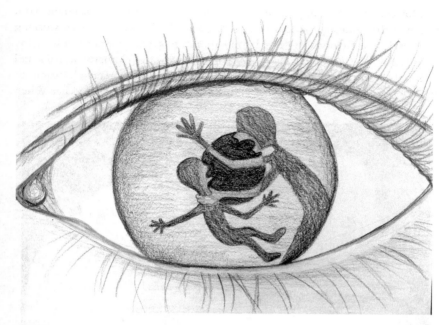

FIGURE 6.3   Witnessing Abuse

Beth Enterkin

During supervision both Beth and I made images as the foundation for our discussion of the scope of her responsibility and the limits of care. The incidents of abuse with many of her clients were ongoing. Although she reported them to child protective services after almost every session, the parent usually did not take action by moving to safety. Until they were ready to accept change, all that Beth was able to offer was her support and her attention to her clients' ongoing ordeals. Beth's response art helped her to manage the intensity of what she witnessed in sessions. It also grounded her as she dealt with the child welfare system and explored her frustration about it in supervision.

Beth described the layers of meaning in her drawing. At first the image represented the eye of a mother as she watched her child's abuse. Then Beth saw the eye as her own as she heard the mother's accounts in session. As I listened to her, grounding myself by working on my own artwork, I was aware that the eye in the drawing is now mine as well, as I have become a witness to the stories.

We explored how she managed such intensely painful work as we discussed her image, exploring harm's touch and the personal cost of providing care. The stories that we witness are hard to bear. Making images during supervision can help to ground both the supervisee and supervisor, facilitating profound communication. Creating response art to help us understand and share overwhelming experiences is an important part of art-based supervision. When we are witnessed as we express how we are touched by harm, we can feel supported and less isolated in our work.

Not everyone has support or handles the content of this demanding work in a way that mitigates its toxic effects. Caroline Heller was an intern working at a residential facility that served children, most of whom were wards of the state. She made *Child Abuse Investigator* (Figure 6.4) out of cloth, twine, nails, and metal blades in response to her encounter with a social worker who came to the site to investigate a client's allegations that a staff member abused her. When

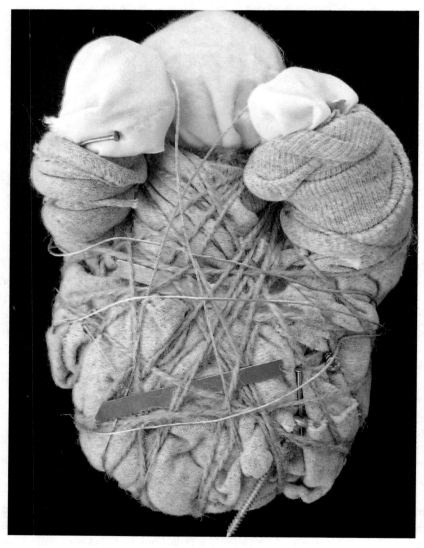

FIGURE 6.4 Child Abuse Investigator

Caroline Heller

we discussed the encounter, Caroline said that when the investigator arrived she seemed burned out. Applying the clinical language often used to describe children in treatment, Caroline told me what she saw. "It was clear that she was very desensitized, as evidenced by her body language and the way she responded verbally to this situation as if it were just another case" (Caroline Heller, Personal communication, April 10, 2015). The image Caroline created was her response to how the caseworker appeared to be "damaged" by all that she saw in her work.

When Caroline shared *Child Abuse Investigator* (Figure 6.4) in supervision class, it led us into a discussion of the requirements and procedures for the mandated reporting of abuse and neglect. These include notifying the site supervisor and documenting the call. We continued to explore the importance of safety in session when supporting clients' disclosure of traumatic material and the value of self-care in sustaining this work. Caroline was concerned that the social worker sent to investigate the child's allegation appeared to be shut down. As we affirmed the important role of mandated reporters as client advocates and witnesses, we also acknowledged the powerlessness many of us feel about the way reports are often handled.

We talked about harm's touch as we looked beyond the required actions called for by Caroline's work as a mandated reporter. We recognized the potential cumulative effects of witnessing trauma. If it is not addressed, harm's touch can leave us numb and burned out. Caroline described how hard it was for her to tolerate hearing the stories of clients who experienced severe abuse. Together we explored strategies for contending with the material and engaging in self-care to remediate how we are touched by harm in our own work.

Response Art Used to Explore Countertransference

Kelly Riddle, an intern in an elementary school program, was working with a young girl whose mother recently died of breast cancer. Her response to the girl's sorrow was palpable. Week after week the child talked about her sadness and how her father was beginning to move on, dating someone new. Kelly was concerned about the child and often discussed their work together in supervision.

Dream (Figure 6.5, Plate 7) is response art that Kelly made and brought to supervision to process a dream that she had about her client after their session. The client had been distraught during therapy as she talked about her nightmares about her mother returning from the dead. As the girl struggled to make sense of her new reality, Kelly felt overwhelmed.

When our clients find their way into our dreams it is often an indication that we have been touched by harm and that there is countertransference needing to be processed. Bringing her response art to supervision helped Kelly to share the meaning of her dream and hone the direction of her work with the child. Kelly said the piece depicts her carrying the girl away from her isolation and sorrow, represented as the woods. After she shared her drawing and described her dream, we talked about the intensity of Kelly's feelings and her rescue fantasy about the

FIGURE 6.5 (PLATE 7) Dream

Kelly Riddle

girl. Together we discussed the challenging work of supporting grief and how it is tempting to move away from difficult feelings before the client is ready.

Kelly's countertransference ran deeper. Subsequently she told me that her own mother suffered a life-threatening injury when she was a young adult. Her experience with the possible loss of her mother intensified her identification with her young client's loss. Although I did not know about this at the time, her drawing brought the supervision group's attention to Kelly's strong reaction to her young client. It helped her regain realistic footing while she supported the girl in therapy as she processed her loss.

Interdisciplinary Use of Response Art

Others who are not therapists or counselors may also be affected by harm's touch as they witness the ordeals of those they work with. Geraldine Gorman, a nurse with extensive experience in hospice, invited me to introduce response art to the student nurses she supervised as a faculty member at a university college of nursing. I came to the nurses' biweekly postclinical conferences that supported their first experiences with patients. During the conferences, the student nurses gave traditional verbal presentations. After class everyone was asked to respond to the presentations by making images and bringing them back to share the next week. These were not elaborate pieces of art but instead profound expressions made from whatever materials the students had at home. The class discussions deepened as we shared the artwork, helping the nursing students to open up about the intensity of their involvement. As they shared their work they received support from one another, recognizing the value of their reflections to ground their work and help them feel less isolated.

Making images to explore how we are affected by our work can be helpful for those at any artistic skill level. The willingness to intentionally explore a situation, feeling, or reaction through imagery is all that is necessary. *Response to Stem Cell Unit* (Figure 6.6) is Geraldine Gorman's work with her patients. She created it

And so ends
another day
on the stem cell
unit . . .
4 casualties
and counting.

FIGURE 6.6 Response to Stem Cell Unit

Geraldine Gorman

at home after a day's work at the hospital. The piece represents the patient surrounded by machines and medical staff. On it she wrote "And so ends another day on the stem cell unit . . . 4 casualties and counting" (Geraldine Gorman, Personal communication, March 14, 2014). When she brought the piece into the group, she modeled the use of response art to communicate the intensity of her experience for the nurses she supervised.

Response Art Used in Consultation

I experienced harm's touch when I consulted to residential facilities struggling to provide therapeutic services for youth. While at an agency, I met a teenager with a bone-chilling story. As I walked the grounds I saw a girl sitting on the steps of one of the homes with a childcare worker standing at her side. She was about fifteen years old and wore shorts, flip-flops, and a man's soiled, sleeveless tee shirt as she perched on the stoop in front of the house. I introduced myself and she told me that she was the only girl living in the home. When I asked she told me why. She said that several weeks before many girls lived in the home. There was lots of fighting and running away. She said that fights happened frequently and there weren't enough staff to break things up, especially on the night shift. One night when she was asleep, her roommate returned to the home after being "on run." Coming into their bedroom, her roommate jumped on her while she was asleep, punching and biting her. She was startled awake, turned over, and bit the aggressor violently, disfiguring her. Now she was charged with assault and lived alone in the home, away from the other girls. She waited to see if the court would send her to serve time in juvenile corrections. "There weren't enough staff to break up the fight" rang in my ears as I walked away.

I painted *Despair* (Figure 6.7) because I was so disturbed by the girl's story. The tragedy that she related, describing desperately aggressive youth, was hard to bear. I had to find a way to manage how I felt about it before I would be able to look for its value for informing my work. In my role as consultant, this and other examples of unchecked violence that I observed concerned me deeply. The children in care came from violent and unstable pasts where trauma and aggression were the norm. How could they heal and learn to manage their emotions safely when they were in environments where those caring for them did not intervene in trauma? I considered the limited number of staff who were available to support clients, as well as the training, support, and supervision that was given to those charged with the bulk of the interactions with the clients.

The story gave me information from the client's perspective. Making the image helped me to stay with the horror of the experience that she described and deconstruct it. This made it possible for me to find helpful feedback and suggestions to present to the agency's administration, calling for support and training for staff to facilitate their ability to establish and sustain a safe, therapeutic environment.

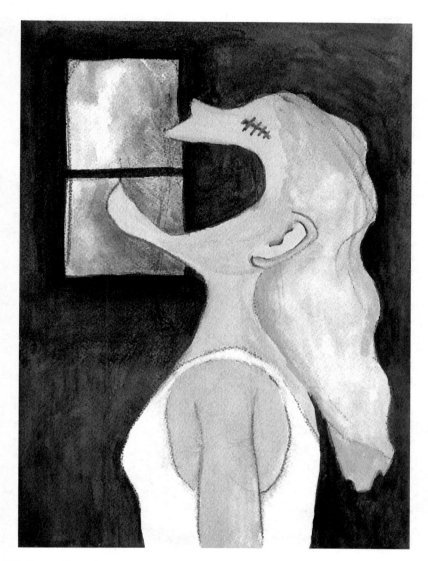

FIGURE 6.7   Despair

Barbara Fish

I began this chapter with a discussion of *Restraint* (Figure 6.1), a drawing that I made to contain and explore my feelings about what I saw during my training as an art therapy intern. I turned to response art because I could not get the image of it out of my head.

Thirty years later, I drew *Witnessing Restraint* (Figure 6.8) about an incident that occurred at a hospital where I consulted. I created this image at home on the

FIGURE 6.8   Witnessing Restraint

Barbara Fish

same day that the incident occurred, just as I had many years before. This time, I was not an intern but a consultant. I was advising hospital staff in need of training and direction to improve their treatment of youth with severe mental illness and trauma. As I watched the restraint happen on an adolescent girl's unit, I was concerned that excessive force was used. I was struck by the size, blank gazes, and mechanical appearance of the male staff as they immobilized the adolescent girl who thrashed against them, trying to regain control. My only impact on the restraint itself was to redirect the men holding the girl.

This piece enabled me to engage as an activist. I took the image to my team and to the hospital administration to stress the need for improved training and supervision for the staff. In addition to helping me to contain my feelings about the incident, it described my concerns as I advocated for reform that I believed would lead to improved patient care.

When I drew *Restraint* (Figure 6.1) during my training, I started to think about questions that I have continued to ask throughout my career. These include striving to understand the balance between autonomy and external control, the role of power, and the use of physical control in therapy and in the treatment of mental illness. There are times when hospitalized patients must be stopped from hurting themselves or others. These encounters are fraught with opportunities for the abuse of power. I advocate for humane and therapeutic ways to keep those I work with safe. As I reflected on the personal impact of these experiences, I realized that being touched by harm helped me to question my own ideas about power, control, and agency as well as why I have been drawn to work in environments that require extreme interventions to ensure safety.

My ongoing questions about the use of power in therapy supports the reflections of those I supervise who struggle with similar issues in their work. An art therapist in postgraduate supervision painted *Pile* (Figure 6.9) as he investigated his own questions after he participated in a violent restraint in the adolescent unit at a hospital where he worked.

> It was chaotic and excessive and I complained about it. . . . These things happen in institutions. It's a reflection of the work place. I like to think that I'm loyal to the work place but my loyalty to the children trumps all of that. That's why I did the painting, to clarify that in my own head.
>
> *(Anonymous, Personal communication, July 1, 2015)*

After reporting his concerns about the restraint to his supervisor, and reviewing the triggers that led to the restraint in postrestraint discussion with staff, the therapist met with the patient individually. Together they talked about the incident and the issues that led to his outburst, the importance of safety, and the strategies that could help him to avoid resorting to aggressive behavior in the future. The therapist's work with this image helped him to reflect on the situation, understand it, and work with it to inform his actions and make a difference. He realized that he had a responsibility to support the patient and to process what happened as well as to report the occurrence to ensure patient safety.

When we met for supervision, we reflected on the incident together. We talked about the intensity of working with youth who have endured complex trauma and the importance of staff support. We went on to discuss larger systemic issues

FIGURE 6.9   Pile

Anonymous

that may have contributed to the situation, including the necessity of sufficient numbers of staff and the availability of training and supervision for them. Finally, the therapist questioned his own use of physical power. What is the role of a male therapist when a patient requires physical intervention? Should he participate in the physical management of aggressive patients? What is the impact on the therapeutic relationship? By investigating these issues with response art in supervision, the therapist was able to look at how he was touched by harm, understand its importance, and move beyond it to renew his focus on how to intervene effectively and advocate for the children.

Beyond helping us to look at interpersonal dynamics with clients, response art helped the therapist manage reactions to agency and systemic issues and allowed us to explore them in supervision. In addition to helping him process his experience of the restraint, response art offered a way to communicate his concerns about the system of care where he worked. The therapist could see that the agencies where we work are sometimes themselves barriers to treatment. Understanding his frustration with the dysfunctional system became the focus of supervision.

This challenge confronts new therapists as well as seasoned professionals. By making this image, the therapist was able to represent his attempt to provide effective treatment for his client in the face of the system's dysfunction. Making response art in this way allowed him to express and look at the paradox in his work as we explored his struggle.

Art for Peace

As therapists and supervisors, we are intentional witnesses to trauma. We are also exposed to the pain of others in our daily lives, unintentionally and without our consent. We are affected by what we experience at any time, inside and outside of our work. Part of professional development is learning to engage with and help your community in times of tragedy, crisis, and stress. Supervisors facilitating the professional development of others sometimes have the opportunity to be leaders in these endeavors. This was the case when I started Art for Peace in response to the events of September 11th. This is not a therapy or supervision group, but began with the intention of holding a space for art therapists and others to come together as a community to make art and become peaceful and grounded, supporting our efforts to be responsive instead of reacting out of fear.

I watched the live broadcast of the towers in New York City falling on September 11, 2001, from my home in Chicago. After I called my family on the West Coast, I began to think about the welfare of friends, colleagues, and students. As I experienced waves of anxiety, I thought about the well-being of those in my community. I realized that my fieldwork supervision group at the school would be cancelled the next day, and I knew that most of my students were far from their homes. For that reason I decided to hold the class in my home-studio, giving us a chance to make art with the intention of calming ourselves and connecting with one another.

When we met the next day, we lit a candle and made imagery together for the entire three-hour session. Some of us talked quietly, but most of us focused on working with our imagery, letting it hold all that we felt. At the end of our time, we decided to meet again the following Friday evening, inviting neighbors, other therapists, and friends to join us. This is how Art for Peace began. Since then we gather on Friday evenings in my home, bringing food to share and art materials to use. We light candles and make art together with the intention of connecting as a community. There is no charge for the group. For me, the gathering is a service that we provide for each other.

I painted *September 11th* (Figure 6.10, Plate 8) during the first Art for Peace group. I began by making a purple border to hold the intensity of all I saw. I felt flooded by the images that I saw reported live and then rebroadcast in seemingly endless repetition. Applying the watercolor to the page comforted me as I thought about all that happened the day before. This sensory experience with materials and others' focused artmaking helped me calm myself and feel connected again.

Mary Ann Tunnell, another early member, painted *September 11th* (Figure 6.11, Plate 9) during one of the first meetings. She worked quietly, focusing on her image. This was one of many pieces she painted over weeks, providing a focus for the intensity of her experience.

Dissanayake (1988), an anthropologist, examined the uses of art across cultures to manage world events. She said that "by short-circuiting the analytic faculties, art connects us directly to the substantial immediacy of things—we feel the direct impact of color, texture, size, or the particularity and power of the subject matter" (p. 67).

FIGURE 6.10 (PLATE 8) September 11th

Barbara Fish

FIGURE 6.11 (PLATE 9) September 11th

Mary Ann Tunnell

Dissanayake (1988) went on to point out the value of art and ritual to help us access and relive intense events, recalling them to make sense of what happened.

> At times of violence—natural disasters, wartime—ordinary life for a time acquires a dimension of excitement, however terrifying or poignant, that in normal time is lacking. It is significant that individuals who experience

these occasions often commemorate them in the future, not only to give witness to the seriousness of their sufferings but to reexperience the heightened sense of personal meaning that permeated the time.

(1988, p. 139)

My own experience with response art supports Dissanayake's belief that art has the potential to literally handle, as well as to bring back, the intensity of an event. I felt the power of an experience and relief from it while making images as part of Art for Peace as well as when I made them in supervision. Response art can help manage current feelings by holding them. Later, the piece may be revisited to investigate the "heightened sense of personal meaning that permeated the time" (p. 139), offering deeper understanding of the experience.

Art for Peace met weekly for five years and continues to meet as world events move us to do so. *Art for Peace 2012* (Figure 6.12) is a photograph of one of our gatherings. Born out of a desire to calm myself and to support those I supervise, Art for Peace has become a gathering that supports students, new graduates, seasoned professionals, and others as they make art together, share experiences, network, and inspire each other. Our joint intention remains the same: *We make art as part of a community to become peaceful so that we will be responsive instead of reactive in our lives and in our work.*

FIGURE 6.12 Art for Peace 2012

Barbara Fish

Conclusion

Sound supervision helps to sustain healthy practice by supporting the development of tools for managing and exploring our work. Therapists who address harm's touch in art-based supervision add a valuable dimension to verbal discourse about the intensity and impact of therapy on the therapist. Without a strategy for managing and learning from harm's touch, we may leave sessions and other experiences filled with stories of trauma, unable to think of or attend to anything else. Over time, as stories and images made about them accumulate, they can load us with unprocessed material, having emotional and physical impact.

Response art is an opportunity for supervisors to model healthy strategies for managing and learning from the work as they engage in their ongoing use of imagery in supervision. Students and new therapists are often overwhelmed by what happens in therapy. Art-based supervision affords an opportunity for both supervisor and supervisee to engage their imagery as a resource to support and deepen the understanding of their practice. Response art can be made to address harm's touch at any time before, during, or after session and brought to supervision. Response art holds layers of content and can be revisited over time, reminding us of important information and bringing new resources from the experience.

Leigh Ann Lichty, an art therapy intern, explored the concept of harm's touch through response art that she made about her placement working with children in residential care. She began *Harm's Touch* (Figure 6.13, Plate 10) early in her internship to reflect her feelings of being "completely overwhelmed with my responsibilities as a therapist, coupled with my personal life challenges" (Leigh Ann Lichty, Personal communication, February 22, 2015).

She didn't complete the piece at the time but set it aside, knowing it needed something more. When she finished the piece at the end of her internship, she described how her understanding of her work had changed over time.

> My connection with my clients had deepened. I recognized how much they affected me and I affected them. That is the basis of my understanding of harm's touch. . . . In the piece there is a three-dimensional hand, which I cast from my own hand. Beneath it, there is a painted shadow of a hand. Originally I intended for the shadow to represent the children I worked with and how they touched me—the back and forth, the give and take, the dance of therapy. I have since considered the idea of the shadow also being akin to Jung's shadow, where it represents everything about myself that I bring to a therapeutic relationship. It could be interpreted as both my clients' influence as well as my past, because in tandem, those elements create countertransference. . . . The hand is cracked and imperfect, yet its veins run bright and multicolored. Much like my therapeutic relationships, it's not perfect, but it is rich and meaningful.
>
> *(Leigh Ann Lichty, Personal communication, February 22, 2015)*

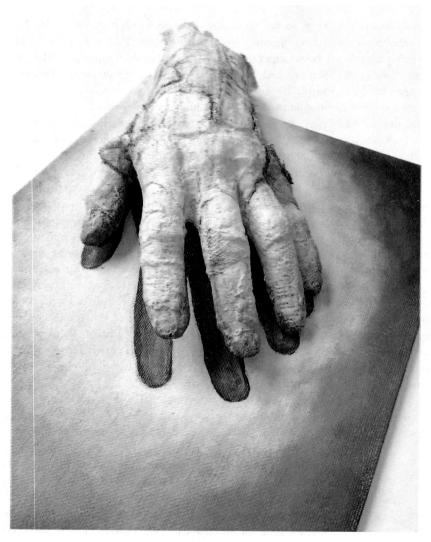

FIGURE 6.13 (PLATE 10) Harm's Touch

Leigh Ann Lichty

Learning to successfully work when we are touched by harm requires an appreciation of harm's toxic effects as well as the opportunities it offers to support our growth. We are touched by harm throughout our careers and in our lives outside of treatment. Harm's touch comes to us through opportunities to be fully engaged with another as a witness, allowing ourselves to be changed by the experience.

The intentional practice of making response art to understand and grow from harm's touch is a kind of self-care that is a form of therapist hygiene. It can support resilience and sustain healthy practice as we avoid accumulating the toxic material that we witness.

Harm's touch is an opportunity to recognize the universal value of our experiences beyond our initial encounters, deepening our capacity for empathy, understanding, and sense of purpose. New therapists, as well as veteran professionals, are touched by harm. Response art has the ability to help both supervisees and supervisors learn from these encounters and care for themselves by managing and letting go of the toxic effects of harm's touch. It also has the potential to help us to focus our responses effectively or soothe us into inaction, derailing our socially responsible reactions. The utility of response art depends on the clarity of our intention.

This chapter presents the concept of harm's touch, understood as how we are affected by what we witness, and suggests the use of response art as a resource for containing, investigating, and communicating our experiences. These narratives include examples of images employed to address harm's touch. Making and exploring the artwork helps both those I supervise and me to gain personal insight and deepen our capacity for empathy while offering awareness, enhanced communication, and resources to help us to let go of the toxic effects of harm's touch.

References

Baker, E. (2003). *Caring for ourselves: A therapist's guide to personal and professional well-being.* Washington, DC: American Psychological Association.

Dissanayake, E. (1988). *What is art for?* Seattle, WA: University of Washington Press.

Figley, C. E. (1995). *Compassion fatigue: Coping with secondary traumatic stress disorder in those who treat the traumatized.* New York, NY: Brunner/Mazel.

Fish, B. J. (2006). *Image-based narrative inquiry of response art in art therapy.* (Doctoral dissertation). Retrieved from Dissertations & Theses database. (UMI no. AAT 3228081).

Pearlman, L. A., & Caringi, J. (2009). Living and working reflexively to address vicarious trauma. In C. A. Curtois, & J. D. Ford (Eds.), *Treating complex traumatic stress disorders: Scientific foundations and therapeutic models* (pp. 102–122). New York, NY: Guilford Press.

Pearlman, L. A., & Saakvitne, K. (1995). *Trauma and the therapist: Countertransference and vicarious traumatization with incest survivors.* New York, NY: W. W. Norton.

Trippany, R. L., Kress, V. E. W., & Wilcoxon, S. A. (2004). Preventing vicarious trauma: What counselors should know when working with trauma survivors. *Journal of Counseling & Development, 82*(1), 31–37.

FIGURE 3.3 (PLATE 1)   Moving On

Sangeetha Ravichandran

FIGURE 3.5 (PLATE 2)   Sock Animals

Emily Allbery, Barbara Fish, Julie Krause, Leigh Ann Lichty, Ashley Melendez, Kelly Riddle

FIGURE 4.1 (PLATE 3)   First Day

Kelly Riddle

FIGURE 4.6 (PLATE 4)   Tornado

Barbara Fish

FIGURE 5.2 (PLATE 5)   Gone

Barbara Fish

FIGURE 5.4 (PLATE 6)   Breathing In and Breathing Out

Lisa Thomas

FIGURE 6.5 (PLATE 7)   Dream

Kelly Riddle

FIGURE 6.10 (PLATE 8)   September 11th

Barbara Fish

FIGURE 6.11 (PLATE 9)   September 11th

Mary Ann Tunnell

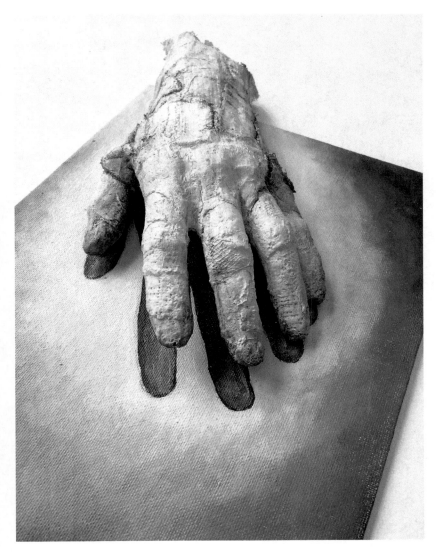

FIGURE 6.13 (PLATE 10)   Harm's Touch

Leigh Ann Lichty

FIGURE 7.5 (PLATE 11) Failure

Noel King

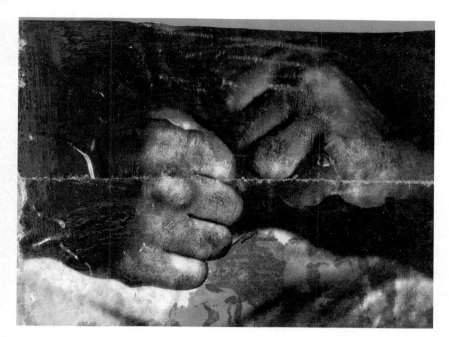

FIGURE 7.7 (PLATE 12)   Fists

Leigh Ann Lichty

FIGURE 7.9 (PLATE 13)   Response Art About Group

Kelly Riddle

FIGURE 7.10 (PLATE 14) Reality

Jen Kirkpatrick

FIGURE 7.11 (PLATE 15)   Telling Trauma

Elissa Heckendorf

FIGURE 8.4 (PLATE 16)   Spreading Tendrils

Julie Ludwick

FIGURE 8.9 (PLATE 17) Sword

Anonymous

FIGURE 8.11 (PLATE 18) Untitled

Sangeetha Ravichandran

FIGURE 9.11 (PLATE 19)   Rage

Barbara Fish

FIGURE 9.12 (PLATE 20)   Not Manipulation

Barbara Fish

FIGURE 10.3 (PLATE 21) Termination

Anonymous

FIGURE 10.4 (PLATE 22)   Supervision

Barbara Fish

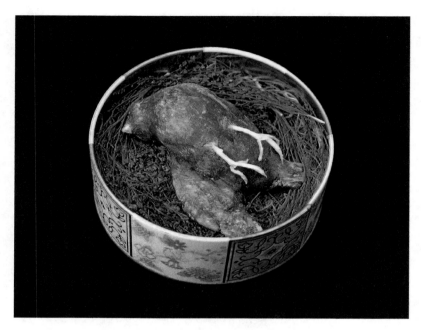

FIGURE 10.6 (PLATE 23)   Bird With Broken Wing

June Dondlinger

FIGURE 10.8 (PLATE 24)   Supervision Nest

Elissa Heckendorf

FIGURE 10.10 (PLATE 25)   Fieldwork Response Art Composite

Barbara Fish

FIGURE 10.11 (PLATE 26)   Beginning Supervision

Barbara Fish

7

SUPERVISION DURING GRADUATE EDUCATION

Supervision supports three areas of the new therapist's work, all of which are rooted in the profession's ethical code and standards of practice. First, it facilitates effective therapy for the client by providing opportunities to evaluate and conceptualize treatment. This supports the development of client goals and facilitates an appreciation for the meaning of client behavior including aggression and resistance.

Second, supervision supports the effective functioning of the therapist. This is a place where the critical evaluation of client services is balanced with fostering students' and new professionals' confidence and use of intuition. Supervisees learn the importance of understanding the use of their own power, cultural sensitivity, and competency and of finding resources for understanding and managing new situations. They untangle their personal responses to therapy, including countertransference and counterresistance, as they explore their first professional encounters with psychopathology and trauma.

Third, supervision is a forum for helping students and new professionals navigate the systems where they work. They receive help understanding models of treatment, procedures, and documentation. Supervision provides direction and support as new therapists navigate the ethical and technical aspects of treatment, including the importance of informed consent, the utility and implications of diagnosis, and the use of medication. It is a place to sort out the new therapist's appraisal of the course of treatment, fostering an appreciation of effective communication of clinical issues to clients, treatment team members, and coworkers.

Art-based supervision incorporates imagery and metaphors into traditionally verbal work. In Chapters 3 and 4 we discussed some methods for engaging images during supervision. Chapters 7 and 8 delve more into examples of how imagery is used to support practice, demonstrating a range of issues that may be addressed by employing imagery in supervision. Chapter 7 provides assignments that I use in my group supervision classes. The use of art materials in class can help ground and focus students. Art-based projects, created outside of class and processed during fieldwork supervision groups, provide a venue for exploration, insight, and understanding. Chapter 8 consists of examples of more advanced practice by those in individual postgraduate supervision.

Supervisory Support and Direction

Those who are supervising student therapists during their training are introducing them to their first experiences of providing therapy. It is the supervisor's responsibility to guide the process, being mindful of the requirements for sound treatment and the student therapist's learning style, strengths, and challenges. It is important for the supervisor to help students develop strategies for understanding their work and sustaining sound practice. The supervisee's responsibility is to come with an open mind and heart, willing to listen to and integrate direction and feedback while resonating deeply with the material to find insight.

New therapists often experience anticipatory anxiety as they begin their new internships. I often tell students that the hardest day of an internship is the day before it begins. Learning ways to conceptualize, reflect on, and communicate about clinical work will serve therapists throughout their careers. Those in training learn what they can expect from supervision. It is a forum for developing skills, articulating concerns, problem solving, and learning the value of collaboration and support. Students are developing a professional repertoire that will serve them in their careers. Habits formed early in practice can become either a resource or an impediment to later work.

During training, supervisees working in fieldwork placements receive supervision on-site from a therapist employed at the agency as well as from a faculty supervisor from their school. Art-based supervision can be used in both venues. Making art during and outside of class allows the emerging professional to find containment for their nervous energy and a focus for their investigation as they learn to support clients with difficult clinical material, build empathy, and develop patience with themselves.

Art-based supervision plays a critical role in graduate therapy training by providing imagery as an interactive resource for shedding light on the subject at hand. Many supervisors have their own favorite assignments. These are designed to help students conceptualize treatment, explore and deepen their understanding of themselves and their work, and support their practice. Art-based supervision offers ways of understanding in addition to standard supervisory assignments such as case presentations, written reflections, progress notes, and other forms of documentation. Sharing some of the art-based projects that I use will stimulate the reader's own ideas for using imagery in supervision.

Art-Based Assignments

On the first day of supervision class, as students shuffle paperwork communicating fieldwork site information, I shift the focus from practical matters to the core of who they are as artists and therapists. I ask them to bring one of their own images to the next class to introduce themselves. The images that they bring can be created recently or be one from the past. They may choose any media or form of imagery. Students-in-training usually know each other fairly well as classmates. This exercise gives them the opportunity to revisit their artist selves in a new forum, beginning to understand what value this aspect of their persona holds for them as therapists. This assignment is designed to help those in training engage their artist selves. Used early in the supervisory process, it brings the images of new therapists into supervision and supports the development of the group's art-based culture.

I participate in this exercise along with the students, bringing one of my images to introduce myself and to demonstrate how I use imagery as part of my practice. My involvement begins an interpersonal foundation for image-based engagement with the students. As discussed in Chapter 4, bringing the supervisor's imagery into supervision should be done mindfully. The work must be explored first by the supervisor to unpack its personal meaning and then shared only if it is in the best interest of the supervisee. Used this way, the response art of the supervisor adds an additional resource to the art-based and verbal discourse in the supervisory relationship.

In addition to this first assignment, I use a number of other art-based projects in supervision during graduate training. In Chapter 4 I described two ongoing directives that bring a steady flow of imagery into supervision throughout the semester. Here are examples of these assignments in more depth. A weekly assignment is a response art project asking student therapists to make a piece outside of class about some aspect of their internship. They return to each of the following classes with their imagery and process it within the group. Another project follows a student's formal presentation of case material. I ask those witnessing the presentation to make response art about it after class as feedback and bring it with them to supervision the next week for discussion. In addition to providing valuable feedback for the presenter, it often holds insight for the student who made it. In addition to these regularly scheduled assignments, there are projects that I give once a semester. The fairy tale assignment asks students to write, illustrate, and present a story in which one of his or her clients is the protagonist. This work helps the student think of the client and his or her challenges through the lens of metaphor. This aphoristic frame focuses on client strengths and possibilities for change. In an in-service assignment, students are asked to provide art-based experiential training for their colleagues at their internships. For a project that is unique to the School of the Art Institute of Chicago, Graduate Art Therapy program students participate in the Art of Connection Exhibition. This annual art show explores the relationship between the client and therapist through their imagery. Reflecting on the meaning, ethical considerations, and manifestation of each student's contribution to this exhibit in supervision is an important part of our work together. Although most students will not have a similar exhibition opportunity, the issues that this project raises are rich resources for supervisory discourse.

Methods and Reasons for Making Imagery in Supervision

There are many ways to use images and the image-making process in art-based supervision. Clients work with materials during art therapy as they discuss important issues, helping them to manage the intensity of the interaction. Similarly, handling materials can help student therapists cope with the powerful content that they investigate in supervision. Using materials calms and absorbs anxiety, allowing student therapists to participate and attend to the conversation of often traumatic and potentially disturbing content. Now we will look at students' engagement with media during fieldwork supervision class. Having personal experiences with materials used in this way offers us a visceral awareness of their value in therapy.

Students are encouraged to participate in supervision in the way that supports their focused attention and involvement in the fieldwork discussion. Each supervisee makes his or her own decision whether or not to work with art materials and, if so, which media to use during class. As some students engage materials and others sit with still hands, we create an emotionally safe environment that supports the work to come.

Imagery made in class as students explore their practice can be created with any available media. From week to week many students bring their own supplies or work on an ongoing project. Their work ranges from doodling with pencils or markers to more elaborate images or constructions made with art materials or recycled and found objects. As they handle the materials, they discuss their practice with clients and contribute to their peers' discussions.

Annie Tabachnick was an art therapy intern working in a program that served children who were under twelve years old with recent sexual trauma. She created *Toothpick People* (Figure 7.1) as she talked about her work addressing the complex trauma of her young clients. As she bound the toothpicks together with embroidery floss, forming the structure for each figure, she described how she facilitated the children's use of art and play to address their trauma, helping them to feel safe again.

Caroline Heller, an art therapy intern working in a residential agency for children with behavioral and emotional disorders, appliquéd a bird onto translucent fabric (Figure 7.2). As she sewed the cloth into place, she talked about her clients and the problems that they faced, including their fragile and complex family environments and the interpersonal and systemic issues that became snags in the fabric of their treatment.

FIGURE 7.1 Toothpick People

Annie Tabachnick

FIGURE 7.2 Applique

Caroline Heller

Manipulating media without it resulting in a formed expression can be an end in itself. While this use of materials may be pleasurable, it also holds significant value when used as a backdrop while focusing on challenging content from sessions. Perry and Szalaviz (2006) recommended sensory patterned involvement to quiet the brain that has been exposed to trauma. Perry elaborated that the same sensory interventions that help to regulate the traumatized brain are also helpful for those who are touched by the trauma of those they work with and the environments where they serve (Perry, 2008).

Finger knitting is a way of working with materials that we discussed as an example of skill-sharing. Cate Barrington-Ward, an art therapy intern working in a psychiatric hospital serving patients who struggled with chronic mental illness, poverty, and substance use issues, knitted long colorful scarves (Figure 7.3) using her fingers instead of knitting needles. Finger knitting eliminates sharp tools and puts the yarn directly into her hands. Week after week she brought yarn and worked with it as she described her interactions at the hospital to the supervision class. Cate's discussions focused on the specific needs of this acute group of patients as they cycled in and out of short-term treatment. She sought encouragement and ideas of how to use the creative process to support them.

FIGURE 7.3 Finger Knitting

Cate Barrington-Ward

Making Art Outside of Supervision to Process in Class

In addition to imagery made in class during supervisory conversations, students in training make response art for specific assignments and bring it to class. I share imagery made in response to my work, demonstrating my use of creativity to reflect on my practice. Here I am offering some of the projects that I use to inspire supervisors to employ these and their own assignments in their work with new therapists. Response art can help to hold experiences and the reactions that come with them, investigate interpersonal and systemic dynamics, gain insight into professional issues, and communicate effectively with others.

Weekly Response Art Practice

In addition to investigating clinical work directly through discussions and reviewing sessions with clients, I ask students to make response art each week and bring it to class to explore their internship experiences. These pieces are made before supervision class to help supervisees begin to process and reflect on their experience. Response art made after their work with clients can help new therapists hold difficult material until they can bring it to supervision. Once shared with others, imagery can help them to effectively communicate the intensity of the experience.

Supervisees are asked to make this imagery outside of class to afford them the ability to determine the allotted time, media choice, and environment for creating their imagery. Ranging from visual images to poetry and performance pieces, this work may investigate an internship issue of their choice, including the therapeutic relationship, a conflict with a coworker, or any other facet of their work.

Bringing response art into supervision helps supervisees to communicate concerns from session, deepening the discourse and enriching the conversation for all involved. By making and presenting their pieces as part of the class, interns commit to discussing concerns with the group. This way of working supports a wide range of individualized expressions and creates a visual record of therapists' growth. It also requires that the new therapists hold themselves accountable to make time to reflect on the issues at hand in a meaningful way outside of class.

Each student displays his or her imagery in turn to open the discussion. The student describes the issue or concern from therapy and the group engages in the process of challenging, problem solving, and supporting the student as he or she reflects on the work. Students request the kind of feedback and support that they want from the group. One may pass the art piece around the table, asking each person to hold and view it. Another may ask the class for comments and full engagement with the image. Still another may ask people not to comment about the piece, instead focusing on the verbal description of the work with clients. In each instance supervisees practice articulating their intentions, clearly stating what they hope to accomplish in supervision and asking for what they need from the group. The artwork may commit the student to addressing a concern or it may act as more of a backdrop. Either way, the image helps to hold the frame for the discussion, creating a rhythm as we move from student to student, conceptualizing treatment and addressing clinical issues.

Maia Hubbard, an art therapy intern in my class, brought *Feeling Separate* (Figure 7.4) to supervision to help her describe her second week at her internship working in an empowerment program for adolescent girls housed in a high school. During her first days at the school, the students clumped together in groups and hostilely resisted her attempts to engage them. She said that she was discouraged and felt like an outsider. Her image depicts a chair separated from a group of chairs by a jagged yellow line. The students' behavior troubled Maia as she worked to fit in at the school.

Together we talked about the importance of trying to understand the students' behavior and what their attitudes toward Maia might mean. There are times when resistance is the only power that people feel that they have. The students might have been testing Maia's resolve for the work and whether she intended to stay. Their distancing actions might have been their way of staying interpersonally safe. Maia was new to them. They understood that she was an intern and would be leaving at the end of the year. It would take time to decide if the potential relationship was worth the risk necessary to let her into their lives. Encouraging Maia to look at the dynamics and understand how the behavior might be serving

FIGURE 7.4 Feeling Separate

Maia Hubbard

the girls helped her not take their rejection personally. She felt clearer about the situation as she returned to her internship and continued to work to engage the young women.

Noel King drew *Failure* (Figure 7.5, Plate 11) in response to a situation at her internship at a middle school serving youth who were struggling with their

FIGURE 7.5 (PLATE 11)   Failure

Noel King

behavior in class. Noel drew this image after returning from Christmas vacation when two of her young clients told her they wanted to end therapy. They became argumentative when she tried to explore their wish to terminate, walking out in the middle of their sessions. In supervision, Noel told us that she didn't understand. She said that she had such good relationships with the students before the vacation.

Failure (Figure 7.5, Plate 11) is a two-page spread in an altered book that contained her response art from each week and chronicled her internship experiences. Noel is a woman who is deaf and uses sign language with her clients. In the image, she represents herself with limp arms and a broken heart, holding a heavy weight. The word "Failure" clearly communicates her disheartened reaction to her clients' wishes to end therapy.

Noel presented her drawing to the supervision class as we talked about what happened at her internship. It started a class discussion about clients' reactions to their therapists' absence. Clients are often ambivalent about reengaging in treatment after time away from therapy. This resistance can manifest as hostile and even aggressive behavior. The feelings that can result from a therapist's time away can be a fruitful forum to rework abruptions from past relationships. Instead of leaving the supervision group feeling as though she had failed, Noel gained understanding of what happened as a predictable part of therapy that could be processed with the clients and used in treatment.

Ashley Melendez put her drawing *Overwhelmed!!!* (Figure 7.6) on the table in front of her as she began to talk about her internship at a continuing care facility for older adults. She told the class about her frustration and how overwhelmed she felt. The drawing depicts Ashley balancing stones inscribed with all that she was managing resting heavily on her head. Her challenges included managing the financial ramifications of working at an unpaid internship; the hours that she spent at her site writing notes; her responsibility for forming relationships with clients, leading groups, and creating directives for lower functioning residents; providing in-service training; obtaining informed consent forms; writing her master's thesis; coursework; and coming to supervision. Support was the last thing on her list. In her drawing Ashley stands with her eyes closed and her hands in her pockets, overwhelmed and alone.

Ashley shared her response art with the group as she told us about her work. The lively conversation engaged her peers, all of whom felt similar pressures. The image supported the discussion, giving the students a chance to vent about the pressures that they all felt, finding resonance with each other's concerns and considering creative solutions for managing their own internship workloads. Problem solving and developing the time management strategies to handle the stress of graduate training is a topic often discussed in supervision. Ashley returned to her placement with the assurance that we understood and resonated with the challenges of her work and that we appreciated the difficulty she experienced balancing everything.

FIGURE 7.6 Overwhelmed!!!

Ashley Melendez

Exploring Countertransference

Response art brought into supervision can help new therapists and supervisors explore personal responses stirred by treatment and supervision. Overly intense reactions to the client or feeling foggy or unclear may be signs that countertransference should be investigated. The classic analytic definition of countertransference describes it as the unconscious response of the therapist toward the client (Kahn, 2002). Recent definitions are more inclusive, encompassing all of the responses that the therapist has toward the client, whether they are unconscious or not (Corey, Corey, & Callanan, 2011). Countertransference may manifest in the therapist's positive or negative response to the client. Both must be addressed to avoid interference in treatment. Once the therapist has a lucid understanding of the relationship, therapeutic work becomes unencumbered by his or her personal reactions.

Art-based supervision offers imagery as a way to reflect on and understand countertransference so that it may be clarified and understood. This use of imagery in supervision supports the therapist's realistic view of the client, alleviating confusion from the therapist's personal issues that interfere in clinical work (Fish, 1989; Lachman-Chapin, 1983; McNiff, 1989; Moon, 1998).

Experiencing countertransference is part of providing therapy. Although countertransference is challenging, it is also an indication that the therapist is deeply engaged in the work. For me, discovering and resolving countertransference issues is like eating wasabi, a form of Japanese horseradish. The experience itself is very intense, but afterwards I feel clear, sharp, and keenly focused.

Investigating Treatment Issues

The traumatic stories that clients relate in session can be shocking and deeply disturbing to veteran therapists as well as to those who are new to this work. Leigh Ann Lichty, an art therapy intern working in a residential program for children, created *Fists* (Figure 7.7, Plate 12) to help her describe her experience witnessing a young boy's struggle to manage his past trauma. Following a session early in her internship she made this mixed media piece.

Describing what she saw in session and the piece that she made in response, she wrote:

> You gripped the back of the chair as you ground your teeth and bit the inside of your cheeks. Your eyes batted furiously, trying to make sense of it all. I don't know why there are bad people in this world who do unspeakable things and I wish you didn't have to think about them.
> *(Leigh Ann Lichty, Personal communication, February 22, 2015)*

As the mother of a one-year-old, Leigh Ann worked to manage her countertransference. It was hard to see the impact of early trauma at her internship and then return home to her own child. Making imagery, and exploring it in supervision, helped her to hold the impact of what she heard and saw while sorting it all out, finding a way to stay effectively engaged with her client and care for herself.

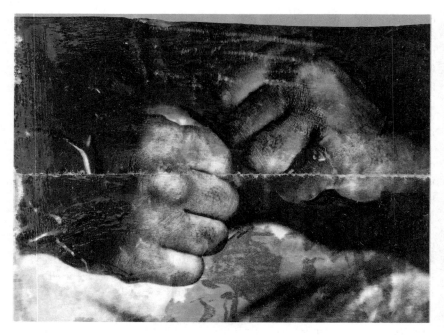

FIGURE 7.7 (PLATE 12) Fists

Leigh Ann Lichty

Emily Allbery's work is another example of response art made to reflect on and describe her experience. She drew *Childhood* (Figure 7.8) while interning in a child life program in a medical hospital. She shared her drawing with the class when it was her turn to explore her work.

> After a while you start to notice that the patients who have to spend a lot of time in the hospital incorporate their own wardrobes and personalities from home. Compared to the schemas I had regarding a typical childhood, the term "childhood" means something entirely different to a kid who has spent theirs in a hospital. This specific patient began to be the protector of her parents. She remained strong for them, whereas in the beginning of her treatment, as an infant, they were taking care of her. Now the roles were reversed. I remember feeling as if I wanted to take care of the patient, but came to realize that her form of coping was to take care of those around her.
> *(Emily Allbery, Personal communication, April 29, 2015).*

The image depicts the patient growing up in the hospital, first as an infant and then as a child. Drawing it helped Emily describe how she felt after spending

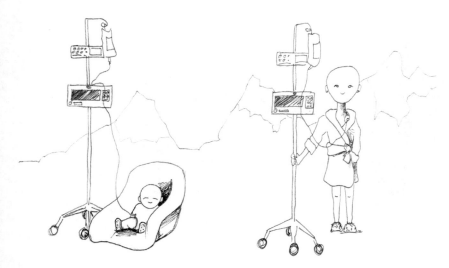

FIGURE 7.8   Childhood

Emily Allbery

hours with frail and vulnerable children, supporting them as they endured a different experience of childhood from what she had known. She discussed the challenges of learning to appreciate her patients' unique ways of coping with the impact of their illnesses. By sharing her artwork, Emily was able to look at her role in supporting the patient and strategize about resources for self-care to help sustain her work.

Kelly Riddle was an art therapy intern in a public elementary school working with children who struggled to pay attention and control their behavior in their classrooms. After working with the children for several months, she looked for a way to use positive interventions in her work with them. During one of her group sessions the students made a collaborative quilt that incorporated positive affirmations. Kelly made a drawing, *Response Art About Group* (Figure 7.9, Plate 13), at home to help her reflect on the group's process. The piece portrays the children gathered around the mural, contributing their positive statements.

Kelly took her response art to show the students the next time the group met. The children were delighted to see themselves acknowledged for their positive contributions the week before in the drawing. Later Kelly brought her image to supervision, sharing the impact of the focus on the children's positive interactions. Kelly began an ongoing practice. At the beginning of each group, she shared the response drawing that she made after meeting with them the week before. Her images helped to shift the focus from setting limits on negative behavior to engaging the children by recalling and recognizing their positive work together.

FIGURE 7.9 (PLATE 13) Response Art About Group

Kelly Riddle

Although response art may be made to communicate about the work, the therapist must consider his or her intention for using it with clients. It should be used only to support the therapeutic relationship and further clients' treatment. Kelly's practice helped her engage the children by showing them how she saw them in session through her imagery. People who are accustomed to criticism and gain attention from their negative behavior often respond well to reflection on their positive interactions. In Kelly's group, the focus on positive reinforcement made them want more. This became a creative intervention that she wove into her practice. Although it is not always possible to make imagery to respond to clients, it can be a powerful way to demonstrate the quality of your attention to them. This is a potent way to communicate how you are affected by clients' stories or their behavior by physically showing them your response.

Imagery Made to Give Feedback

Imagery is a powerful tool for communicating what we think and feel about our experience. To sharpen this skill I ask students to use their imagery to demonstrate their understanding of one another in supervision. In Chapter 4 I described the art for feedback assignment. Supervisees make response art inspired by one of their peer's presentation of case material. This assignment is designed to give feedback to the presenter. I make my own response art to present along with the students. During our next class meeting we arrange our images next to each other and explore them one by one with the presenter. This leads to further discussion of issues brought up by both the initial presentation and the artwork created about it.

Jen Kirkpatrick's image *Reality* (Figure 7.10, Plate 14) is an example of response art made to give a peer feedback. During class, one of the students

FIGURE 7.10 (PLATE 14)   Reality

Jen Kirkpatrick

presented her work with a woman from an art therapy group in a community counseling program. As part of the presentation, the student said that the woman appeared to be so "normal." After group she was surprised to learn that the client suffered from chronic schizophrenia and continuously heard self-deprecating voices. As she worked with the client, the intern had not seen a sign of the thought disorder. Jen, one of the other students, painted *Reality* (Figure 7.10, Plate 14) and brought it to class to demonstrate her understanding of her peer's experience.

Our discussion in supervision about the case presentation was supported by Jen's response art as well as images made by others. We discussed the importance of having clinical information about the clients we work with before providing services. Information is critical to ensure safety as well as to support effective treatment. We also talked about balancing clinical information with an interpersonal appraisal of the client. It is important to see clients with fresh eyes, not only through the lens of psychopathology. Our discussion shifted to focusing on schizophrenia and other thought disorders. We explored the differences between ego syntonic and ego dystonic hallucinations and how to differentiate between hallucinations and delusions. Then we talked about ways that these symptoms may manifest interpersonally, such as irritability, distraction, or inattention.

Finding ways to help student therapists comprehend their first experiences with psychopathology is an important part of supervision. Diagnosis and other coded terminology, used to support efficient communication in treatment planning and consultation, often baffle students. The alien nature of this kind of communication, in combination with new experiences with people contending with mental illness, can leave new therapists reeling. Although there are certainly insensitive uses of terminology that limit and objectify clients, it is important to help new therapists understand the meaning of psychiatric classifications. The purpose of diagnosis is to make communication more efficient.

Elissa Heckendorf drew *Telling Trauma* (Figure 7.11, Plate 15) to respond to the case presentation given by another student who was an intern in a community counseling program serving adults with chronic mental illness. During her presentation, the student therapist described how she felt flooded by the forceful feelings that her client shared during session. Elissa's response art represents the literal wave of emotion that her peer described. This image led us into a class discussion about how to help clients disclose trauma safely in therapy while maintaining our own equilibrium. There are instances in therapy when people begin to share painful information and are unable to regulate how much they disclose. Afterwards, many feel unsafe and withdraw from the therapist as a reaction. Holding the frame for the safe discussion of traumatic material requires attending to the feelings of the client as well as our own. When we feel flooded in this way it may be an indication that the client is feeling it as well and unable to stop the flow.

FIGURE 7.11 (PLATE 15) Telling Trauma

Elissa Heckendorf

We talked about how to help clients slow and focus their narratives. Saying something simple to help shift and hold the focus can be helpful. I often tell clients that what they have already shared is important and deserves our focused attention; there will be time to share more.

I have developed a consistent approach for the response art that I make for this assignment. I draw each piece with colored pencil within a 5½" square. I do this for two reasons. The first is practical. The format offers a consistent method for creating the many images that I make in response to student supervisees' work. The second reason is that the consistent size and shape of the pieces allows me to group them together as modular units into a class composite at the end of the semester. I will discuss how I use these pieces as part of closure for termination in Chapter 10. The images that I make are little windows into clinical experiences. They are powerful tools for feedback and are important resources in guiding my own work as a supervisor.

Paying close enough attention to make art about another's experience builds astute observational skills and empathy while providing colleagues with profound witness. These pieces demonstrate active listening and provide powerful feedback for the presenter. They also offer insight for the student or supervisor creating the image. Sometimes this concludes the assignment; other times we continue to explore the imagery.

Response Art Engaged With Witness Writing

In Chapter 4 I discussed my use of witness writing to explore my response art to reframe the work of one of my supervisees. The following example shows the use of witness writing to clarify the countertransference that I experienced about a student supervisee, helping me to understand my response and support her work effectively.

At times I work with witness writing (Allen, 2005) to shift and deepen my understanding of the imagery that I make for supervision. When time permits I share this process in supervision class, demonstrating its use for reflecting on the work. I begin by writing an intention that clearly states what I hope to learn or accomplish by working with the image. My investigation is guided by my intention as I continue to engage the piece. When I facilitate this process with others, we also work with our images through witness writing. Then those who choose to, read their writing aloud to the group as the others listen without commenting.

During a supervision class we shared response art, giving feedback to the presenter from the week before. We decided to continue to engage the images in deeper investigation through witness writing. I chose to work with the piece that I created with the revised intention of understanding the intensity of my reaction to the way that the student engaged with patients at her internship. I hoped that the process would bring me insight into my reactions and inform my supervisory work with her.

The interaction that led to my work began with a site visit where I observed the art therapy intern facilitating a group on an inpatient psychiatric unit serving adults. As I watched the group, I was disturbed that the intern seemed to be shut down, withdrawn, and distant from the patients. She appeared to be unable to easily interact with them and did not quickly respond to them to support their process. The intern provided them with little structure, support, or processing. She was so inactive that it seemed as though the patients were almost on their own.

I was surprised. The student and I had worked together for several months and I had not seen her like this before. I considered that she might be nervous about being observed by me. Even if this was a part of it, her blunted interaction worried me. I wondered if her inability to engage fully was because she was afraid, overwhelmed, or put off by the patients. When I discussed my concerns with her after the group she was vague and unclear about the problem, but earnestly promised to do better.

Weeks later the intern presented her work with a different group to the supervision class. As she discussed her involvement, her description of the process felt limited. She did not have background or contextual information about the patients. When asked about it, she said that she tried but was unsuccessful in her attempt to access the milieu report and patients' charts before running the group. Because the intern had so little information to support her work, the presentation felt thin, and I had a hard time picturing the group's process. I felt frustrated. As she presented her recent group to the class, I envisioned the session that I had observed her doing weeks before.

After class as I made a drawing to give her feedback, my memory of her site visit added to the intensity of my response. As I drew *The Chasm* (Figure 7.12), a crevasse appeared in the floor of the image, separating the intern from the patients in the group. When I showed my drawing the next week in class, I told her once again that I saw her holding back from fully engaging with the patients. After talking about the response art, I engaged in witness writing along with the supervisees to demonstrate this mode of investigation.

I began by writing my intention: *I learn what the image has to offer about supervising this student.* I went on to engage the image in imaginal dialogue. An excerpt from that dialogue follows.

The crack in the floor said:	Brittle. Everything is brittle. Don't push so hard. Flexibility takes time.
I said:	I'm looking for openness not flexibility.
The crack in the floor said:	It takes time and trust to be open. If you move too fast you will break. This is true of you and true of others. Build trust. Build, don't push. Listen more than speak and you may all learn something.
I said:	Thank you.

Although I had worked with the student for some time, our supervisory relationship still felt new. The image reminded me that resistance is usually rooted in fear

FIGURE 7.12 The Chasm

Barbara Fish

and helped me to soften to the student's struggle, reengaging my role as one who encourages instead of one who pushes. Had I not listened to my image, I might have continued to confront the new therapist about her hesitance to engage instead of supporting her. Sometime later I asked the student if my response art and witness writing about her experience during supervision was helpful to her.

> Yeah, absolutely. Even if at the time it seemed like I was shutting down in response to the art that you made, I was able to be reflective on that art piece, what was discussed, how I functioned within that group and your observation of me. A lot of knowledge comes in reflecting back on what you've done. So I think stepping back from it and being able to see the whole picture helped. I think I already knew what was going on in this instance. But it is still whether or not you want to recognize it. That's where the inherent difference lies, right?
>
> *(Anonymous, Personal communication, July 2, 2015)*

Engaging my drawing in this way helped me to realign my supervisory direction. As I interacted with my image, I recognized how intimidating inpatient psychiatric treatment can be for new students. I was reminded to hone my expectations so that they were consistent with the experience and ability of the new therapist. The patients in the image appear to be calm and unthreatening to me. However, a new therapist's perception of the patients might be quite different. Confronting the student and pushing her to be more interactive was not productive. Supporting her at the level where she was functioning and working to help her to understand her reticence was a more productive use of supervision. True supervisory collaboration can take place when the relationship becomes a safe place to be vulnerable.

Fairy Tale Assignment

As I discussed earlier, the fairy tale assignment is one that I find useful. It helps interns challenge and shift their perceptions of clients through metaphor by retelling their story through an imaginal lens. I ask supervisees to write and illustrate a fairy tale in which one of their clients is the protagonist. Students present the stories to the class in graphic book form. Through this assignment, interns see their clients with fresh eyes, assessing strength, capabilities, and resilience as well as noting limitations and challenges. Creating the story often brings up countertransference and other responses to clients that are important for supervision.

Julie Krause was an intern working within a behavioral health program in a psychiatric hospital when she wrote and illustrated this fairy tale about a scared little turtle. She painted a tiny box to hold the story (Figure 7.13).

> *Once upon a time a scared little turtle lived near a lake in a valley nestled between huge mountains.*
> *What the turtle didn't know was that he had once been a happy little boy with a family, and a house with his very own space.*

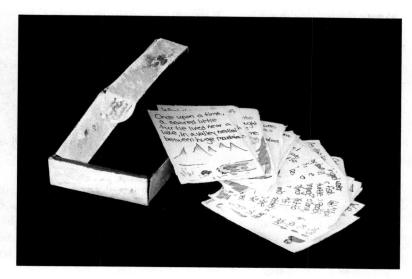

FIGURE 7.13   Scared Little Turtle Fairy Tale

Julie Krause

One day, the boy wandered deep in the forest. He thought he heard someone calling out his name.

Indeed, someone was calling him . . . It was an angry, lonely magic monkey, jealous of the boy's life.

He gave the boy no chance. Swiftly the boy had been turned into a scared turtle. The monkey took the turtle high up in the tree, and flung him past the mountains, stealing his memories before he left.

The only memory he left with the boy was this: That if he could climb the highest mountain, the boy could have his life back.

After months & months of trying, the scared turtle gave up.

You see, his shell was far too heavy to allow him to climb so long & high.

So the turtle lay down next to the pond, weeping because he missed his life even though he couldn't remember it.

As the tears tripped into the pond, all of a sudden the water began to swirl . . .

Out of the water came a magic fish. He asked the turtle "Why are you crying?" The turtle replied "My shell is too heavy. I can't climb the mountain to get home!"

The fish replied: "You have been so good, and waited so long, but never thought to ask for help, until today. I've watched you struggle up the mountain. Let me fix your shell, and then you can go home."

POOF

And with that the turtle's shell was aluminum, strong enough to carry everything, but light enough to get over the mountain.

The turtle thanked the fish and began his journey home . . . It took months of climbing
but finally the turtle crossed into his yard. He became a boy again!
With that, the boy's family ran to him hugging him and crying for they had missed
him so. From that day on, the boy learned to ask others when he really needed help.
Finally, his life could begin again.

The End

Looking back on her fairy tale, Julie said that she could identify herself as well as the patient she had worked with within the story.

> Growing up I felt very much on my own. I learned how to take care of my own needs for myself. I tended to stay in the background. I was a good student and I didn't really cause a lot of problems. So it's interesting that I wrote the story and then, after reading it, I realized this about me. I did not know it when I was making it. Aside from being about the patient, it's definitely about me too.
>
> I kept things to myself when I was growing up, not as much now. I let people in to a point. But there were protective walls and fences that I built and I knew very clearly that they were there. As a young adult I had somebody come into my life who was very important to me. This person helped show me how to actually trust people and that let some of those walls come down. That was a huge turning point for me and the way that I interact and function with people.
>
> I've never seen the physical place I've lived as home. Even today it's not home. I realize that my home is with people, certain people in my life. It's not a physical place. It's an interesting response to the story as well. The turtle itself really is its own home. I think that's always the way that I'll be. I may have a space that's a place that I sleep at night. But that's not necessarily my home.
>
> *(Julie Krause, Personal communication, July 7, 2015)*

Julie's fairy tale raises issues that we can all relate to. The protagonist faces loss and fear while dealing with issues of trust and vulnerability. When in despair, he asks for and receives help, finds resilience, lightens his load, and is able to go home. The message in Julie's tale is about balancing self-sufficiency and trust and asking for help. Once the little turtle stopped steeling himself with his heavy shell and reached out to ask, he was able to get the support that he needed. This is a good lesson for supervisees and supervisors alike. Asking for support and sharing resources can lighten the load for all of us.

In-Service Assignment

During the course of graduate therapists' training, I ask students to provide an experiential in-service at their internship. This gives site supervisors and colleagues a firsthand experience of the way that students work with clients. I find that this kind of participation, led by those in training, can help others gain confidence in their work. This often results in enhanced collaboration and referrals. It is also a fruitful tool for new graduates looking for employment, allowing them to literally show others the way that they work. Students develop their original in-service idea and bring it to class for discussion and feedback before implementing it at their site.

Experiential in-services are opportunities to help colleagues to engage in image-based work through participation in art-based directives and to discuss examples from therapy. I advise students to describe their work with clients concisely, saving time to allow participants to work with media, talk about their experiences, and ask questions. This is not the time to lecture about art therapy or other approaches to treatment. I recommend providing reference lists and articles as handouts for participants to read later.

Those designing an in-service should think about what they want to accomplish. Do they hope to help others understand how they work in order to gain appreciation for the value of art-based practice? It is important to remember that an in-service is not a therapy group. This is not the time to probe colleagues for personal issues. Participants should be made to feel open and at ease. For that reason a nonthreatening, art-based experiential directive should be chosen. Provide a range of materials including those that are easy to control as well as looser, more sensory media. Encourage participants to choose media that they feel comfortable with. People are often working with art materials for the first time since they were children. Some will be guarded and need to be put at ease. Allow them to choose whether or not to participate. They usually will. Remember to be flexible. The experience should allow for questions throughout and provide accommodations for participants coming in late or leaving early.

When designing the in-service, consider how much time is allotted. Find out how to schedule the in-service and how to communicate scheduling information to the staff. Be sure to give people enough notice so they can plan to attend. Communicate special instructions about anything that they should bring such as an old shirt or apron. Try to determine how many people will attend in order to plan.

Think about space. How many people will the room accommodate? What materials are feasible? Are there tables and a sink? What kind of materials will people be comfortable using there? Is it possible to bring materials and arrange the furniture or set up the space ahead of time? Do you want participants to help you set up the room as part of the experience? Where will people clean up after the in-service? Be sure to choose materials that can be easily cleaned with the available resources. Participants shouldn't risk embarrassment or ruin clothes by engaging in the process.

When designing the in-service, think about who will be in the audience. Consider the participants' power, privilege, and agency in the system where they work. In-services may be presented to any number of people from any discipline that the interns interact with. Do you plan to invite people from one discipline or have an interdisciplinary gathering? Be sure to address how people from other disciplines may look at your work from their perspectives. What do you want them to understand about the way that you work? What about your practice with clients will be valuable to them? A social worker may have different concerns about patient issues than a nurse. A social worker may want information about how you use metaphor to address problems on the treatment plan or how you work with building interpersonal skills through cooperative projects. A nurse may want to know how you ensure safety when working with materials.

If you include people from a variety of disciplines, how will they work together? Will a psychiatric resident feel at ease making imagery with milieu workers? Finally, remember that clean-up is an important part of closure. Don't neglect its significance in your in-service. Help those involved become ready to leave the in-service symbolically through clean-up and verbally through answering questions and discussion.

Experiential exercises I have asked coworkers to engage in during in-services include: make an image of yourself at work; find a partner and develop an image together without talking; make an image of yourself with a client you felt successful with; and create a problem symbolically out of clay and then create a solution. All of these art-based experiences give others the opportunity to engage materials, imagery, and metaphor to reflect on their work. It is a useful way to help them see the value of art-based practice.

I encourage student therapists to consider these and other factors as they create their in-services. I hope that this assignment will be a productive experience that will lead them to provide additional interdisciplinary training in their future roles as professional therapists.

Exhibiting Client and Therapist Imagery

An unusual and valuable part of fieldwork supervision at the School of the Art Institute of Chicago is participation in the Art of Connection Exhibition (Vick, 2000). All of the logistical planning for the show takes place outside of supervision; the essential element that we explore in class is the use of creativity within the therapeutic relationship. The exhibit includes client and intern artwork from a wide range of settings. Whether or not the clients participate in the show is considered to be a part of the clients' treatment and is integrated into treatment goals. Their involvement may include active participation in the exhibit. The participation can include collaborative pieces created by the therapist and the client. At times the supervisee may participate in the exhibit without the clients' active involvement or imagery, sharing response art that explores and communicates how he or she understands the relationship. Some clients attend the opening reception for the exhibition. Other clients do not.

Clinical and ethical aspects of the show are nuanced therapeutic components that we discuss in supervision. Whether the client's artwork is displayed in the exhibition or the supervisee's response art exploring the relationship and issues in treatment is the focus, we discuss informed consent for participation and releases for the exhibition of imagery as part of the clinical oversight. We explore whether or not the client will benefit from showing his or her work and attending the opening of the event.

As I stood at the opening of the Art of Connection, I overheard two adolescent boys who came to the show from a residential substance abuse program where they were court ordered for treatment. As they looked at their pieces on display, one told the other that it was the best day of his life.

Conclusion

Therapists in training have intense experiences in settings that challenge them on many levels. The skills cultivated during training serve as a foundation for the therapist's professional practice to come. Art-based supervision provided during graduate training supports students in their early encounters working with clients as they bring theory into practice. Using imagery to deepen their understanding and communicate their experience to others is an important resource in the collaborative practice that supports supervision.

There are seemingly unlimited ways to incorporate images into supervision. Each supervisor must assess the needs of the supervisee and their clients, helping to direct and focus sound practice. Art-based supervision offers images as a way to hold issues that call for our attention. We have discussed a variety of art-based assignments used to support the investigation and communication of treatment issues during training. Now we will turn our attention to the art-based supervision of postgraduate work.

References

Allen, P. B. (2005). *Art is a spiritual path*. Boston, MA: Shambhala.

Corey, G., Corey, M., & Callanan, P. (2011). *Issues and ethics in the helping professions* (8th Ed.). Belmont, CA: Brooks/Cole, Cengage Learning.

Fish, B. J. (1989). Addressing countertransference through image making. In H. Wadeson, J. Durkin, & D. Perach (Eds.), *Advances in art therapy* (pp. 376–389). New York, NY: John Wiley & Sons.

Kahn, M. (2002). *Basic Freud: Psychoanalysis for the 21st century*. New York, NY: Basic Books.

Lachman-Chapin, M. (1983). The artist as clinician: An interactive technique in art therapy. *American Journal of Art Therapy, 23*(1), 13–25.

McNiff, S. (1989). *Depth psychology of art*. Springfield, IL: Charles C Thomas.

Moon, B. L. (1998). *The dynamics of art as therapy with adolescents*. Springfield, IL: Charles C Thomas.

Perry, B. (November, 2008). *Applying the neurodevelopmental model of therapeutics to performance arts therapies.* Master class presented at the meeting of the American Art Therapy Association, Cleveland, OH.

Perry, B., & Szalaviz, M. (2006). *The boy who was raised as a dog and other stories from a child psychiatrist's notebook.* New York, NY: Basic Books.

Vick, R. M. (2000). Creative dialog: A shared will to create. *Art Therapy: Journal of the American Art Therapy Association, 17*(3), 216–219.

8

POSTGRADUATE ART-BASED SUPERVISION

New therapists experience all of the intensity of therapy without the supportive environment of graduate school and the supervision that they received there. Postgraduate supervision offers an additional focus on the therapist's practice. It takes therapists beyond the work they were capable of doing during training. At this phase of their professional development, new therapists take on more responsibility with clients. Now they function within the agency's oversight, following policies and procedures without academic support.

This chapter features the art-based reflections of new professionals, made as they investigate challenges in their work. These therapists have stepped out of the relative comfort of graduate school, where clinical encounters can be viewed as temporary "academic" problems, and into the "real world," where they bear a different level of involvement and accountability. Just as it is in graduate training supervision, postgraduate supervision is multifaceted. It focuses on the conceptualization and oversight of clinical work, ensuring the quality of care while reflecting on the systems of care in which it is delivered. It also supports the supervisee's personal understanding and management of his or her work.

The supervisor of new professionals maintains the dual role of administrative and clinical oversight. In some settings, the on-site supervisor's administrative responsibilities may take on a primary role, focusing on schedules, programing, and workload, leaving the novice therapist to more independently contend with the complexity of his or her clinical work. In some settings, the new professional may have a supervisor from another discipline who is not able to provide feedback about the profession-specific nuances of his or her work. For these and other reasons, many therapists seek additional supervision outside of their agency. Many new therapists have a combination of supervision from supervisors on- and off-site.

New therapists seeking supervision outside of the agency where they work choose their postgraduate supervisor based on their relationships during training, information gained through networking, or the knowledge of the supervisor's work by word of mouth and through his or her professional presentations and publications. Some return to supervisors they have worked with during training, while others move to another professional to advise their work. Their choice is guided by the experience and approach of the supervisor and the type of format that they are looking for. Whether the new therapist decides to go to group or individual postgraduate supervision, he or she is wise to look at the supervisor's expertise in his or her area of practice.

Those seeking licensure and credentials in their field look for supervision from professionals licensed in the area of their training. New therapists choosing supervisors outside of their agency select group or individual supervision. Group supervision provides a format similar to that which student therapists experienced during their training. New therapists benefit from listening to the challenges and experiences of others. The cost of group supervision is often an additional incentive to make that choice. Individual supervision affords the opportunity to intensify the focus of the session on the new therapist's work. More time can be tailored to address details of the supervisee's practice. Many new therapists begin their postgraduate oversight in group supervision and later move to individual supervision as their work intensifies or their peer group moves on.

In addition to administrative and clinical oversight, the content of postgraduate supervision focuses on the new therapist's professional growth and development. Some come for advice before seeking or accepting a position. At that juncture we explore job search strategies and approaches to interviewing. We discuss the importance of clarifying expectations when accepting a position, including finding out if work hours are flexible, if compensation time is given for extra work, whether the agency pays for licensure, or if there is compensation for off-site conferences and training. Those who are already employed look for assistance conceptualizing and processing their clinical work. Newly employed therapists also seek support clarifying and establishing the boundaries and limits of their practice. As part of their professional development, I help supervisees to find networking opportunities and support their involvement in professional associations, encouraging them to serve on committees and attend programs and conferences. If they are interested, I help them with their efforts to present their work and write for publication.

I am presenting examples from new therapists' postgraduate individual supervision because this is primarily the way that I provide this level of professional support. New therapists face challenges with their clients and the systems where they work that requires intense, focused, and customized attention. I find that sharing time within a group setting often does not allow for adequate time to address the individual therapist's unique concerns.

Because therapists gain important support from their peers, I also encourage new professionals to become involved in local and national professional associations as an additional resource. This provides them the chance to develop resonance with one another's work, find inspiration, and gain personal and professional support.

During art-based supervision we work with materials, grounding ourselves during discussion or creating pieces over many weeks to explore issues related to practice. There are times when I suggest that the new therapist make response art to investigate a concern that he or she has raised. However, most of the time imagery manifests organically during or after supervision in response to the content of our discussion.

Working With Materials for Grounding

Postgraduate supervision is supported by careful attention to space, time, and ritual. I work to create an inviting and creative space to hold the content that new therapists bring. I begin and end sessions on time, ensuring that our meeting has a beginning, middle, and end, modeling respect for others' schedules. I intentionally start and end supervision the same way each week. At the beginning of each session, I offer coffee or tea and set up the requested materials. At the end, we clean up the materials, set up the next appointment, address payment, and walk together to the door. The discussion of the therapist's practices is held by this opening and closing ritual.

Because of the depth of the work in postgraduate supervision, the use of imagery to ground the discussion becomes even more valuable than it was during training. Making imagery offers a sensory experience that can help to calm our brains, allowing us to focus our attention as we delve into material that is often traumatic and personally difficult. Supervisor and supervisees reach for endless combinations of materials to handle and steady themselves as they talk about the content and challenges of their sessions. Media use for grounding can range from organizing materials such as sorting beads to finger knitting or working with clay. This use of materials supports but is not the focus of supervision.

This way of engaging materials to support the supervisory conversation is important for the supervisor as well as the supervisee. As a supervisor, the way that I engage materials models their use for those I work with. Sometimes I use materials without a formed expression in mind, as a backdrop to help hold my attention on the discussion. More often I engage in working on an image over several weeks, as seen in *The Supervisor's Artwork* (Figure 8.1). Feeling the brush pull paint across the paper and seeing the paint flow and soak in steadies me as I focus on the supervisee and his or her story, engaging in the content that the supervisee presents. This use of materials supports my sustained attention. I frequently work on images over time. Supervisory sessions often begin

FIGURE 8.1 The Supervisor's Artwork

Barbara Fish

and end as I continue to work with the same painting, helping me to hold the space for each therapist in succession. Being in the flow of one piece helps me reengage with it without disruption as I focus on the next supervisee's work. When supervision begins, I sit down and resume working on one of my images that is in process or begin to work with some other piece as a sensory resource.

As I pick up materials and begin to work with them, the supervisee often does too, mirroring my actions.

Chance Ramirez made *Untitled* (Figure 8.2), carefully preserving seedpods by gluing them into rhythmic forms with acrylic medium, as she talked about her work in a psychiatric hospital. She described complex and difficult interpersonal contact with patients on chaotic hospital units where she was called to participate daily in physically restraining patients. Chance gently manipulated the seedpods into order as she described the fragile relationships she formed with her patients. As she worked she told me about the challenges they faced in treatment and in their lives outside of the hospital. Chance reflected on her process.

> What I like about it is the juxtaposition. I'm manipulating these gentle, fragile seedpods and talking about the non-fragile aggressive thing that I am a part of at work. I didn't know what I was doing when I was making it. I was just talking and doing something with stuff I found on the ground. In the hospital patients come and go and then come back again. Just like all of these cycles that I feel caught in and also trying to change somehow.
>
> *(Chance Ramirez, Personal communication, June 17, 2015)*

Adrienne Lewis also used materials to support the content she brought to supervision. She drew abstract images with colored pencils, such as *Drawing During Supervision* (Figure 8.3), to ground herself while discussing the details of the work she did with women and children in a domestic violence agency. As we talked about the complicated situations that her clients encountered, she stroked

FIGURE 8.2 Untitled

Chance Ramirez

FIGURE 8.3   Drawing During Supervision

Adrienne Lewis

the paper in her notebook with rhythmic lines of color. Adrienne described how doing her drawings helped her to engage fully in supervision.

> I need something instant when I process or make a piece of art, especially while I'm talking about the actual work that I am doing at the shelter. There is something soothing about using colored pencils. Drawing this way gives

me a place of calm to get centered when I'm talking about things that are not very centering and calming, things that are distressing, uncomfortable or difficult to process. It's the opposite of the shelter experience. I think that's what I need.

(Adrienne Lewis, Personal communication, June 9, 2015)

There are times when the therapist's method for approaching media reflects the way that he or she practices. This is the way that Julie Ludwick engaged with materials as she talked about her work in an art therapy program within a therapeutic equestrian center. Julie and I worked together in supervision as she envisioned and developed the program during her graduate training. We continued to work together during her postgraduate work when she was hired to implement the program, eventually taking on and supervising her own interns and postgraduate art therapists.

Julie sees participants with a variety of issues. These range from physical disabilities, including cerebral palsy and traumatic brain injury, to intellectual disabilities and communication disorders, such as social communication and autism spectrum disorders. Many clients have impediments that challenge their ability to effectively move and communicate with others. As part of her strengths-based approach, Julie adapts media and develops art-based communication tools to support the social and emotional growth and self-esteem of her clients.

Serving as the artists' "third hand" (Kramer, 1986), Julie creates images with clients with limited mobility, guiding them hand over hand to manipulate media according to their direction. Client artists without speech use their eyes and their fingers to communicate through word boards and other adaptive communication methods, spelling out their intentions for their process and articulating their own artist statements.

In addition to her work with participants, Julie's professional development includes her work as a new supervisor, supporting the learning of student therapists and new professionals. This challenge has offered Julie new opportunities to reflect on her practice.

Julie created *Spreading Tendrils* (Figure 8.4, Plate 16) during supervision as she discussed the challenges that she faces with clients, the system where she works, and her role as a new supervisor. Here her image-making process spanned weeks and employed watercolor, scissors, and a glue stick. Over time she created a complex watercolor painting. Once it was finished, she cut the painting into tiny pieces and reconfigured the shapes into a new image. She made *Spreading Tendrils* through her process of creating, deconstructing, and reconfiguring to explore her work. She described it as creating a safe space and boundaries for creative work. She reorganized it to find clarity. By working in this meticulous way, Julie used the image-making process to ground her and help her focus during our discussion. As she worked, Julie talked about problem solving and reconfiguring her approaches to clients and to her career.

FIGURE 8.4 (PLATE 16)   Spreading Tendrils

Julie Ludwick

Response Art Used to Explore Clinical Content

Imagery made with the intention of holding or investigating clinical concerns has a different role. We also turn to imagery to explore supervisory content and to demonstrate empathy and understanding.

Mary Usdrowski is a therapist who was working in a group home for adolescent boys with behavioral issues and who were wards of the state. *The Wall*

(Figure 8.5) represents one of her clients standing behind his crumbling interpersonal wall. She peers around one corner while her client watches her cautiously from the other. The once formidable wall now holds both hope and danger as it shows signs of collapsing. Mary painted this piece as we talked about the meaning of the young man's actions. As she made the image, she tried to understand why his resistance to change often took the form of defiance or aggression. Our work

FIGURE 8.5 The Wall

Mary Usdrowski

helped Mary remember that behavior has meaning and that the way to work with resistance is to understand how it serves the needs of the client.

Frederica Malone worked with me in supervision during her graduate training and continued to see me during her postgraduate work at a community-based agency serving children and their families. Over weeks she talked about aspects of her work while she slowly fashioned two small sculptures, *Client in Foster Care* (Figure 8.6) and *Self Portrait* (Figure 8.7), out of masking tape and aluminum foil, painting the pieces once they were formed.

FIGURE 8.6   Client in Foster Care

Frederica Malone

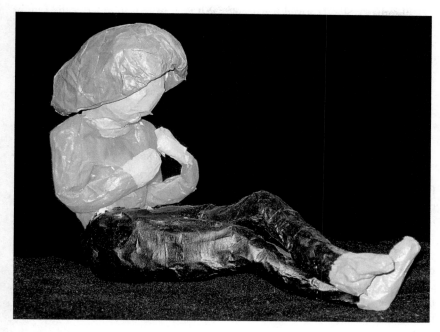

FIGURE 8.7 Self Portrait

Frederica Malone

Reflecting on the figures, Frederica talked about a seven-year-old girl who was small for her age. Abuse and neglect had resulted in failure to thrive, stunting her physical and emotional development. Frederica met with this child for therapy while the child resided in the latest in a series of foster homes with her two younger brothers. This foster home did not provide adequate support, nurture, or treatment to deal with the child's current needs and the impact of her history of trauma and neglect.

Frederica met with the child in the home because the foster mother wouldn't bring her to the office for regularly scheduled therapy services. Describing the foster mother as harsh and neglectful, Frederica said that it seemed like the woman was providing foster care just to "collect a check." She clarified her statement.

> This was not an emotional response aligned with unsupportive thinking about foster parenting. In actuality, I struggle with both sides of foster par-enting, but my perspective in this case comes from what I observed in the home. She framed all of her foster care licenses (many of them) in the center of her living room wall surrounded by pictures of herself and her biological family. But one could not see any evidence of the foster children who graced her home, including the ones she cared for at the time (my client and her

brothers). She displayed her licenses as if they were trophies. But the care of the foster children in her home was not reflected with any pride, or at least not with the same sense of pride she had for her own biological family.

While I was in the house, the foster parent spent most of her time in her room and strange men would run in and out from the back door. The girl's brothers were always told to sit in a corner. I was not allowed to go in the girl's room. She was not allowed to sit on the furniture in the living room. I could sit on the furniture, but she had to sit either in the dining room on a hard chair or on the floor.

(Frederica Malone, Personal communication, March 27, 2015)

Frederica, as well as others, reported neglect as well as the dangerous and inappropriate activity in the home. In response, all three children were eventually moved to another foster placement.

While Frederica made these sculptures, she told me of her feelings about the child. *Client in Foster Care* (Figure 8.6) is a carefully crafted piece representing the girl. Frederica paid close attention to the figure, representing the flowers on her shirt and the trim on her pants and tenderly forming braids decorated with beads in her hair. As Frederica reflected on *Self Portrait* (Figure 8.7), she described sorting out her feelings of countertransference.

My perception of the quality of the care informed how I approached my client. It increased my desire to give her a more validating experience, some recognition of her in my world, even if it was through the response art that I created. This piece was about when she was still in that troubled home. [I wanted to] protect what she could have, like her potential. Because, in the midst of it, we didn't know what was going to happen. If she stayed in that home what risks could come to her? If she were moved from that home, where would she end up? So I wanted to protect what could be for her, what would help her.

(Frederica Malone, Personal communication, March 27, 2015)

Frederica described her use of response art to reflect on her work with this client in supervision.

I think [it is helpful] when I am able to take out of me what I'm feeling and put it into the image and confront it, have it witnessed, and ask questions about it. Because sometimes if it's just in my head I might not see all the way around it. It is really helpful in supervision to have your perspective on it and what you witness to get me to go into it deeper. And see how I'm connecting to it, or even if I'm not fully connecting to it, to try to bridge me to that. Even the process of creating it in the space with you makes it feel safer. If I'm trying to problem solve something, getting some help and feedback with that feels safer. If I get frustrated with it, you'll ground me in the process and give me ideas or feedback.

(Frederica Malone, Personal communication, March 27, 2015)

Frederica used her imagery in art-based supervision to ground her while we engaged in the difficult work of supporting the client as she struggled to heal and grow within the child welfare system. In addition to sustaining a therapeutic relationship with the child, Frederica advocated for services and more appropriate foster care for the girl and her brothers. Her sculptures helped Frederica recognize and understand her countertransference, supporting her work for and with her client.

Beth Enterkin was a therapist working in a program serving those who have experienced domestic violence when she drew *The Anger Monster* (Figure 8.8).

FIGURE 8.8 The Anger Monster

Beth Enterkin

Her client was a seven-year-old boy who, after witnessing violence in his home, had explosive and aggressive behavior toward his sister and his mother. While he discussed his rages in session with Beth, the client drew a figure that he described as the "Anger Monster" to depict the rage inside of him.

Later, in supervision, Beth recreated *The Anger Monster* (Figure 8.8). She added a figure representing the boy sitting curled at the monster's feet as we explored how Beth might help the boy find new ways to express his anger and his fear. When she met with her client again, Beth encouraged him to think about how he could manage the anger monster by expressing how he felt in therapy with her and with other people.

Working with this client and others like him led Beth to develop an innovative, trauma informed treatment group at her agency. It was designed to help young boys process their feelings about the domestic violence that they witnessed at home. By addressing their experiences in this way, she helped them make conscious choices about the kind of men, fathers, and husbands they might become.

Even though the image drawn by Beth's client helped him to express his rage, it is not a threatening piece. That is not always the case. Images made in therapy come from powerful and deeply personal work that may be misunderstood if viewed out of context, outside of session. Graphic, violent imagery is common when working with those who have experienced trauma. I talk with new therapists about the difference between private and public art. Private art is work that represents sensitive, violent, or provocative issues that are processed in treatment. These images are best held in session by the therapist to protect the vulnerable material that they represent. This way of supporting concrete expressions in therapy can be a form of containment that supports closure. Public images are created for interaction beyond therapy. These may be made to process material from session or to communicate feelings and issues beyond treatment. Both the therapist and the client should agree that public images are safe to share. Therapists who understand the distinction between private and public images are able to help their clients navigate this challenging terrain.

It is important to carefully assess imagery that holds the content of session. In reaction to terrorism and increased violence in public places, many schools and other agencies have adopted a "zero tolerance" policy toward guns and other weapons. Participants are met with metal detectors at the entrance to their programs in hopes of ensuring safety for those within.

A therapist I supervised made the response art *Sword* (Figure 8.9, Plate 17) during supervision to understand her client's use of media to make weapons in session as she worked to help him safely explore and express the violence he felt. She provided therapy for children with social and emotional disorders at a residential agency. Having experienced trauma caused by abuse and neglect, many of these children aggressively acted out their conflicts. However, this client internalized his anger, entertaining aggressive fantasies without acting on them. He was withdrawn. He looked like the Grim Reaper, wearing a hoodie and dressing in black. Although he acted like he wanted to appear menacing, he was not aggressive.

This 14-year-old boy was a ward of the state who came to the residential agency from a failed foster home. He was interested in medieval weapons, which he researched in books from the library. As he walked back from school, the client found pieces of rope, chain, plastic, and metal to use for his projects. He combined them with aluminum foil and other materials in the art room, holding them together with duct tape to make weapons.

FIGURE 8.9 (PLATE 17) Sword

Anonymous

The therapist worked to ensure the clinical wisdom and safety of her decision to allow him to express his aggressive feelings in this way. While assessing his ability to use the materials safely, she collaborated closely with the treatment team and the unit staff about which pieces could or could not be kept safely on the unit. After checking with the unit supervisor, she let him keep some of the soft ones in his room. She kept most of the weapons in her office. It was not easy to convince the team that there was value in this intervention. The therapist discussed her reasons for supporting this way of working.

> Making weapons was very important to him. The client had a history of past physical abuse and was treated terribly. He had rageful thoughts and feelings in response. He needed to express the kind of imagery that was inside of him in a relationship where the content was accepted and he was able to process it. When he brought it up in other interactions he was shunned and told that it was bad. Our work challenged me to accept this part of him, his real thoughts and feelings. It helped him to feel like he wasn't a bad kid because he had bad thoughts.
>
> *(Anonymous, Personal communication, July 24, 2015)*

The client made swords, maces, slingshots, whips, and other weapons each time he came to therapy. His imagery was not always about hurting other people. He also made shields for self-protection. The therapist said that she thought that making the weapons made him feel powerful at times, helping him have more sense of self-control. To ensure physical safety with the projects, the therapist often had to take some of the objects away or supplement the materials that he used with duct tape or something softer to keep the pieces from becoming dangerous. The foundation that supported this very complex and sensitive work was built on the trust they developed in their therapeutic relationship. The therapist said that they established an understanding early in their work together.

> He agreed that when he kept a weapon that he made in his room, that he would never use it with anyone in a threatening way. He never abused that. So there was an element of trust between us about him using things in the right way.
>
> *(Anonymous, Personal communication, July 24, 2015)*

The therapist described why she thought it was important for him to make weapons.

> Although the weapons were violent imagery, I never felt that he would be aggressive. He held it all inside of him. Making these pieces helped him feel like he could let these thoughts out without hurting anybody. I hoped that this work would help him to hold them or regulate them without actually

acting on them. If I had not let him make weapons, it would have given him the message that those feelings are unacceptable, that it is not safe to talk about them or let them out.

(Anonymous, Personal communication, July 24, 2015)

Before the client left the agency, the therapist and the client took pictures of all of his weapons because she did not think it was safe for him to keep most of them. They compiled the pictures into a book that he took to his next foster care placement.

Our work was about looking at the violent imagery that was inside of him and him learning how to protect himself. We worked to help him to feel empowered by containing the violence in the artwork that he made.

(Anonymous, Personal communication, July 24, 2015)

The therapist painted *Sword* (Figure 8.9, Plate 17) as she discussed her work during supervision. Her image helped her to describe the power of her intervention, working to support her client's mastery over his thoughts and feelings. As her supervisor, I agreed. I would rather have a client make a sculpture of a gun and process his or her feelings than sit silently thinking about it. If we will not help our clients express the frightful and aggressive thoughts that they hold inside, what hope do they have for understanding and being able to manage them safely?

Seeley Cardone came for supervision for her work at her first job as an in-home counselor at an agency supporting children in foster care. One of her clients was a 12-year-old girl whose long-term relationship with her foster mother was strained. The client's "roller coaster episodes" eventually led to her hospitalization. Seeley's work focused on decreasing the girl's emotional outbursts and supporting a secure attachment with her foster mother. After visiting her client in the hospital, Seeley sat in her car and drew *Untitled* (Figure 8.10) to express the frustration and disappointment that she felt. Later she brought it to supervision.

I had my expectations of what that hospital visit would be and what it would be like to be in a psych hospital. It surprised me to see how comfortable she seemed in the hospital and how she did not appear to take this event as a set back. She laughed and was silly throughout our visit. I was naive about how sick she was. I was so eager to go in there and set up a plan and "fix the situation" and angry that she didn't take my offer of help or want to be helped. It was so confusing for my young therapist self.

(Seeley Cardone, Personal communication, July 31, 2015)

Seeley drew response art to capture her conflicting feelings about the hospital visit. When she brought her drawing to supervision, she talked about how she felt about her client. We discussed the child's history and attachment issues and

FIGURE 8.10 Untitled

Seeley Cardone

how they might manifest interpersonally in her current relationships, including therapy, to understand why the girl might behave the way she did. We considered how these patterns of behavior were defensive, developed over many years of the young girl's life. Finally, we talked about Seeley's rescue fantasy and helped her adjust her expectations.

The use of imagery to hold and explore issues related to the systems where we work is presented in *Untitled* (Figure 8.11, Plate 18), a piece made by an art therapist who worked at a shelter for immigrant women and children. She painted colorful stripes on a postcard-sized piece of watercolor paper as we talked about her challenges at work. After she filled the paper with striations of color, the therapist covered the stripes by writing her thoughts and the fragments of our conversation. She worked steadily throughout the session as we discussed systemic issues, the use of power, and the supervisory challenges that she encountered in her work in an agency dedicated to addressing gender violence.

Erika Molina, a new professional, sketched *Raven* (Figure 8.12), her personal symbol, with chalk as she discussed her disappointment with her new job in a school that she thought held more promise of professional growth and satisfaction. As she drew and talked about the situation in supervision, she clarified her intention to begin to search for another position. Art-based supervision used in this way supports supervisees as they chart their professional trajectory, providing imaginal guides to help them envision their futures.

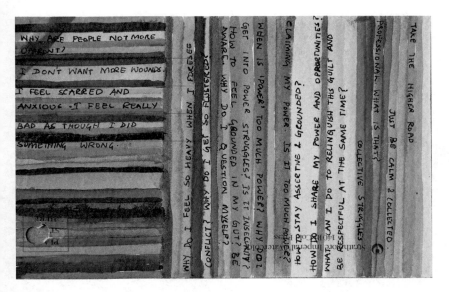

FIGURE 8.11 (PLATE 18) Untitled

Sangeetha Ravichandran

Ryan Noble came to supervision and began to paint *Window* (Figure 8.13) about a child he saw while he was on a job interview for a therapist position on an inpatient psychiatric unit. While touring the facility, he saw a young boy looking out of the window at the end of the hallway. Months later, Ryan reflected on how the image had been useful to him. He said that it helped him to investigate his countertransference and his experience of harm's touch by holding the encounter. The painting also supported the multifaceted communication of his concerns.

> I was exiting the elevator with my soon-to-be supervisor when I saw him, silhouetted in front of the window, with his hair tussled and wearing loose scrubs. I remembered continuing on with the interview process even though the sight of him was sticking with me. I could tell that there was something there but I couldn't let myself feel it. When I left the hospital the impact stayed with me, in my bones, my cells or something. Somewhere between there and supervision I knew that this would be my next painting. I kept seeing it in my head and feeling it in my body.
>
> Even though I'm a father, when I work with kids I find myself reflecting more on my own childhood. This piece helped me look at my counter-transference. Like how am I acting with this child and how is it related to my own upbringing? What's appropriate? What's my role? What is this child bringing up for me?

FIGURE 8.12 Raven

Erika Molina

I like art-based supervision because you actually contain and hold the experience. Making art is a way to remove the spur from our psyche and be able to refer to it again. It helps me manifest it in supervision so that we can look at it. I really like making things concrete, especially emotions. They're so layered and slip away so easily. The image helps me attach words

FIGURE 8.13 Window

Ryan Michael Noble

and feelings to the experience more than if I had to recall the experience with only words. It not only helped me to remove the spur but it also gave me a concrete way to put it out there in front of us.

When I made this piece, it helped me to make the decision to take the position at the hospital. Since then I've used the image in presentations and

I've shared it with my own interns. It not only helps to process my clinical encounters but it is also a professional resource to communicate to other people about how I experience my work.

(Ryan Noble, Personal communication, June 30, 2015)

Ryan demonstrated the utility of the image over time. This piece helped him recognize countertransference even before he began working at the hospital, allowing him to make the decision to work there and to engage with his patients with clarity.

Distance Supervision

Distance supervision can supplement local supervision or provide support for those without local access to professionals in their area of practice. Distance supervision brings its own set of complex issues requiring consideration. It must be provided in compliance with state and federal law including the Health Insurance Portability and Accountability Act (HIPAA), ensuring client confidentiality. Before agreeing to engage in distance supervision, both supervisor and supervisee must have a clear understanding about the eligibility of distance supervision hours when applying for professional credentials.

When I work with supervisees at a distance, we do not send client information over the Internet. We discuss issues during video conferencing to ensure confidentiality. The use of e-mail and video conferencing is helpful when sharing response art to reflect on the work. Supervisees make response art before supervision and send their imagery by e-mail so we can look at it together when we meet online.

As new therapists graduate and relocate, some turn to supervision for help with career development, seeking support and direction for their job searches. Kelly Riddle moved to another state after graduating from a master's program. Soon after we began distance supervision for art therapy as she worked in a community-based program for adults with intellectual disabilities. After several months she found herself moving again. In her new home she drew *Untitled* (Figure 8.14). She e-mailed the image to me before our supervision video call. As we looked at the drawing together, Kelly discussed her job search and a potential position that she was excited about. Although the ground she stands on is colorful, she is not certain of what is next for her and is interested in sorting out the possibilities. Kelly's use of imagery helped to calm and focus her as she explored what is next. By engaging in creative exploration, she began to look at her options imagining her next job as she worked to find it.

Elissa Heckendorf, an art therapist working in a psychiatric hospital in another state serving adults with chronic mental illness, used response art to

FIGURE 8.14   Untitled

Kelly Riddle

explore her work with patients. Together we looked at her response art online during video supervision. She drew *Empty* (Figure 8.15) to reflect on how she saw one of her patients.

> This patient disclosed on several occasions a significant loss in creativity. She was able to connect with peers through drawing repetitive, structured images and giving them away. Her images were always the same and spoke to the surface level connections the patient was comfortable with. By seeing this patient struggle to connect, and by reading the patient's admission notes, I got a feeling of emptiness. This image helped me to describe the feelings that I had difficulty expressing verbally and gave me a deeper understanding of what the patient might have been experiencing.
>
> *(Elissa Heckendorf, Personal communication, June 27, 2015)*

FIGURE 8.15 Empty

Elissa Heckendorf

The response art pieces that Elissa sends to me prior to supervision serve as the starting points of our discussion about her work with patients. They provide a metaphoric point of entry, adding to our shared communication and understanding of her practice.

Cate Barrington-Ward works in New Zealand at an assisted care facility for the elderly, where she is a new supervisor. She e-mailed *Untitled* (Figure 8.16) to me just before our scheduled video supervision. Cate was taking on the challenges of supervision for the first time. She was not only a new supervisor for the two women on her team, but she was also new to the agency. Her drawing helped

FIGURE 8.16 Untitled

Cate Barrington-Ward

me to understand her dilemma as a first-time supervisor attempting to build a cohesive team. It opened and oriented our discussion as we explored the situation during our video call.

Her work took place in the context of the month-long Cricket World Cup Tournament in New Zealand. The competition was the theme of the week for the residents' program. As the supervisor of her team, Cate tried to rally her staff to enthusiastically engage in the project, helping to orient the residents with this focus on current events. Cate's efforts were thwarted by her supervisees' resistance. Her drawing represents them frowning, standing with arms folded behind the wickets from the cricket game. Next to the two women, behind the wicket barrier, Cate wrote, "NO I IN TEAM." She depicted the facility's residents as butterflies swarming overhead.

Cate and I discussed ways that she might approach her supervisees as they worked to build a team of their own. I suggested that she recognize the strengths and skills of the staff while clarifying her expectations for them, reviewing the objectives of the program and how they support resident services. We talked about how this might help those she supervised feel more involved in the event, supporting their improved enthusiasm and involvement in the project.

Conclusion

Postgraduate supervision supports new therapists at the gateway of their careers. Their early experiences are formative as they move into the professional arena. Imagery used in art-based postgraduate supervision helps to deepen reflection on the work, providing vehicles for problem solving and insight into the complexities of therapeutic practice.

New therapists often experience mixed feelings as they transition from graduate school into their careers, striving to establish their professional identities. Beyond looking for support for their clinical work, many look for supervision to facilitate their transition from student to professional as well as document their postgraduate hours to qualify for credentialing and licensure. As a teacher, supervisor, and mentor, I work to support new professionals in their practice and in their efforts to work effectively as part of the therapy community. I encourage those I supervise to participate in professional associations and conferences and to present their work and writing for publication.

Once therapists earn their professional credentials, many maintain their supervisory relationships to access additional support and collaborate about new challenges. Therapists continue to seek supervision for working with complex clients, exploring systemic issues, and developing new projects. They often seek consultation with me when they take on supervisory roles of their own or consider career changes.

We have looked at the use of response art in art-based supervision during graduate training and in postgraduate work. The next chapter expands this use of imagery beyond those who provide art therapy, demonstrating the use of art-based supervision for people working in related fields.

Reference

Kramer, E. (February, 1986). The art therapist's third hand: Reflections on art, art therapy, and society at large. *American Journal of Art Therapy, 24*(3), 71–86.

9

INTERDISCIPLINARY ART-BASED SUPERVISION

Making and reflecting on imagery presents valuable opportunities for reflection and communication for those working in disciplines beyond art therapy. This practice is useful for those in any field who are working to gain therapeutic insight. Counselors, social workers, psychologists, and other clinicians may turn to their imaginations to access deeper meaning. Art-based reflection can also be useful for paraprofessionals without extensive training who are working with clients.

When I offer and support the use of materials to process treatment experiences, other professionals find unexpected resources for deepening insight and clarifying communication. This chapter describes some of the interdisciplinary art-based supervision and consultation that I have provided for medical and social service professionals. I have worked with people from a wide range of disciplines and demonstrated the value of images to clarify issues and communicate treatment concerns. I facilitate others' use of response art and share my ideas about harm's touch through examples of work from consultation and training sessions with nursing students as they engaged in their first clinical experiences, veterans who are nursing students, and a range of mental health professionals working with children in residential care. I describe how I cultivate image making in these venues. The role of the supervisor's response art to help explore and communicate clinical concerns is also discussed.

Student Nurses

While continuing to investigate the uses of response art and the impact of harm's touch, I had the opportunity to work with nurses studying at the College of Nursing at the University of Illinois. The use of response art was part of their supervision seminar during their first clinical experiences.

Student nurses, who work in a wide range of settings, meet some of the same personal and professional challenges as counselors and other therapists. Many feel anxious, overwhelmed, and pressured by the immense workload, the seriousness of their responsibility, and the emotional challenges of caring for those who are suffering. Some seek and find help from supervisors and others at work. Still others experience their training without sufficient support, feeling that they are expected to work independently in their first encounters as student nurses.

I attended the nurses' bi-weekly postclinical conferences throughout the semester as an invited faculty member along with Geraldine Gorman, the nurse faculty supervisor from the college. Each week that we met, two of the student nurses presented their work from their placement. Early in the semester I introduced the process of making response art and explored the concept of harm's touch by making my own images about their presentations. Each week, after an initial class demonstration, we went home and made response art to demonstrate how we understood the challenges of the material that was presented. I shared my images in the next class along with the others in the group.

I drew *Hospice Care* (Figure 9.1) as a response piece to a student nurse working in a hospice program who told of providing comfort for a family while the father died. The student nurse had been clearly moved by what happened as he related his experience. He spoke about sitting with the family, holding the space while they waited, as time seemed to stand still. Through my image, I reflected on and shared my sense of how important the nurse's presence had been as he tended to the family at this difficult moment.

I drew *Aphasia* (Figure 9.2) to demonstrate my understanding of a student nurse's work. The piece is shown in succession and consists of an image with a moving component that changes its effect. The first configuration of the drawing represents the student nurse standing at the bedside of a woman who struggled with this communication disorder, affecting her ability to speak to him. The patient is hidden behind a curtain, allowing only small glimpses of her to be seen. The student nurse stands next to a clock hanging on the wall, holding his list of things to do. I drew these symbols to represent the pressure to work quickly and efficiently with the patient that he described during his presentation. The next view of the image represents the same drawing with the curtain lifted, allowing the patient's unencumbered communication with the student.

As I drew the piece, I thought about how the student presented his work in the group. He described feeling pressed for time because of his numerous responsibilities as a student nurse and how long it took for the woman to find the words to tell him what she needed. I thought about the frustration that the woman must have experienced as she struggled to communicate. The drawing helped me to feel empathy for the student's struggle as well as that of the patient behind the curtain. It also helped me to communicate my understanding of the encounter to the student who had experienced it as well as to the rest of the class.

FIGURE 9.1 Hospice Care

Barbara Fish

Under There (Figure 9.3) is a piece made by another nursing student to demonstrate his understanding of his peer's experience. The drawing consists of a hospital worksheet titled "Aphasia Exercise" that lists statements that the patient might use to communicate about his or her care. These include: "Would you help me find my glasses?" "I think the medication you gave me is making me itchy." "Please close the door while I use the bed pan." To demonstrate aphasia, the student nurse obscured the statements with pencil, leaving only disconnected words and phrases that impaired the communication. This piece, which the student nurse made at home to reflect on another's experience, demonstrates that it is not necessary to have artistic training to communicate powerfully with imagery.

FIGURE 9.2 Aphasia

Barbara Fish

Student nurses brought their images each time we met, spreading them on the table as feedback for their peers (Figure 9.4). Because of the intensity of their work, and the need for practical discourse and problem solving, our class discussion of the imagery was brief. However, the imagery was an ongoing presence and support throughout the semester. The student nurses' response art helped them

FIGURE 9.3   Under There

Anonymous

to demonstrate their understanding and empathy for one another's stories, while sharing their early nursing experiences.

Working with imagery was challenging for many of the nursing students. Most of them had not made imagery since they were children. Art materials felt alien and hard to work with articulately. Some students were self-critical and shy about the appearance of their finished pieces. Nevertheless, many of them reported that

FIGURE 9.4 Student Nurses' Response Art

Anonymous

they appreciated being required to make time outside of class to reflect on their work despite their busy schedules. They said that they also valued having others reflect on their work through imagery. In an informal survey at the end of the semester, several of them commented on the process. One said, "I felt humbled by my classmates' thoughtfulness. It was so refreshing to see and feel empathy in a form that wasn't just an 'I'm sorry'—words get innocuous after a while." Another explained that "it was an outlet for letting feelings percolate and build into something, even if the problem or issue can't be resolved. Creating something to make it real seemed to help."

Veterans' Creative Strengths Project

I have had other opportunities to provide interdisciplinary art-based supervision. One of these occurred while I was working in the Psychiatry Department at the University of Illinois, where I collaborated with the university's College of Nursing and the Disabilities Studies program to develop the Veterans' Creative Strengths Project. This program, funded by a grant from the University Council for Excellence in Teaching and Learning (CETL), provided support for returning veterans who were students in the College of Nursing. The group met weekly and employed visual art, creative writing, and performance to provide an outlet for veterans as they encountered the stresses of readjusting to civilian student life.

I facilitated art-based supervision to support this work. The leaders who participated in it included Geraldine Gorman, a nurse on the faculty of the College of Nursing; Carrie Sandahl, a performance artist who was a faculty member from the university's Disabilities Studies program; Stephanie Ezell, a student nurse from the College of Nursing; Elissa Heckendorf, an art therapy student from the School of the Art Institute of Chicago, and myself. During our planning and ongoing reflective work in supervision, we each chose our preferred mode of expression, deepening the discussion of our ideas through visual imagery and creative writing.

The veterans came to the group looking for community and support. We offered a consistent, predictable format, a nonjudgmental forum for creative expression, and snacks. We structured our time using the Open Studio Process (Allen, 2005), which I describe in Chapter 4. Each meeting began with writing our intentions; we proceeded to offer artmaking, creative writing, and performance opportunities and ended with writing and reading our witness writing. Each participant chose whether to share his or her writing with the group or to keep it private.

We framed our creative work with intention and witness in our facilitators' meetings as well. Due to time constraints, the meetings were not as frequent as we had hoped. The facilitators reflected that, while they could not truly comprehend the veterans' experiences, engaging in creative work along with participants helped them to empathize with the veterans. One facilitator reflected on her process by saying, "It was a grand leveler and a community strengthener." Another commented that she wished she had more time to engage in making art about her experience. "When we did response art it was helpful. We didn't anticipate our own fatigue level or lack of time."

I made *Veterans' Nest* (Figure 9.5) at home and brought it to one of our facilitators' meetings to express how I felt about the group that we created together. I started making the piece by writing my intention, repeating it over and over again: *I hold this space for creativity in community.* I printed, trimmed, and glued the statement into a long strip. Next, I formed people by modeling and twisting aluminum foil to represent the veterans who came to the group each week. I carefully covered each figure with strips of masking tape. I thought about painting them but I decided against it, keeping their uniform appearance. I took wool roving in several colors and softly formed it into a nest, weaving my written intention throughout. After securing the nest with a felting needle, I gently sewed the tiny veterans into the nest, carefully securing them in place.

I made this piece late in the semester, after our work together had progressed for some time and the group was well established. It helped me to express my gratitude for the experience. While we created a safe community for the veterans as they reentered student life, we created a safe space for academic collaboration and support as well. My response art gave all of us impetus to discuss what we received, as well as what we accomplished, as we worked to support the veterans.

FIGURE 9.5 Veterans' Nest

Barbara Fish

Art-Based Supervision in Residential Care

While working at the University of Illinois, I was part of an interdisciplinary team that comprised the Mental Health Policy program. This group was charged with instructing, supervising, and evaluating hospital and residential treatment programs serving children who were wards of the state to improve the quality of their care. As part of that group, I helped to develop and implement the Center for Child Welfare Training. The project's mission was to instruct and consult with a wide range of professionals including childcare workers and milieu staff, psychologists, social workers, counselors, expressive therapists, and administrators in the course of our five-day intensive programs.

My role consisted of presenting images and narratives to deepen participants' understanding of the nature of the problems that faced the children and the possible meanings of their behavior. In addition to showing imagery made by youth, and the response art that I made about my work with them, I facilitated image-making sessions for participants to help them explore and communicate how they felt about their work. The interdisciplinary group processed their experiences through making art and discussion.

Social workers, therapists, counselors, psychologists, and facility administrators participated in image making. But the majority of participants in this program were milieu staff. Many had years of direct-care experience with little formal training or supervision. With changes in services and the increased need for trauma informed treatment, all levels of staff struggled to manage their workload, maintain safety, and function effectively with residents. This use of imagery helped them to express their feelings about their work.

Each time that I provided the training, the process was the same. I offered paper, pencils, markers, pastel chalk, and oil pastels, asking everyone to create an image about how they saw themselves at work. I explained the directive, saying that there was no expectation for artistic skill and that any attempt would be a success. I said that there would be time for discussing the artwork and how the process felt after the images were complete. I stressed that no one would be asked to talk about his or her work who did not volunteer to do so.

My coworkers and I drew images alongside those in training. There was the usual nervous laughter after the initial silence that followed the directive. Then one by one those in the training chose their materials and began to draw. The group became quiet as they worked. I knew we were ready to discuss the process and the drawings as the participants began to mill around and talk. I asked everyone to tape their images on the wall so that we could see them. Then we talked about their experiences.

What Hat Do I Wear Today?! (Figure 9.6) presents all of the "hats," or roles and responsibilities, that the childcare staff member is expected to take on in the

FIGURE 9.6 What Hat Do I Wear Today?!

Anonymous

course of her work. These include police officer, firefighter, artist, and clown. The next drawing, *How? Why?* (Figure 9.7), depicts another staff member with her hands reaching in five different directions and surrounded by her responsibilities, represented by clients, her cell phone, her "To Do" list, and her psychology book. Another worker drew *Untitled* (Figure 9.8). It showed his face, without a body, with the residential homes where he worked sprouting out of his enlarged head. He wrote his work roles on the four corners of the page: "Enforcer," "Problem Solver," "Supporter," and "Positive Male Influence."

A facility administrator drew *Untitled* (Figure 9.9), representing herself as a stick figure holding a large box with arrows pointing to the words and symbols inside of it. These include: "safety," "future," "outcomes," and "DCFS," as well as images representing training, clients, staff, money, time, the agency policy book, and the residents' privilege board. The image *Untitled* (Figure 9.10) was drawn by a therapist who had recently been attacked by one of her clients.

Most of the discussion about the images happened among participants at the small tables where they sat together and drew together. Extensive discussion of the images as a larger group was not possible as the training groups consisted of more than fifty people. When we came together to discuss the experience,

FIGURE 9.7 How? Why?

Anonymous

FIGURE 9.8 Untitled

Anonymous

everyone was invited to comment on his or her work. Those who were reticent were not pushed, but many people talked about the images that they made as well as how they felt about making them. With and without discussion, the images were powerful, and the participants expressed positive feedback about the process.

FIGURE 9.9 Untitled

Anonymous

This experience became a powerful team-building component that supported the training process in addition to helping those involved express the challenges they faced. As they described the images representing their struggles, they resonated with one another, decreasing their feelings of isolation. This began productive discussions that continued throughout the training, addressing the nature of the children's disorders, strategies for treatment, and how the team can work to understand and support one another.

FIGURE 9.10 Untitled

Anonymous

Consultation

The final component of the Center for Child Welfare Training took place after the formal training was over. We accompanied participants back into their agencies, providing ongoing consultation and supervision and solidifying learning by reflecting on it within clinical contexts. For months we helped staff to implement the ideas that we presented during their training experiences. While I did this work, I encountered the real-life challenges that confront those working with youth in residential and hospital care. Response art became an indispensible tool that I used to hold what I saw, helping me to support others as they worked with youth in these settings.

Sometimes the intensity of the interactions that I have with those I work with takes my breath away. I have been frightened, intimidated, and brought to tears in the course of my work. When I have reflected on these interactions through imagery, the artwork brought valuable information for treatment as well as for my own personal growth. I painted *Rage* (Figure 9.11, Plate 19) when I worked as a consultant for an agency serving adolescents who were aggressive, impulsive, and engaging in dangerous behavior. When I walked into the group home where the girls lived, a young woman ran up to me and screamed obscenities in my face, telling me to get out of her house. Her behavior did not change over time. No matter what I did, she shrieked at me; I recoiled in response. I painted this piece to hold my fear of her hostility while I tried to understand the dynamic between us.

The image represents the young woman in a fiery red environment with pointed teeth and knives flying from her open mouth. I was intimidated each time I encountered her. All I could feel was rage coming from her. It took painting and working with the image to help me understand her sadness and see the tears that fell from her eyes.

FIGURE 9.11 (PLATE 19) Rage

Barbara Fish

Making the painting did not lessen her ability to intimidate me or ease our interaction. However, it did help me recognize what might contribute to her reaction to my presence. I focused on the image held on the page as I reflected on our encounter. I am a White woman with privilege who has the ability to come and go as I please. I was walking into her home. Why would she expect that my presence would be safe, let alone helpful?

As I looked at the painting, I thought about the girl's circumstances. She was a ward of the state with a long history of abuse, neglect, and delinquency. Her experiences had taught her that attacking first was the safest way to protect herself. Although I couldn't comprehend her experience, painting about her helped me to hold a space to consider that there was a complexity to her rage beyond what I first saw. I worked to understand her stance and respect her space while trying to make the agency a more therapeutic and humane environment.

At the time, I used this piece as a tool to work with the childcare staff. It helped me cultivate my empathy for the girl as well as for the staff as they tried to work with her. I continue to share this painting with therapists I supervise to support reflexive practice and promote understanding about aggression, the potential meaning of behavior, and how to manage our own responses to it.

I have also served as a consultant to hospital programs where I provided training and supervision for staff from various disciplines who treated children, adolescents, and young adults. As part of that work I regularly met with the hospital administration, making recommendations for improved patient care.

While consulting at a hospital, I found the staff struggled with a lack of resources and support and supervision. This led to interactions with patients that were stressful rather than therapeutic. The staff frequently understood the patients' behaviors as willful instead of an entrenched pattern developed to survive trauma. In this venue I used my imagery to guide my work and communicate my concerns with the staff. I painted *Not Manipulation* (Figure 9.12, Plate 20) as a response to an incident that took place at the hospital. It demonstrates how I used my imagery to clarify and support my work with staff as well as to help manage the affects of harm's touch.

When I walked into the hospital's adolescent girls' unit, I overheard the nurse and several other mental health workers talking about a patient who sat on the floor of the quiet room with the door open several feet away from them. Their voices sounded tense and frustrated from a distance. The girl had found a screw on the floor and pushed it deep into the bloody furrow of the self-inflicted wound on her thigh. She sat staring at her wound, waiting silently for a new dressing. This was not new behavior for her. Self-harm was a problem listed in her treatment plan. She was hospitalized again and again and her behavior was always the same.

The staff and nurses were frustrated and angry about the patient's ongoing self-destructive acts. There was implied negligence on the part of the staff for not having watched her more closely. They were tired of the extra scrutiny and

FIGURE 9.12 (PLATE 20)   Not Manipulation

Barbara Fish

paperwork required for treating "cutters." Their frustration was clear as they talked about how she "did it again, cutting herself to manipulate us into paying more attention to her." After all, they said, she was "attention seeking." Reminding the staff that the patient could hear them talking about her, I tried to reframe her actions as a symptom of her psychiatric disorder and the primary reason for her hospitalization. The staff deflected my feedback, insisting that the patient was manipulative.

New therapists may be shocked or put off by what appears to be the calloused attitudes of veteran staff. Although some of these staff may be burned out, theirs is often a realistic assessment of mental illness, the ensconced patterns of recidivism, and the limited resources of both the patient and those who work within the system. Differentiating burnout and frustration from an accurate assessment of the behavioral manifestation of the patient's symptoms is a topic for discussion in supervision.

When I sat down beside the girl in the quiet room, what I saw was entirely different from what I would have expected from the staff's perceptions. I saw a sad and defeated child with a vacant stare. I was shocked by the contrast between the conversation of the people who were charged with caring for the girl and my view of her.

As I sat beside the girl, waiting for the nurse to put a dressing on her open wound, I knew I was experiencing harm's touch. I tried to reconcile the disturbing discrepancy between the staff's harsh approach and the desperate and poignant condition of the patient. I understood the staff's frustration, but it was clear that they did not understand the girl's mental illness and what drove her to inflict such violence on herself.

I painted *Not Manipulation* (Figure 9.12, Plate 20) at home over several days. It depicts the patient sitting in the quiet room with screws, instead of tears, falling from her eyes into the wound in her leg. This work gave me a place to contain the gruesome witness so that I could find the value and utility in the experience. My painting helped me to realize that we were all angry, although the patient took the brunt of it. Staff members were frustrated because the patient's ongoing behavior caused increased scrutiny of how they monitored her and caused them so much extra work. I was concerned about the patient's care and frustrated and angry that the staff members were unwilling to accept my feedback. We all felt powerless and were faced with the challenge of keeping the patient safe from her need to hurt herself.

Realizing that my anger came from feelings of powerlessness about having such a limited effect on the circumstances helped me to see that the staff members were having a similar reaction. As I softened my own response to the situation, I was able to help some of them soften theirs. I showed my painting to the staff as we had earnest discussions about the meaning of the girl's symptoms and how to respond therapeutically to her. It helped us discuss the dynamics that underlie the actions of people who cut themselves.

This patient had endured abuse that left her vacuous. Having to shut down her feelings over and over again to survive, she harmed herself to manage them. Cutting herself was a desperate attempt to numb her emotional pain and to bring herself back from her dissociative fog. The girl's history of abuse set the stage for a life of tangled and confusing interpersonal conflict. Many children learn early that negative attention is better than no attention at all. The painting helped the staff to consider that the girl's behavior might be a manifestation of her inner pain instead of manipulative behavior. It helped them to soften their approach to working with her. I explained that her "manipulation" was a way of surviving; it was not aimed outward but inward to soothe a desperately unhappy soul.

Conclusion

Interdisciplinary art-based supervision provides opportunities to reflect on work with fresh eyes. The use of creativity and imagination offers new perspectives of clinical work. Supervisors guiding the practice of others may find their own imagery to be a valuable tool for conceptualizing and communicating about treatment. Supporting the use of response art to reflect on practice brings new dimensions to clinical reflection. Response art is a tool for exploring and communicating. It can deepen the understanding of experience and offer ways to share it. The utility of this practice depends on the willingness of participants to engage in art-based reflection.

Artistic training is not a prerequisite for making and learning from artwork. However, those facilitating the experience should be familiar with the media and the image-making process that they offer in order to support successful practice. People without formal creative training made many of the images that I presented in this chapter. Many were tentative about their artistic abilities. The images and materials provided grounding as they explored their concerns. The student nurses made response art outside of class about their experiences and brought their work back for discussion. Veterans who were nursing students made imagery in groups to manage academic stress and form an empathic community. Response art supported the facilitators and helped us to manage harm's touch. The social service professionals made images during workshops as part of their training, expressing their challenges working in residential care. I engaged my imagery throughout to guide my clinical course and give interdisciplinary support and supervision to others.

The interdisciplinary work that I did with art-based supervision did not afford me the opportunity for lengthy relationships. During the training with those working in social service, I worked with groups of about fifty people for less than two hours. Facilitating the use of images to explore facets of the work done by nursing students and mental health professionals afforded them the opportunity to look at their work in new ways. Through their artwork they were able to reflect on their practice and express their feelings about it to one another, finding support and commonality in their concerns.

Reference

Allen, P. B. (2005). *Art is a spiritual path*. Boston, MA: Shambhala.

10

TERMINATION

Finding Closure

There is nothing more important than a good goodbye. This is as true in therapy and in supervision as it is in other significant relationships (Wadeson, 1989; Wilson, Riley, & Wadeson, 1984). Saying goodbye helps us bring closure to interactions, supporting our transition to what is next. This chapter brings us to the end of our discussion of art-based supervision.

In the same way that it is helpful to review treatment to support closure, it will serve us to review where we have been. We have talked about creating a space for art-based practice, being mindful of the use of time, space, and ritual, and explored strategies for engaging imagery in supervision. We have looked at the use of power in supervision and considered ways to process, understand, and manage harm's touch. We have examined the work experienced by new therapists and supervisors during graduate training and the early stages of professional development as well as some of the responsibilities facing new supervisors.

We have examined the varied uses of response art in art-based supervision to hold, investigate, and communicate with others about our practice. We have looked at examples of supervision assignments used to reflect on graduate training and postgraduate practice to stimulate creative ideas and encourage the use of response art in practice. We have discussed examples of the use of imagery in interdisciplinary art-based supervision as a resource for others who provide treatment and advocated for its wider use. Now we will turn to the use of imagery for closure in the end phase of treatment and in supervision.

Termination is an unfortunate term for the end phase of treatment. Chords from personal experiences reverberate for clients, therapists, and supervisors alike as we end therapeutic and supervisory relationships. Therapy, supervision, and personal relationships benefit from intentional focus on closure.

Imagery employed in art-based supervision provides a vehicle to reflect on the course of the work, affirming the value of the experience while serving as an experiential example for the parallel practice of terminating therapy. Whether it is the end of a single interaction or a therapeutic relationship that lasted years, conscious attention deepens our appreciation of the experience. New therapists benefit from support during the important phase of termination, whether they are engaging in brief therapy or long-term treatment. Consciously reflecting on closure in supervision can help supervisees appreciate the significance of this stage of their work.

Endings are often messy, leaving unspoken feelings and unresolved issues from current relationships as well as echoes of past losses. Sometimes we have the opportunity to facilitate thoughtful closure, and sometimes we do not. Whether the end of therapy is carefully planned over time or abrupt, leaving no time for a personal goodbye, supervisees benefit from discussing closure in supervision.

Looking at termination through an art-based lens can help new therapists recognize the value of a productive goodbye. Reviewing imagery created during the course of treatment and supervision allows supervisees to learn firsthand the importance of this reflection on past work. It can also help supervisees to process and come to terms with endings that leave them without the ability to say goodbye to their clients, helping them to find their own closure.

There are endless ways that clients leave therapy. These include terminating without discussion, canceling their last appointment, or transferring to another agency. In some instances clients are hospitalized or die. There are also opportunities to carefully plan the course of treatment, giving attention to closure. Bringing intentional focus to this work helps us to deepen our appreciation of the value of what has gone before.

I remember seeing youth leaving residential care for their new homes, after years of treatment, with their belongings in garbage bags. They said a quick goodbye to the staff on their way out of the door. Recognizing the importance of saying a good goodbye and that rituals are valuable for bringing closure, I helped develop practices at the agency to help end treatment. One of these was an art-based termination project. It began about a month before a child was scheduled to leave to reunite with his or her family or to go into foster care. The youth and his or her therapist walked around the agency, taking digital pictures of favorite staff and important places. Being mindful of the Health Insurance Portability and Accountability Act (HIPAA) regarding client confidentiality, they did not photograph other residents. As they walked they discussed their memories at the site and their work together. The therapist combined the pictures into a CD for the child to take to his or her new home. This review of important relationships helped both the child and the therapist reflect on their experiences of treatment, find closure, and move on.

Termination brings to mind associations to past losses for clients and supervisees. Managing feelings that accompany the close of treatment can be complicated and can benefit from supervisory support. The imagery of both the supervisor and the supervisee can be helpful as new therapists strive to manage the profound nature of this work and the effects of harm's touch.

A student supervisee made angels during her sessions with a hospitalized terminally ill patient. *Holding On* (Figure 10.1) is an image that I made to give feedback to her after she presented her work to the supervision class. I brought this drawing the following week to show her how her presentation helped me understand her wish to hold onto her patient as his illness made him slip away.

Used beyond therapist training, response art can continue to help new professionals find closure for relationships with clients. During postgraduate supervision, Rebecca Israilevich took a small assemblage out of her bag as she described her work at a nursing home serving patients with medical and mental health issues. Her piece was our focus as she talked about a client who

FIGURE 10.1 Holding On

Barbara Fish

had multiple sclerosis. The client was bedridden and unable to speak or use her hands easily. Rebecca described sitting at the woman's bedside, helping her to make a pair of earrings with beads. The woman indicated the order of the beads by looking at each one that she wanted to add as Rebecca strung them on wire. They worked together in this way until the earrings were finished. Finally, she helped the woman put on the earrings and held a mirror so she could look at their work. She asked the woman how she felt about the experience and seeing herself wearing the earrings. The woman looked at Rebecca and said, "Uplifting."

The next time Rebecca went to work, she learned that the woman had died. Later she made *Uplifting* (Figure 10.2) as her response art to honor their time together and to say goodbye. By making the image and bringing it to supervision, she was able to share the story and have it witnessed. This helped her find closure for her work with this client.

Another new professional, working for an in-home counseling service for children in foster care, contended with the abrupt ending of her relationships with four boys, ranging from ten to sixteen years old. She painted *Termination* (Figure 10.3, Plate 21) during postgraduate supervision as we discussed their complex situation. The boys lived with an elderly foster mother who was recovering from a stroke and struggled with socioeconomic challenges. The woman,

FIGURE 10.2 Uplifting

Rebecca Israilevich

FIGURE 10.3 (PLATE 21)   Termination

Anonymous

who was often confused and overwhelmed, had difficulty providing sufficient care for the boys and dealing with their complex behavioral problems. "She loved them but she couldn't take care of them" (Anonymous, Personal communication, July 24, 2015). After several of the boys were hospitalized, the foster mother decided to end services with the therapist, choosing to have them seen through the hospital where they had been treated. This happened quickly, leaving the therapist without a chance to say goodbye.

Because the foster mother really couldn't manage them, the therapist thought that the boys would probably be taken away from her and placed into a different foster home. Either way, she was worried that the situation would be bad. In their current home, the foster mother loved them but was confused and neglectful. If they were moved, the therapist wondered where they would go and if they would be able to stay together.

> The painting was my way of letting them go, of releasing them, which I had to do on my own without being with them in person. It was especially hard for me because they were some of my first clients at the agency and that was my first job as a therapist. They were going to fly away and there was nothing I could do to stop it.
>
> *(Anonymous, Personal communication, July 24, 2015)*

There are often times when clients move on, leaving the therapists invested in their treatment and powerless to help. This therapist was able to use her response art in supervision to find closure after her clients left treatment. The work helped her to reflect on her unresolved concerns, acknowledge her inability to have an effect on their situation, and to let them go.

I use response art to share the depth of my experiences of supervision with those I supervise. As I painted *Supervision* (Figure 10.4, Plate 22), I looked back over a year of working with two new professionals as we developed an art therapy program serving children in a public elementary school in Chicago. The momentum we gained as we collaborated had sustained us as we engaged in the enormous task of developing the program from the ground up. The work included developing contracts with the Chicago Public Schools, providing in-service training to introduce the program, consulting with teachers and parents, ordering and maintaining materials, soliciting referrals, obtaining informed consent from parents, assessing and determining treatment priorities including who would benefit from group or individual treatment of 137 children, and communicating with parents and teachers while overseeing the quality of care during the academic year.

After painting the piece, I gave prints to the therapists at the end of the program to express how I felt about working with them. In the image, I stand on the precipice of this new adventure, supporting them and balanced by the energy they return to me. Supervising these new professionals inspired me, reminding me of our unlimited creative resources and the potential that they bring. A productive supervisory relationship engages and supports all of those involved in growth and learning. This piece helped me to process and close our work together when the year ended and we moved on.

FIGURE 10.4 (PLATE 22) Supervision

Barbara Fish

Reviewing the Work

Beyond supporting nuanced and layered communication in supervision, the images we make are tangible records of the material we have handled. Just as it is valuable to review the course of the client's treatment before terminating therapy, it is important to reflect on the path of supervision. Response art is a physical representative of the work. Reviewing imagery made as part of supervision over time can affirm our efforts and consolidate our gains, bringing new insights.

This way of reviewing supervision can be seen in the reflections of June Dondlinger, a student supervisee working as an intern in a psychiatric hospital program. She constructed *Bear* (Figure 10.5) at the beginning of her internship to express how she felt about her practice at the hospital. As with many student therapists, June was anxious and apprehensive when she began her internship. She entered the hospital feeling out of context. Immersing herself in the medical model at the hospital left her feeling unprepared, without the confidence or the skills she relied on in her life outside of her internship. Her piece depicts a bear standing in a small wooden structure with its claws and teeth scattered on the floor at its feet. June discussed the meaning of her piece.

> Initially the bear represented disempowerment. I felt like the disturbing loss of teeth and claws were about resistance and fear in this new, strange and confining environment. I struggled with being in the scariest place I could think of. Not because it was a mental health hospital, but because I was in the one place where I perceived everyone to be superior to me. Putting myself in that situation was about as scary as it gets for me. So if you

FIGURE 10.5 Bear

June Dondlinger

think about that one thing that you are most afraid of, and for me it's being around people that I perceive to be smarter and superior to myself, then try to imagine performing a new and complex skill, that you have only just learned, which requires your full attention and absolute presence. It seemed an impossible task for me, and was by far the most difficult thing I have ever done in my life. Forget about nursing my mother's death. Forget about having three children. Forget about helping my husband start seven businesses. I can't think of anything else in my life, past, present or future, that could possibly be more challenging than that was for me.

(June Dondlinger, Personal communication, June 10, 2015)

As she engaged in and reflected on her work at the hospital, June's understanding of the bear changed.

Then later, when I looked at it, I realized the bear was not disempowered, but simply evolved. Softening, it was losing its means for reactive aggression, allowing for other abilities to surface and resonate. Now the bear is more of a guide than a source for distancing from difficult emotions. Letting go of that need for defensive power made room for different kind of strength; not aggression, not defense, but an inner truth where there's no need for teeth and claws.

(June Dondlinger, Personal communication, June 10, 2015)

Midway through her nine-month internship, June created *Bird With Broken Wing* (Figure 10.6, Plate 23) as a reflective assignment to depict how she saw herself at this stage in her professional development. The image represents a bird resting in a nest of lavender that pads the bottom of a decorative tin. June said that she experienced supervision as a nest, where she was able to rest and heal old wounds. She used her time in supervision to reflect on her skills as a therapist while she navigated the hospital system, its hierarchy, and its use of power. She struggled to see the value of her understanding of patients in relation to the hospital's medical classifications and clinical approaches to treatment. Because she was used to depending on herself, asking for supervisory support challenged June. *Bird With Broken Wing* showed how hard it was for her to ask for help.

This was a kind of surrender, the broken wing, surrendering to the nest, surrendering to being helped. Which was a huge big deal for me. I'm still not good at asking for help. First admitting that you have a broken wing, admitting you can't fly, and then allowing somebody to hold you while you try to process. That is a very challenging place to be. The transition from feeling disempowerment to viewing it as evolution, change and growth was pivotal. It was a different kind of power that allowed me to surrender to this, because you can't get to that liminal space, which is really scary too, if you don't surrender.

(June Dondlinger, Personal communication, June 10, 2015)

FIGURE 10.6 (PLATE 23) Bird With Broken Wing

June Dondlinger

Working within intense treatment environments often stirs personal and professional responses. Supervision can help therapists to untangle countertransference from other treatment issues and guide them to the most appropriate forms of support. Used in conjunction with her own therapy, June was able to reflect on her past and current experiences and how they impacted her practice as a new therapist. This awareness helped her to understand and be more effective as she provided treatment for adult patients dealing with psychiatric issues.

At the end of her internship, June created an image about a dream that she had, *The Wood and Also the Space Between the Wood* (Figure 10.7). She brought it to supervision as her final response art piece, sharing it as she described her dream to the class.

> [In the dream] I was called as a member of an important council and I was to speak on behalf of wood. The other members of the council were all very knowing and very wise about their own specific things. At my turn to speak I stated: "I am here as the representative of wood". Then, somebody more knowing older and wiser than myself interrupted, and said "you are not only the wood, you are also the space between the wood."

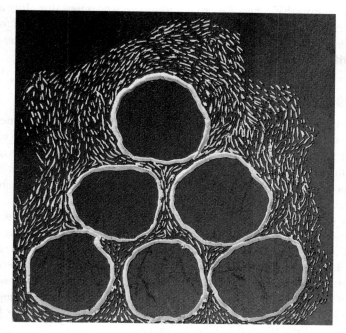

FIGURE 10.7   The Wood and Also the Space Between the Wood

June Dondlinger

[The council in the dream saw me as] bigger than the wood. I was also the space between the wood. It was about accepting myself at the level of the council and also having room to learn and be told more. This is a different situation from the one with the bear where I was in a hospital with people who were older and wiser than myself, but feeling disempowered, feeling less than, feeling other than. This dream was not of feeling less than, feeling other than. As a response to my personal work and growth through supervision, I was confident to say, "I am the knower of wood."

(June Dondlinger, Personal communication, June 10, 2015)

Reflecting on these pieces as part of termination from her internship and field-work supervision class helped June acknowledge the enormous personal and professional challenges she had taken on. She saw how far her efforts had brought her. Beginning as a powerless bear and ending up with the strength of wood, she found self-acceptance and recognized her true power. Arriving in what she identified as a liminal space, she was willing to give up her old ways of knowing without having fully established a new way. June was now able to be more open to the discomfort that is necessary to move into new situations that challenge her to grow and change. Her imagery, reflected on in supervision, helped her to access and apply her newfound confidence and tolerance for unknowing, as she moved beyond this threshold of her work as a therapist.

Holding a Space for Closure

Both clients and therapists experience termination every time a client finishes his or her work and moves on. Student therapists leave their internships according to academic schedules, frequently leaving their sites before their clients are ready to end treatment. This kind of ending also occurs when a therapist leaves his or her job to move to another position. All of these forms of closure warrant attention in supervision.

As we discussed in Chapter 3, rituals help us to pay attention to what is important. They can help us to hold space and deepen our appreciation for the closure phase of treatment and supervision. Processing termination with clients can happen quickly in short-term work or over time, depending on the course of treatment. Intentionally using the time available to focus on termination allows both the client and the therapist the space to bring important issues into therapy. Those involved may not be happy with ending the relationship. But over time, feelings of anger, abandonment, and loss can be processed, leaving a sense of resolution and closure.

The work that I did with a boy in residential care is an example of intentional termination. I saw him for four years, ending when he was ten and I moved on to a new position. Initially, he had no visible reaction when I told him that I was moving away to take another job. Days later, I was called to the cottage where he lived to help calm him during a violent outburst. I found him being held in the physical restraint by staff. He looked at me and said, "I don't care if you leave. I don't care if I die." Over the next weeks, we processed my departure. At first he was distant, then he was angry, and finally he was sad. In our last session we walked by the lake and told one another goodbye.

During supervision class we investigate art-based ways that therapists can process the close of treatment with their clients and site supervisors. Imagery used for termination is useful for recalling the course of the work as well as holding meaning, serving as a transitional object. The artwork can involve creating elaborate collaborative pieces or simply making a card or exchanging pieces created in the last session. This focus on imagery used for closure increases the potential for the experience to be a good goodbye for all of those involved.

A student therapist working in a clinic with child survivors of sexual abuse prepared to leave her clients at the end of her internship by creating a calendar for each child. She made colorful paper butterflies and attached them to the calendars to represent her appointments for her last month of sessions. At the end of each session, she gave her client the butterfly that signified that day. At the end of the month, when it was time to say goodbye, each child had a handful of butterflies and his or her calendar was empty.

Therapy is a professional relationship with boundaries that must be clearly defined. Students and new therapists often yearn to stay in contact with clients whom they must leave behind. This is a supervision matter that warrants close attention. Termination is a time that is rife with countertransference and other issues. It is important for new therapists to consider the ramifications of this decision. Is staying in contact in the client's best interest? What are the agencies' policies? Is maintaining contact sustainable for the therapist?

Ending contact with the client at the close of treatment allows the client to use what he or she has learned from the therapeutic relationship and apply it beyond treatment. In the same way, closing the relationship enables the therapist to make a full commitment to his or her next client. Helping new therapists understand the value of this ending is an important part of supervising the end of treatment.

A Spanish-speaking supervisee leaving her first internship wanted to continue to work with one of the clients as a volunteer. She had a good connection with the client, who spoke Spanish. He would not have access to Spanish-speaking services once the supervisee left. She got permission to see the client beyond the end of her internship from the agency and asked for my advice.

I asked her to consider the time that her next internship commitment would entail. I encouraged her to think about her new clients at her next site and her upcoming academic obligations. I reminded her of the time it would take to commute to the agency to see the client for one hour a week. I asked her to consider how the other clients at the agency would feel, seeing her work only with this one client. Would she take time to talk to all of them? I encouraged her to use this point in her training as a natural time for closure. I reminded her that if she has to stop seeing the client later on, it would be for her personal reasons and not because of the academic schedule. That situation would be more difficult for both of them to process. The supervisee decided not to see the client beyond her internship and terminated with him, as well as the other clients at her site.

By paying attention to the ending of supervision, we bring it into conscious focus and recognize its meaning. Though students have ongoing relationships that reconfigure into other combinations in classes and beyond school, the specific grouping and intention for the gathering that takes place in supervision will never be the same. Those who are leaving postgraduate supervision may be ending the relationships but may move on as a professional colleague or friend. After that transformation, I often remain a supervisory resource, periodically meeting with therapists for consultation. Regardless, the relationships change as they move beyond supervision and its accompanying responsibilities and expectations.

Using experiential methods to support closure in supervision provides a parallel process to that of termination in therapy. In addition to providing a vehicle for reviewing the course of supervision, imagery made to commemorate this stage helps to acknowledge the value of the work as it comes to a close. Planning and reflecting on this phase of the therapists' work with clients offers experiential learning that can inform supervisees' art-based closure with clients.

Imagery is at the heart of the closing ritual in my fieldwork supervision class. We prepare outside of class for our last meeting by making images to give to one another to say goodbye. As we create these pieces we reflect on our experiences together in supervision. At the end of our last class we take turns presenting the images to one another, explaining their meaning. This art-based ritual helps us to review our work with clients, acknowledging our relationships, closing our time together, and helping us to say goodbye.

Elissa Heckendorf said goodbye to her fieldwork supervision class by casting a nest out of wax. She perched seven wax birds of various colors, representing each of the students and me, in the nest (Figure 10.8, Plate 24). As we ended our last group together, Elissa gave a bird to each supervisee and presented me with the nest with the last bird remaining in it.

Kelly Riddle made the small quilt squares that comprise *Termination Quilts* (Figure 10.9) to symbolize each class member. She distributed them to each of us at the end of our last session.

FIGURE 10.8 (PLATE 24) Supervision Nest

Elissa Heckendorf

FIGURE 10.9 Termination Quilts

Kelly Riddle

Termination is a useful time for supervisors to turn to their own imagery to review their work in supervision. Beyond its value for supervisory insight and closure, it serves as an experiential example of art-based work. At the end of supervision class I revisit the response art assignment that I discussed in Chapter 7. For that assignment, the students and I made response art outside of class after each student's case presentation to give him or her feedback. These pieces help me to understand the students' practice and to inform my work with them. At the beginning of the next class, we view and discuss the pieces to explore the treatment issues and interpersonal nuances that manifest in each student's case presentation.

I use a consistent format for the images that I make for the assignment. I initially developed this approach to my images to reflect the rhythm of the work, seeing the images as aphoristic windows into treatment. Over time I saw these modular pieces as an opportunity to reflect on the course of supervision. At the end of the semester I look back over the drawings as part of my own termination. The following example demonstrates how I worked with these images, further engaging with them, with a revised intention for closure.

I drew the six individual images as my responses to students' presentations that took place throughout the semester. The combined image, *Fieldwork Response Art Composite* (Figure 10.10, Plate 25), is my visual expression of the work we did together in supervision. I recalled my work with each student, their practice with clients, the obstacles they navigated, and the changes that they made throughout the semester. When I fashioned the drawings into one piece, I thought about my experiences with each student and the supervision group as a whole.

I made this composite response art piece and others in the same format as part of my self-reflective practice as a supervisor. They bring insight into students'

FIGURE 10.10 (PLATE 25) Fieldwork Response Art Composite

Barbara Fish

clinical work and supervisory relationships. These pieces are windows that hold the experiences we shared in supervision, documenting my years of work with student supervisees.

We end supervision with an art-based ritual, reflecting on and affirming our work together. For this practice we make an image for the other members of the group and distribute them to one another. For my part of the ceremony, I present each supervisee with a print of my fieldwork composite drawing as a visual record of my feedback. This gives them a tangible record of how I witnessed their experiences in supervision. Image-based reflection helps new therapists appreciate the value of imagery used as a part of termination in therapy.

As a supervisor, I use my response art privately to reflect on the course of supervision as well. At the end of a two-semester fieldwork supervision class, I looked back at a painting that I made at the onset. Revisiting *Beginning Supervision* (Figure 10.11, Plate 26) helped me remember how the group started. I made the piece after the first class, when the students and I were new to one another. I was excited about getting to know them and I anticipated the challenge of productive work. As I painted the image, I remember thinking about us at the beginning of the journey, perched on the edge of our experience. I hoped to lead the way for new supervisees to turn to their imagery to reflect on their experience. Now when I look at the painting, I see birds sitting still in an energetic spiral.

FIGURE 10.11 (PLATE 26)   Beginning Supervision

Barbara Fish

As I look at it from this point in time, I recognize the fundamental value of establishing interpersonal safety to support the supervisory process.

Although I made the piece to explore how I felt about the group's start, I did not share it with the class at the time. I brought it to supervision class weeks later, after unpacking the piece's significance for me. Then, it demonstrated to the supervisees how I use response art to reflect on our process. The painting helped me to think about the moment of beginning, when relationships were not yet formed and we were held by our intention to investigate together.

Conclusion

An intimate understanding of the use of response art, developed during supervision, serves the therapist well throughout his or her career. Early experiences with response art foster its use in therapy and support therapists as they take on the challenges of providing supervision. Imagery used for closure in art-based supervision may capture a shared journey or demonstrate a witnessed experience. Images can be simple objects made quickly, such as a painting of a personal affirmation on a stone, or more elaborate pieces designed and created over time. There are endless possibilities.

As I support others, I learn more about my own work. I encourage other supervisors to enlist images in supervision as important resources for cultivating insight, supporting communication, and managing the effects of what we witness. Art-based supervision invites creativity into the supervisory relationship. It supports supervisor and supervisee as they face the challenges of their work. These range from the uncertainty of new therapists, weathering and contending with harm's touch, and the task of facilitating meaningful closure.

Graduation is a time to celebrate; it is also a moment that often brings bittersweet reactions. At the close of the final semester of supervision, before student therapists graduate, I make a piece for each of them to commemorate his or her transition from student to new professional. As I form each piece, I think about each supervisee, remembering his or her challenges and hoping for a smooth transition into the work to come.

I often make key amulets (Figure 10.12) for this purpose because of their symbolism for me. As I work I remember the skeleton key that I used when I worked at the state hospital. I can still hear the substantial sound it made as it turned the lock in the door, opening the art room where so many thoughts and feelings were set free. The key is a talisman that carries my hope that these new professionals will discover creative resources of their own. As students close the door on their training, they unlock another to their professional lives and careers. I envision them wearing the key or putting it in their pocket as they go to a job interview, work with clients, or give a professional presentation.

When I began writing this book, I intended to share my experience of art-based supervision. As I look back over the text, I am struck by how much I have

FIGURE 10.12   Termination Amulet

Barbara Fish

learned as I held the space for the images and the stories of others. At every turn
supervision challenges us to understand and to help address situations in treatment
that are not our own. Supervision affords unending opportunities for professional
and personal growth as well as an obligation to hone our clinical and perceptual
skills and our ability to pay attention and to feel empathy. Response art used in

art-based supervision offers both supervisors and supervisees ways to deepen our practice, explore and communicate about treatment to one another, and process the impact of the work. I hope you will use art-based supervision as a key to unlock creative resources in your own supervisory relationships, opening new possibilities to inform and support sound practice.

References

Wadeson, H. (1989). The art therapy termination process group. In H. Wadeson, J. Durkin, & D. Perch (Eds.), *Advances in art therapy* (pp. 433–451). New York, NY: John Wiley.

Wilson, L., Riley, S., & Wadeson, H. (1984). Art therapy supervision. *Art Therapy: Journal of the American Art Therapy Association, 1*(3), 100–105.

GLOSSARY

The following words and phrases are used in art-based supervision and in art therapy.

Active Imagination   A method of inquiry developed by Jung that involves engaging in imaginal work and processing it through writing and image making.

Art   An image made in the context of therapy and art-based supervision regardless of the level of esthetic sophistication, technical expertise, or ability to communicate to others outside that relationship.

Art-Based Supervision   Supervision that uses response art as a primary mode to explore internship issues and professional concerns.

Art Therapist/Therapist   *Art therapist* and *therapist* are terms used interchangeably. Art therapists are master's prepared clinicians. Supervision is required for registration and certification with the Art Therapy Credentials Board, Inc. and licensure with state boards of professional regulation. The work of art therapists often resembles that of traditional verbal therapists. Art therapists may serve as primary therapists and as case managers in a wide range of mental health settings.

Counterresistance   The unconscious distancing attitude and resulting behavior of the therapist that is brought on by the distancing behavior of the resistant client.

Countertransference   The unconscious feelings of the therapist toward the client based on the therapist's prior relationships.

Duty to Warn   State laws mandating that mental health professionals disclose confidential information about clients who may become violent, including warning third parties of an imminent threat to their safety. The law provides professionals with protection from both civil and criminal liability for failure to maintain confidentiality in the event of a report if they act "in good faith."

Harm's Touch An original concept describing how we are affected by what we witness. It is not a clinical syndrome, like vicarious trauma, but an embodied experience offering benefits as well as risks.

Image Any formed expression of a thought, feeling, or idea. It may be two-dimensional, three-dimensional, video, or new media. Images may be manifested in a variety of ways, including visual pieces and performance.

Image-Based Narrative The story of an image that relates how and why it was created and the purpose that it served. Its context and meaning are determined by the image's life story as described by the artist and through direct engagement with the image.

Image-Based Resonance When an image is inspired, created, or recalled as a response to another image or story.

Image Making The process of creating images that focuses equally on the process and the product.

Image's Life Story The history of an image beginning with what inspired it and ending in the present.

Imaginal Dialogue A way of engaging imagery that involves conversing directly with images as a way to find deeper insights.

Intention A statement written in the present tense that clearly articulates what one hopes to explore, accomplish, or learn from an experience.

Intern Graduate student engaged in fieldwork and site supervision during his or her therapy internship.

Media Anything used to make images. This consists of traditional and nontraditional art materials.

Narrative Inquiry A postmodern, qualitative research methodology in which the inquiry evolves as a written or verbal story.

Narrative Therapy A postmodern treatment model that draws from a feminist therapy philosophy, addressing issues of gender, power, and privilege. This method strives to empower clients whose stories reveal that they are marginalized by the dominant culture.

Patient/Client Terms used interchangeably to indicate the recipient of therapeutic services.

Process Time spent engaged in image making.

Processing Reflection and discussion of the experience of image making and the product.

Product The object made through the creative process in therapy or supervision.

Referencing Being inspired by or incorporating aspects of another's artwork into one's own.

Response Art Art that is made by therapists to contain, explore, and communicate about their work.

Response Writing   Creative writing that is written by therapists to contain, explore, and communicate about their work.

Ritual   Intentional actions designed to bring meaning to an event or situation.

Self-Soothe   To participate in something to calm and ground the therapist or client. Depending on the precision of our intention, self-soothing can help us sustain clarity during stressful encounters or act as a distraction and means of avoidance.

Space   The physical and emotional environment in which an important interpersonal exchange takes place. It refers to both the seen and unseen elements at play.

Student   Trainee in a clinical placement under supervision.

Supervisee   Therapists engaged in postgraduate supervision.

Talking With the Image   Part of the active imagination and witness writing process in which the artist has a dialogue with his or her image, usually transcribing the experience into written form.

Witnessing   Silent, focused attention paid to an image, written piece read aloud, verbal discourse, or performance.

Witness Writing   A writing process involving imaginal engagement with imagery, preceded by a written intention and followed by reading the transcription to others who witness silently.

Word Image   Descriptive words in poetry or prose that elicit images.

INDEX